SOONER THAN YOU THINK

Mapping a Course for a Comfortable Retirement

SOONER THAN YOU THINK

Mapping a Course for a Comfortable Retirement

Gordon K. Williamson

BUSINESS ONE IRWIN
Homewood, Illinois 60430

This book is dedicated to all of my clients.
May they continue to sleep well at night.

This publication is designed to provide accurate and
authoritative information in regard to the subject matter
covered. It is sold with the understanding that neither the
author nor the publisher is engaged in rendering legal, accounting,
or other professional service. If legal advice or other expert
assistance is required, the services of a competent
professional person should be sought.

From a Declaration of Principles jointly adopted by a Committee
of the American Bar Association and a Committee of Publishers.

Senior editor: Amy Hollands
Project editor: Waivah Clement
Production manager: Jon Christopher
Art coordinator: Heather Burbridge
Compositor: Precision Typographers
Typeface: 11/13 Palatino
Printer: Book Press, Inc.

Library of Congress Cataloging-in-Publication Data

Williamson, Gordon K.
  Sooner than you think : mapping a course for a comfortable
retirement / Gordon K. Williamson.
    p.   cm.
  ISBN 1-55623-541-0
  1. Retirement income—Planning. 2. Estate planning. I. Title.
HG179.W53514 1993
  332.024'01—dc20   92-12568

Printed in the United States of America
1 2 3 4 5 6 7 8 9 0 BP 0 9 8 7 6 5 4 3

Preface

Even though 8 out of 10 Americans think they can retire comfortably, less than 20 percent feel highly prepared for that day. Almost a fourth of those who are 10 years from retiring feel that they are not ready. The number of people who feel comfortable about entering their leisure years has been declining steadily.

· You may be wondering if you really need a plan to retire. After all, most people just "let it happen." But as you get older, your options in life become fewer. In addition, planning to do nothing with one third of your adult life is a pretty risky proposition. Retirement can be the most rewarding period of your life. It gives you the opportunity to start a new career, travel, pursue hobbies, participate in sports, and have the freedom to do what you want, when you want.

Retirement planning will force you to: (1) make a realistic assessment of your financial situation now and at retirement, (2) identify problem areas you might encounter in retirement and find solutions before it is too late, (3) examine the possibility of an early, normal, or late retirement, and (4) look at your future anticipated lifestyle during retirement in order to set financial goals and objectives today.

In the past, people had few assets during their retirement years. Lifestyles were determined solely by monthly checks from social security and a company pension plan. If the money received was not great, at least it was dependable. Retirees generally lived only a few years after retirement. Today, things have changed. You can now expect to live for an additional 20 years or more. The majority of us retiring in the future will not get monthly checks from our former employers; instead, we will be getting statements from financial planners and brokers. For the past several years, social security has not covered most postretirement expenses, and its role will continue to diminish in the future. And since we are living longer, inflation, which has been positive every year since 1954 (averaging 3.1 percent over the past 60 years and 6.4 percent for the last 20 years), is something that must be factored into our future.

This book gives you the knowledge you need to retire comfortably, whether your goals are lofty or simple. Since you are now in the position of planning ahead, you are looking at from 5 to 20 years down the road until you decide to retire. The chapters will show you what to do and when to do it. First, you will find out exactly where you stand. The second step is to calculate where you want to be when you retire. The final step is to learn about the strategies that will help you get there, along with some tips to protect you and your loved ones along the way.

In a recent Gallup poll, close to half of the Americans surveyed were concerned about the possibility of outliving their retirement assets. This is an indication of the five common myths about retirement: (1) short-term nature of life expectancy, (2) preservation of capital as the primary concern, (3) income taxes and housing costs will drop, (4) medicare will provide all necessary health insurance, and (5) financial help to others will end. Before moving on to the actual process of planning for your retirement, let us first explore these myths.

Myth One

Although life expectancy tables show that the typical American lives for 75 years, this is a misleading figure. The average also includes the 20 percent of the population who die before reaching retirement. A male who reaches age 65 will probably live to 85; a female will likely see 89. This means that you must make sure your income lasts much longer than you originally thought.

Myth Two

The second common myth is that when retirement occurs, you need only be concerned with preservation of capital for your remaining years. Unless you have a net worth, exclusive of your home, of close to half a million dollars or have a pension whose increases are tied to the real rate of inflation, preservation of principal is not enough. With greater life expectancy and some of the other problems outlined below, you need to make sure that your asset base grows every year to offset the effects of inflation.

Furthermore, most people believe that their home will provide the hedge against inflation that will be needed later. The great majority of these people, however, do not ever want to sell their house and begin renting. Even more important, real estate is not expected to appreciate in the future as much as it has during the past two decades.

How you invest your lump-sum retirement distribution and other assets will be the biggest determinant of your future lifestyle. And with the Census Bureau reporting that the great majority of people do not believe they are adequately prepared for retirement, the need for planning beyond the preservation of existing capital becomes clear. More than ever, the quality of your life during retirement will be what you make it. Your company pension plan and social security will play a much smaller role than it did for your older friends or parents.

Myth Three

The third myth challenges one of our most basic assumptions: that when we retire, our income will drop and so will our tax bracket, allowing for the comfort of reduced costs, including housing costs. It is true that you may now be in a lower bracket, but the total amount you put aside for taxes may not go down at all. The total amount of income that you pay in taxes, which is known as the *effective tax rate*, has actually been increasing for most people ever since Congress enacted income taxes in 1913. Although rates may have dropped, the value of exemptions and deductions have also dropped. There have also been increases in local taxes and the taxation of social security benefits.

Most of us like to think that once our mortgages are paid off, housing costs will decrease. But housing-related costs actually increase. As your home gets older, maintenance will increase. Taxes and utility costs will also continue to climb.

Myth Four

Myth four is one of mounting concern for it involves both the increased life expectancy and the ever-increasing costs of medical care in the United States. Medicare will not meet all of your health insurance needs, even if you have a company-sponsored plan that you can take advantage of during retirement. First, medicare covers only approximately half of health care costs and only for those 65 or older. Second, starting in 1993, corporations may be required to account for health-care benefits in a new way. At the very least, changes will occur because of the continued rise in the costs of such benefits, increases that even the most generous employer cannot maintain.

Studies show that the two major concerns of those between the ages of 45 and 65 are inflation and rising health-care costs. Approximately 85 percent of the respondents to surveys worry that nursing home costs could financially ruin them or their families. Over 95 percent of people polled between the ages of 60 and 65 believe that they will not be able to pay their medical bills.

Myth Five

The final myth is that you are the only person you will need to support. Yet, as life expectancy increases, so does the average age of children still living at home with their parents. In fact, in the past 20 years, the number of college graduates returning home has doubled. In the past, most couples were through paying for their childrens' education when they reached their early 50s. This left them with another 10 or 15 years to prepare for retirement. Today, raising children has been postponed by many people. This means that millions will later find themselves on the verge of retirement, still swamped by tuition bills. To make matters worse, college costs increased at twice the rate of inflation during the 1980s.

In addition, only 18 percent of all children in the United States live in households that make sufficient salaried income to pay for even the least expensive two-year public college. In the future, the increasing number of single parents, coupled with inflation, will make this number ever smaller. Efforts by most families to set aside monies for college costs often fail because there is a tendency to invest in conservative assets, "safe" investments that frequently do not keep pace with inflation or taxes. Ironically, parents who wait until the last minute to pay for their kids' education have a retirement problem, not a college problem. Parents in such a crisis-planning stage often must exhaust most of their financial resources, including a home equity loan, to pay for college, leaving little for retirement. In such situations, a loan secured by the child or a college work program needs to be reexamined.

Not only may you be supporting your children longer than anticipated, but you also may be supporting your parents. Approximately 60 percent of the elderly in this country are dependent on their children for partial or full support. Not only may the expenses of raising your children crowd your accumulation years for retirement, add to this the likelihood that you may also have to help your parents or in-laws.

Other Considerations

During the most recent decade, inflation averaged 5 percent annually. At this rate, the cost of goods and services doubles every 14 years. Phrased another way, your income stream will have to more than double every 12 years for you to just keep up. Think of the alternative. If your monthly income does not grow each year, your standard of living will drop by 50 percent every 14 years.

What does this mean to you? Clearly one of three things is going to happen: (1) you are going to have to work to approximately age 70 or older; (2) your retirement benefits will be slashed; or (3) taxes, real and hidden, will increase substantially. We have already seen these events unfold. Benefits are being gradually postponed from age 65 to 67, and social security taxes have been steadily rising for each of the past several years. The combination of higher taxes and delayed benefits will make your social security checks less appealing. According to the Congressional Research Service, a person who retired in 1980 after paying the maximum possible social security payroll taxes for 44 years got all of these taxes back, plus interest, within the first five years of retirement. This made the system a sweet deal. However, in the future, a similar worker who also works until he or she is age 65, will have to live to 100 just to break even (it should be noted that social security payroll taxes also cover workers for things such as disability and survivor's benefits).

Things do not look any more promising in the private sector. Until recently, most employers had what is known as a *defined-benefit retirement plan* for their employees. This type of plan meant that you were assured of getting a specific dollar amount each month after you retired. It was something you could count on. In short, your company assumed any and all responsibility for making sure that you got a monthly pension check. According to the Employee Benefit Research Institute, this type of retirement plan is now the exception and not the rule.

Social Security and retirement benefits are not the only things that are going to be cut back. Employer-sponsored health care benefits are also slated for massive changes, none of which are in your favor. Right now, about 30 percent of retirees receive medical help from their former employers. The costs of these benefits to the company have been doubling every 3.5 years. No employer can continue a medical benefits package with such increases. In the not-too-distant future, you can assume that the costs of such health care will either be eliminated by your employer or you will be asked to supplement the premiums.

There is absolutely no reason why your expenditures on any household or personal item should necessarily decline on the day you retire. Government statisticians have found out that, in real life, persons and families over 65 do not necessarily spend a single cent less on any major category of consumption after retirement, just as common sense might tell you. Health care, even with medicare, will be dramatically higher. The percentage of family income that goes for health care is 50 percent higher for those 65 and over than for those 55 to 64.

The bottom line is simple: if you are between the ages of 35 and 55, changes by Congress, your employer, and the economy will cause your future standard of living to be radically reduced unless you begin to take an active role. The longer you postpone planning your future, the fewer options you will be left with and the greater the likelihood that your retirement years will be less than satisfactory.

This book not only points out areas you should be concerned about, it provides the answers you need. The disturbing figures give us an indication of what we have to look forward to: uncertainty and financial fear. The unknowns that lie ahead result from the fact that most people have not taken the steps to find out what is available to them.

With proper financial planning and disciplined investing, you need not be wary about the coming years. But such an approach will require you to take control of your destiny and rely less on the promises of others. Chapter outlines appear at the beginning of each chapter to give you a general idea of what will be covered. Each chapter concludes with a checklist of things to do. By completing the checklists, you will be on your way to a successful future.

Planning for retirement requires the following steps: (1) setting goals, (2) defining your objectives, (3) reviewing the different investment strategies, (4) implementing the investment plan, (5) estate planning, and (6) reviewing. Chapter One will help you set goals—the first step to an enjoyable retirement. The first chapter will also show you how to determine the value of everything you own and calculate whether or not you will have enough money during retirement.

Gordon K. Williamson

Contents

Chapter One

Setting Goals

The First Step: Answering Some Hard Questions
Your Net Worth
Where the Money Comes from

I have a friend who always seems to know where everything is. I know that when I have a deadline or cannot find something in a hurry I can turn to my friend. He is one of the most organized people I know. His sense of neatness and organization is something to behold. This is one guy I do not worry about because he is always prepared, he is admired by co-workers and friends alike. You probably know someone just like this—someone you respect, someone who has "his act together."

You too can gain this sense of reliability and calm by knowing where all your assets and possessions are located. This chapter begins by raising critical questions that will affect your retirement. It is important that you think about the answers to these questions while you still have time to make adjustments. The second part of the chapter is a lengthy worksheet that will help you determine your net worth. This first worksheet will take you at least a half hour to fill out. Do not skip this section; it is the basis of later worksheets that will determine when you can retire and the amount of money you will have during your retirement years. The next section is a second worksheet; this one will show you how much needs to be saved to retire comfortably. This worksheet cannot be completed without knowing your net worth. The chapter closes with a pie chart that shows the sources of income used by other Americans during retirement.

THE FIRST STEP: ANSWERING SOME HARD QUESTIONS

The first step, identifying your goals, touches on two distinct phases in your life: (1) remaining work years and (2) retirement and estate planning. For most people between the ages of 45 and 65, the overriding goal is usually the conservation of wealth for future use. During this time, income is often stable and predictable. Your largest expense, purchasing a home, has been left behind. The other major expense, educating children, has either been addressed or needs to be taken care of. Strategies and specific investment suggestions for college costs and housing options are discussed in later chapters.

While reviewing your retirement goals, ask yourself the following questions:

1. *At what age do I plan to retire?* The answer to this question will largely depend on your answers to the questions listed below.

2. *What is the least amount of annual income I will need during retirement? How much income would I like to have during these years?* Financial planners often say that retirees should plan on spending approximately 75 percent of their after tax, preretirement income during retirement. Depending on your circumstances, many of which are discussed in a later chapter, you may find that for the first several years of retirement your annual needs will not decline at all.

3. *Are there any anticipated special events or circumstances that will require extraordinary expenditures?* These extra expenses include college educations, trips, weddings, and gifts.

4. *How much health insurance coverage beyond medicare and/or medicaid will be needed?* Later chapters cover medicare and medicaid in detail, as well as the pros and cons of long-term health care and other forms of supplemental insurance. Depending on your particular health needs and family history, extra coverage may be a minimal or a large additional annual expense.

5. *Am I going to remain in my current residence?* If you plan on staying put, look into the pros and cons of paying off any remaining mortgage, obtaining an equity loan, a reverse mortgage, the one-time exclusion you are entitled to (if you are 55 or older, up to $125,000 of the net profit from the sale of your home is free from

income taxes), and/or remodeling your home. If you have decided to move, start looking at different municipalities and states. In particular, research the cost of housing in other areas, the type of weather, job opportunities (if you plan on starting a second or part-time career), local and state sales, property, and income taxes, and the level of crime.

6. *If I own a business, what arrangements for its sale or continued operation will best suit my retirement plans?* If you have a partner, look into what are known as buy-sell agreements and key-person life insurance. If you are a sole proprietor, think of ways of adding value to your business so that it will look more attractive to buyers.

7. *In the event of my premature death or disability, what estate planning have I done?* For many people, this means having adequate insurance. The type and amount of life and disability insurance you should have is discussed in a separate chapter. The subject of death and disability includes other estate planning such as having a will, looking into the advantages and disadvantages of a living trust, as well as having powers of attorney in place in the event that you are unable to act for yourself due to either a physical or mental handicap, temporary or permanent. Again, these subjects are covered at length in later chapters.

Answering these seven retirement goal questions will help you get a grip on what needs to be done. After all, understanding the problems, as it is commonly said, is half the battle. But before we tackle the second half of that battle, you must finish the second part of the first step: identifying your estate-planning goals. For most people, the disposition of their assets involves two concerns: (1) providing for a surviving spouse and (2) setting aside what remains for the children.

For your spouse, try to answer these questions:

1. *What kind of annual income will my spouse need after my death?* Current lifestyle, work skills, and existing employment of your husband or wife will largely determine how much (if any) life insurance or nest egg is needed to support your partner.

2. *What percentage of my estate should go to my spouse?* Consider your spouse's net worth, children from previous marriages, the prospect of remarriage, and the special needs of your relatives. Specific estate planning strategies can help preserve your portfolio for future generations.

3. *Can my spouse manage the affairs of my estate as well as his or her own interests and assets?* If the answer to either part of this question is no, start interviewing money managers and find out how a living trust can help manage your estate when you are gone.

4. *Do I expect my spouse to outlive me? Have I made any provisions for his or her future housing?* Surviving spouses normally want to remain in familiar surroundings. If your home has a mortgage, look into a life insurance policy to pay off any remaining balance. If nursing or senior housing is a consideration, find out how much these facilities cost.

The final aspect of determining your estate planning needs is to decide what you want for your children and grandchildren. To help you establish these goals, ask yourself the following questions:

1. *How much income will my kids need after my death?* Educational costs may or may not be an issue at this point in their lives. In the case of grandchildren, chances are that their parents could use some help in setting up a college fund. In the case of your own children, think about whether or not you want to leave them some money to start or buy into a business and/or purchase their first home.

2. *Can my children manage their own financial affairs?* Whether or not your children are adults, you can still have a say in how their inherited assets are managed. By setting up a living trust, you can determine who will manage the inheritance and how and when it will be eventually distributed.

3. *Are there any special considerations or conditions of my children that need to be addressed?* Younger children may need additional money for schooling. Any physical or mental disabilities need to be provided for by naming a guardian or conservator and/or setting aside special funds.

4. *How much of my estate should go to my children? Should some of this be gifted to them while I am still alive?* You may be in a fortunate position where careful estate planning is required now. Look into any tax ramifications of making gifts while you are alive and any possible estate tax consequences if your children will inherit sizable amounts. An equally important consideration is how will such gifts or inheritance affect the child. You may want to make distributions, either while alive or after death, at certain age intervals such as

when the children reach age 25, 30, and 35 or when they complete their education.

As you can see, a great number of challenges lie ahead. To prepare yourself for these events, you will need a plan of attack. In other words, clearly state your goals, define your objectives, study strategies, implement a course of action, and systematize a process of review to make sure that all of your needs are realized. By reading through this book, you will learn what all of this information means to you and how you can safeguard a comfortable retirement. The guidelines and strategies presented in these chapters will be your blueprint for future success. The first step for tomorrow is to determine where you are today.

YOUR NET WORTH

The purpose of calculating your net worth is to determine your current resources and thereby discover how much these assets must grow or be augmented in order to afford the lifestyle you want at retirement. Net worth is your financial value based on everything you own minus your debts and obligations. Filling out the forms in Exhibit 1-1 will also be helpful in Chapter Ten, Estate Planning.

While filling out the forms try to follow these guidelines:

1. Estimate the value of your holdings to the nearest hundred dollars; do not attempt to use exact values.
2. If in doubt about the value of something, use a low number.
3. If you are married and not planning on a divorce, include assets from both spouses.

For comparison purposes, you might like to see how you compare to the average American household in several of the categories listed above. These figures were taken from 1988 data compiled by the Census Bureau. This represents the most current data available. Exhibit 1-2 shows the percentage of households who own a particular asset and the average value for such owners. The "top

EXHIBIT 1–1
Net Worth Worksheet

General Information

Date _____/_____/_____
      Month / Day / Year

Name _____
         Last   First   Middle

ASSETS

Insurance

Cash (surrender) value of all policies you own $____
Cash (surrender) value of all policies owned by your spouse   ____
   Total cash value of insurance $____

Stocks, Bonds, and Mutual Funds

Current market value of all common and preferred stocks $____
Current market value of all mutual funds (money market, balanced, growth, specialty, international stock, foreign bond, corporate bond, government-backed, etc.)   ____
Current market value of all government obligations (T-bills, T-notes, and T-bonds)   ____
Current market value of all corporate and municipal (tax-free) bonds   ____
   Total stocks, bonds, and mutual funds $____

Bank Accounts and Savings Bonds

Current value of all checking and savings accounts $____
Current value of all CDs and savings bonds   ____
   Total bank accounts and savings bonds $____

Real Estate

Current market value of your personal residence $____
Current market value of all income and business property   ____
   Total real estate $____

Personal Property

Current value of your automobile(s) $____
Current value of your recreational vehicle, boat, and/or airplane   ____
Current value of your jewelry, artwork, and/or antiques   ____
Current value of any collectibles (e.g., gold, silver, rare coins, stamps, etc.)   ____
   Total personal property $____

EXHIBIT 1–1
Net Worth Worksheet (Continued)

Loans Made to Friends and Relatives

Remaining balance owed to you on all personal loans $____
Remaining balance owed to you on all trust deeds you have carried back ____
   Total loans $____

Retirement Accounts and Deferred Income

Current value of all IRA accounts $____
Current value of all other retirement plans, including deferred compensation ____
   Total retirement $____

Business Interests

Value of your business $____
Value of any and all business ventures, interests, and partnerships ____
   Total business interests $____

Miscellaneous Assets

Current value of all limited partnership interests $____
Current value of: _____ (identify asset) ____
Current value of: _____ (identify asset) ____
   Total other assets $____

Summary of Assets

Total surrender value of insurance policies $____
Total stocks, bonds, and mutual funds ____
Total bank accounts and savings bonds ____
Total real estate ____
Total personal property ____
Total loans ____
Total retirement ____
Total business interests ____
Total other assets ____
   Total value of assets $____

LIABILITIES (WHAT YOU OWE)

Remaining mortgage balance on your home $____
Remaining mortgage balance(s) on business or investment properties ____
Balance due on any outstanding life insurance loans ____

EXHIBIT 1-1
Net Worth Worksheet (Concluded)

Balance due on any outstanding installment loans	_____
Balance due on any automobile loans	_____
Balance due on all personal loans	_____
Credit card balances	_____
Value of all other loans you have outstanding	_____
Total amount of liabilities	$_____

TOTAL NET WORTH

Total value of assets	$_____
Less: Total value of liabilities	_____
Equals: Total net worth	$_____

quintile" column shows you how the highest ranking 20 percent of those polled fared in each category.

Retirement Planning Worksheet

The second step is to set a savings goal that reflects the standard of living you expect in retirement and the time remaining before you retire. Such a target will keep you from realizing too late that you have not saved enough. Careful planning is required to secure a steady source of income throughout your retirement. Increased life expectancies mean that Americans may spend up to one third of their adult lives in retirement, requiring substantial resources to finance their nonearning years.

Social security is not designed to be the sole source of retirement income. Generally, you can count on social security to provide no more than 33 percent of your retirement income needs. Considering that, according to the Employee Research Institute, company pension plans may provide an additional 20 percent, you can see that personal planning becomes a crucial factor in maintaining a comfortable lifestyle.

Determining how much income you will need.   The first step when planning for retirement is to determine the amount of

EXHIBIT 1–2
Common Household Assets (1988)

Asset	Percent Who Own	Average Value	Top Quintile
Equity in home	64	$43,100	$61,200
Checking account	48	500	900
Savings (CDs, etc.)	73	3,500	6,700
Bonds and money market accounts	9	10,900	14,800
Stocks and mutual funds	22	4,500	6,500
IRAs or Keoghs	24	9,000	11,400
U.S. savings bonds	18	500	700
Equity in rental property(s)	9	37,400	48,200
Other real estate equity	10	18,100	23,900
Business equity	12	10,400	26,700
Median income	100	23,800	

retirement income you will need. If you're like most individuals, you may find an alarming gap between what you think you will need for a comfortable retirement and the amount of money you will actually have on hand given your current savings plan.

Experts estimate that you will need about 75 percent of your preretirement income to maintain a financially sound retirement. The steps presented in Exhibits 1–3 through 1–6 will help you determine your retirement income gap—the difference between the monthly income needed and the amount you expect to receive. The calculations assume that you will retire at age 65.

WHERE THE MONEY COMES FROM

Exhibit 1–7 shows the most common sources of income used by Americans during their retirement years. The figures are based on a broad sample of retirees at all income levels.

The next chapter covers life insurance. Whether or not you have life insurance, or even if you are certain that you do not want it, at least read the first few pages of the chapter. If, after reading

EXHIBIT 1–3
Retirement Income Needs and Sources

A. *Estimate the monthly income you will need at retirement*

$_____ × _____ .75 × _____ = $ _____
Current monthly   Multiplied   Inflation factor   Estimated monthly
income   by 75%   from Exhibit 1–4   retirement income
                                                                 needed

B. *Determine the sources of your retirement income*

    $_____ Monthly social security benefit × _____ inflation factor
                (from Exhibit 1–5)   (from Exhibit 1–4)

=

    $_____ Inflation-adjusted social security benefit

+

    $_____ Anticipated monthly company retirement benefits

+

    $_____ Anticipated monthly income from your IRA and other investments

=

    $_____ Anticipated monthly retirement income
                (add inflation-adjusted social security benefit with anticipated monthly
                company retirement benefits and anticipated monthly income from
                IRAs and other investments).

C. *Calculate your retirement income gap*

A − B = C $_____ Monthly retirement income gap at age 65

D. *Monthly investments needed to fill your retirement gap before you reach age 65**

If your monthly retirement income gap is approximately $500, $1,000, $2,000, $3,500, $5,000, or $10,000, you would need to start investing the amount shown in the column below the gap amount.†

Age Now	$500	$1,000	$2,000	$3,500	$5,000	$10,000
25	$ 17	$ 34	$ 68	$ 120	$ 171	$ 342
35	40	80	160	281	401	802
45	101	203	406	710	1,015	2,030
50	173	345	691	1,209	1,727	3,455
55	327	653	1,307	2,287	3,267	6,535
60	814	1,627	3,254	5,695	8,136	16,271

*The table is for illustrative purposes only and does not represent the performance of any mutual fund. The results assume an 8 percent fixed return (compounded monthly), a fixed rate of withdrawal for 20 years, and no fluctuation of principal. Income received from most funds is not fixed, and the value per share varies with market conditions. No adjustment has been made for income taxes. Higher monthly investments would be necessary if you plan to retire before age 65.

†Qualified plans, such as IRAs and Business Retirement Plans have maximum annual contribution limits of $2,000 and $30,000 (or 20 percent of earned income), respectively, with the result that some retirement gaps could not be met by relying solely on these plans. In addition, an investment in a mutual fund does not guarantee that you will have sufficient funds to meet a retirement income gap.

EXHIBIT 1-4
Inflation Table

Age Now	Year of Retirement at Age 65	Inflation Factor
25	2031	7.04
35	2021	4.32
45	2011	2.65
50	2006	2.08
55	2001	1.63
60	1996	1.28
64	1992	1.05

these pages, you have determined that you either do not want or need additional coverage for yourself and your spouse, skip to the middle of the chapter and review the life expectancy tables. Knowing the number of years you have remaining will be helpful in developing your financial plan, a topic covered later in the book.

The next four chapters cover nonglamorous topics: life insurance, health and disability coverage, social security, medicare, and medicaid. These are certainly not the most interesting of chapters, but they are necessary reading. The foundation of any financial plan is first making sure that you have adequate protection. You cannot build from this base if the foundation is shaky. Understanding the types of insurance and coverage that you can obtain on your own, through work or by a public agency, *may* be important to you before you stop working and definitely *will* be of value during retirement.

Lack of proper coverage can result in the partial or full loss of all of your investments. It can also mean that a substantial portion of your future earnings will be used not to build for the future, but to pay off obligations incurred by an unforeseen event. Few things in life are as frustrating as having to pay for something that took place a month, year, or decade ago. Do not let this happen to you.

Do not gamble with your future. If you want to make sure that you have done all you can to provide for those future leisure years, read these chapters. If, for some reason, you think that "ignorance

EXHIBIT 1–5
Projected Social Security Benefits

To use this table, find your age and the figure closest to your earnings last year. These figures will give you an estimate of your retirement benefits at various ages.

Retired Worker's Earnings Last Year

Worker's age in 1992	Worker's Family	$25,000	$30,000	$35,000	$40,000	$50,000	$55,000 or more[1]
25	Retired worker only	1,201	1,364	1,450	1,535	1,706	1,801
	Worker and spouse[2]	1,801	2,046	2,174	2,302	2,559	2,701
35	Retired worker only	1,111	1,263	1,342	1,421	1,580	1,662
	Worker and spouse[2]	1,666	1,894	2,013	2,131	2,370	2,493
45	Retired worker only	1,019	1,159	1,231	1,302	1,436	1,491
	Worker and spouse[2]	1,528	1,738	1,846	1,953	2,154	2,236
50	Retired worker only	971	1,106	1,166	1,226	1,334	1,375
	Worker and spouse[2]	1,457	1,658	1,749	1,839	2,000	2,062
55	Retired worker only	924	1,052	1,101	1,150	1,231	1,258
	Worker and spouse[2]	1,386	1,578	1,652	1,725	1,846	1,887
60	Retired worker only	893	1,015	1,054	1,094	1,156	1,173
	Worker and spouse[2]	1,340	1,522	1,581	1,641	1,734	1,760
65	Retired worker only	863	977	1,008	1,038	1,081	1,088
	Worker and spouse[2]	1,294	1,465	1,511	1,557	1,621	1,632

[1]Earnings equal to or greater than the social security wage base from age 22 through the year before retirement.

[2]Spouse is the same age as the worker. Spouse may qualify for a higher retirement benefit based on his or her own work record.

Source: Social Security Administration. Approximate monthly retirement benefits assume worker retires at age 65 with steady lifetime earnings. The accuracy of these estimates depends on the pattern of the worker's actual past earnings and earnings in the future.

is bliss,'' skip these chapters and move directly to Chapter Five, Qualified Retirement Plans.

This ends Chapter One. Before moving on to Chapter Two, look at the checklist opposite. Take action on those suggestions that apply to your situation. A checklist is at the end of each chapter. Sometimes the suggestions are rather specific and you must decide if they are applicable to you. Other times, such as when it is recommended that you order a certain publication, you are strongly encouraged to follow them.

EXHIBIT 1–7
Sources of Retirement Income

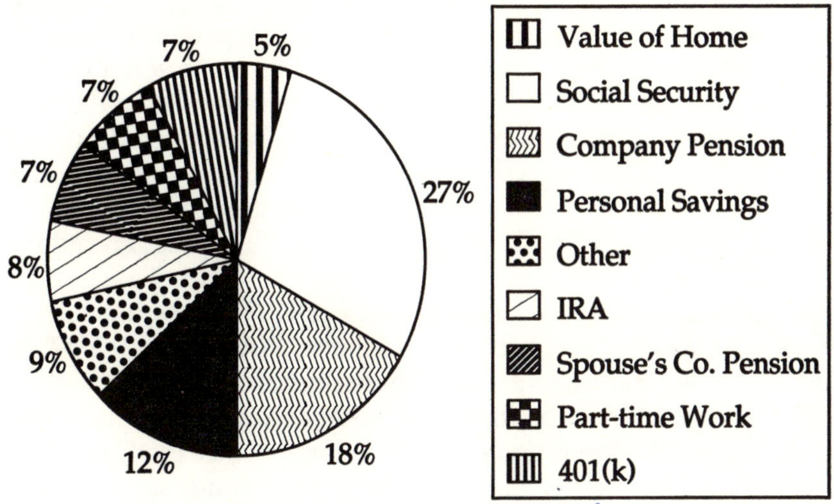
7%
5%
7%
7%
27%
8%
9%
12%
18%
Value of Home
Social Security
Company Pension
Personal Savings
Other
IRA
Spouse's Co. Pension
Part-time Work
401(k)

CHECKLIST OF THINGS TO DO

1. Join the American Association of Retired Persons (AARP) by sending $5 to: AARP Membership Processing Center, 3200 East Carson St., Lakewood, CA, 90712 (or telephone 202-434-3470). Publications of the AARP include *Modern Maturity* and the *AARP News Bulletin*. This nonpartisan, nonprofit organization offers a wide range of publications and services you may find useful. You must be at least 50 years old to join but you do not have to be retired.

2. Spend a few bucks and get a copy of your credit history. The three major credit reporting services are: (1) TRW Credit Data, 505 City Parkway West, Orange, CA, 92668; (2) Equifax Credit Information Services, 1600 Peachtree St. N.W., P.O. Box 4081, Atlanta, GA, 30302; and (3) Trans Union Corporation, Consumer Relations Dept., P.O. Box 119001, Chicago, IL, 60611.

3. Pay off any credit card debt as soon as possible. It makes no sense having a savings account earning 5 percent or owning bonds yielding 9 percent if you are paying 19 percent on a credit card

balance. If you are going to continue paying interest on a credit card, shop around. There are no disadvantages to using an out-of-state bank card. If you are considered a credit risk, you may have to settle for what is known as a *secured* card (you deposit money into an interest-bearing account, the bank then gives you a Visa or MasterCard that has a limit of somewhere between 50 to 100 percent of what you have on deposit). Ask your bank or credit union if they have such a card. You may also want to shop around. For a list of banks that offer secured credit cards, send $3 to the Bankcard Holders of America (560 Herndon Parkway, Suite 120, Herndon, VA, 22070).

4. Make sure your bank is insured by FDIC. For an added sense of security, pay $10 to Veribanc in Woburn, MA (800–442–2657) to find out how financially secure the institution is.

5. Get an interest-bearing checking account that uses the *average-daily-balance* method (versus the low-balance method). You will also want to know if your bank charges for things such as ATM transactions, a monthly service fee, or a per-check charge. As a generality, money market accounts through mutual fund groups offer higher yields. Your bank, however, offers convenience and perhaps a better range of services.

6. Invest in a file cabinet or dedicate a couple of desk drawers for your records. The type of things you will want to store are:

Health and disability insurance policies.

Tax returns for the past three years (six years if there is any chance you have underreported your income by more than 25 percent.

Any tax forms that show a capital loss or gain carryforward.

Any tax return that shows nondeductible IRA contributions.

Copies of cancelled checks for the past three years.

Copies of any checks that show home improvements.

Medical bills for the past year.

Credit card statements for the past two years.

Gold and silver coins or bars.

Prospectuses from any investments purchased.

Year-end brokerage firm statements.

A master list of where everything is (safe deposit box key, your accountant, where securities are held, etc.).

7. Get a safety deposit box from your local bank. Items you will want to store there include:

Your will and living trust.

Life insurance policies.

Securities.

Marriage certificate.

Divorce papers.

Birth certificate.

Military-service records.

Title to your car(s) and property(s).

A list of your retirement accounts and all your investments (account numbers and location).

A list of all major debts and money owed to you.

Make sure that you do not live in a state that seals safety deposit boxes upon notification of the owner's death.

8. Pay off any car loans as soon as possible if the loan rate is higher than what you are getting on other investments. Liquidate any low interest-bearing accounts if necessary. If money is tight, consider a home equity loan.

9. If you have children who will go to college, pick up a copy of *Money's 1993 Best College Buys* at your local newsstand.

10. Contact the IRS and request the following publications: *Your Rights as a Taxpayer* (publication no. 1), *Your Federal Income Tax* (publication no. 17), *Exemptions, Standard Deduction and Filing Information* (publication no. 501), *Tax Withholding and Estimated Tax* (publication no. 505), and *Recordkeeping for Individuals and a List of Tax Publications* (publication no. 552). These free publications may help you reduce your income taxes.

11. If you have a mortgage and want to pay it off in less than 30 years, ask your lender if you can make one or two extra payments each year without incurring a penalty. The extra payments will reduce the term of your loan by 10 to 15 years. This is usually a better way to go than getting a new 15-year loan. A 15-year loan will not give you the flexibility of paying less certain months. Neither will a 30-year loan, but the monthly payments will be hundreds less, and you should have the option of making a 13th or 14th payment each year.

Chapter Two

Life Insurance

Reasons to Consider Life Insurance
The Basics of Life Insurance
Life Expectancy Tables
Canceling a Policy: Tax Consequences
Policy Riders

I know many people who buy lottery tickets regularly. They figure that there is always the chance they will win and end up with thousands or millions of dollars. They know that the chances of actually winning are slim. What these people probably do not know is that there is a greater likelihood of being chosen to fly on the space shuttle than of picking the winning number. Surprisingly, most of these people have no life insurance. Somehow they think winning the lottery is more likely than death. Yet, any rational person knows that the odds of dying are much greater than winning the lottery or orbiting around the earth. Death is guaranteed; so is a life insurance policy. One may not know when or how one will die, but with life insurance at least one knows that family or friends are provided for.

The last chapter asked you to take an inventory of your assets and determine if you will have enough to retire on; several of the worksheet spaces asked you to list your investments. But before you make your next investment or reposition an existing holding, find out if you need any insurance. With proper financial planning and investment selection, only one thing can stop you from enjoying the retirement you deserve—lack of adequate insurance. After all, you will not be able to save much money each year if you suddenly become disabled and are no longer able to work.

Similarly, your family may be robbed of the financial security you were planning because of your premature demise. Most people are insured. The problem is that the coverage usually is not large enough.

REASONS TO CONSIDER LIFE INSURANCE

Life insurance is something that needs to be considered by every adult, whether 18 or 80. This type of insurance is not something that everyone should have, but its place in your retirement planning needs to be examined. You may discover that you need more insurance, less insurance, a different type of policy, or possibly even no life insurance. There are multiple reasons why life insurance may be beneficial to you and your loved ones. The three benefits of life insurance are: (1) as a source of revenue to replace the earning capacity of someone now deceased, (2) as a tax-sheltered investment, and (3) for greater flexibility in estate planning.

THE BASICS OF LIFE INSURANCE

Life insurance comes in one of two basic forms: whole life or term. *Term* insurance is coverage in its purest form. All of the premiums you pay go toward coverage; there is no cash buildup, no investment, and no borrowing privilege. The life of the policy is its term. If you die during the life of the policy, then your beneficiaries receive payment. *Whole life* insurance is simply term insurance coupled with a savings plan. Whole life premiums are more expensive since a portion of each dollar received by the insurance company is used to fund the investment side of the policy. The investment portion of the whole life policy is known as its *cash value*. Furthermore, the amount of each dollar that goes toward an investment that you can later tap into depends on the type of whole life policy and the rate charged by your insurer for mortality, administrative, and other expenses. Thus, although there are only two major types of insurance, whole and term, each comes in several different forms.

The rate of growth of the policy's cash value depends on how the investment side is managed. With some whole life policies, the insured chooses the investment vehicle(s); other types of whole life policies offer no investment options, and the investment portion of the premium depends on the success of the insurance company's portfolio.

If you lack the discipline to save for retirement, then whole life insurance can serve as a forced savings plan. We will discuss later more appropriate ways to save such as the purchase of series EE bonds from a payroll withholding plan or automatic deductions from your checking account that are invested directly into a mutual fund. If you are able to set aside money on a regular basis for your future, then term insurance may be the best choice. If you are in a moderate- or high-tax bracket, certain forms of life insurance can provide you with the necessary coverage and a neat way to have your money grow tax advantaged while still providing you with several different investment options. Since whole life is, initially at least, three times as expensive as similar term coverage, cost can be an important con- sideration. On the other hand, if the family's budget can afford the higher premium of permanent insurance, then the relative merits of both term and whole life coverage should be examined.

Term Insurance

Term life insurance is in effect for a specified period of time known as the term of the policy. Although term coverage is usually renew- able, check to see if it is automatically renewable. Otherwise the insurance company could refuse to provide you with coverage at the end of the term. Renewability allows you to maintain the policy regardless of your health, and no new examinations are required (see next paragraph). Many policies, however, terminate the right of automatic renewability at a specific age, such as 65 or 75. How- ever, another important advantage of term is that most policies allow you to convert to whole life insurance.

Policy illustrations are usually shown with two columns, *reentry* or *without reentry*. Reentry means that the insurance company has the right to recheck your health at the end of the term; the term may be 1, 5, 10, or 20 years. By allowing your insurer this right, the cost of the premium is reduced. Without reentry means the company can only charge you the rate shown, a figure that eventually becomes greater than the figures shown under the reentry column.

Term insurance comes in several forms: straight, yearly renewable, multiyear renewable, to a specific age, and decreasing.

Straight term life insurance. Straight term is not renewable; once the term ends you cannot force the insurer to renew the policy. Initially, this is the cheapest form of insurance. It would be an ideal choice if you were certain that you needed coverage only for a select number of years that coincided with the term you are purchasing.

Yearly renewable term life insurance. Yearly renewable term means that the policy is renewed each year at a higher price. This is only fair since your chances of dying increase each year. The insurer must keep the policy in effect for as many years as you continue to pay the increasing premiums. These policies are a favored choice for someone who plans to shop price every three to five years. You are not overpaying or underpaying for coverage. If you plan on staying healthy and do not mind doing a little work, this may be your best option.

The insurance industry is highly competitive. There can be substantial savings by getting new quotes every couple of years. The renewal rate with your existing insurer may be several hundred dollars greater than coverage from a different company that is aggressively seeking new business.

Multiyear renewable term life insurance. Multiyear renewable term means that you have coverage for a block of time, ranging anywhere from 5 to 25 years. The premiums remain level during the entire term. At the end of the term, if the policy is renewable, your premiums will increase. If annual rising prices upset you, then this is for you. Premiums on these policies do not change during the term period. Comparing one policy against another is easiest when this type of policy is selected.

Term to a specific age life insurance. Term to a specific age policies last until a certain age is reached, usually 65 or 70. The amount you pay each year for coverage does not change. This type of coverage usually is not renewable. If you are only concerned about being covered until a certain event occurs (pension payments begin or the house is paid off), then this type of policy would be a good choice.

Decreasing term life insurance. Decreasing term insurance means that you are buying less coverage each year. The premium does not change, but the death benefit goes down. Mortgage insurance is a form of decreasing term insurance. This type of insurance is usually expensive and is not recommended. It certainly sounds appealing, particularly when described as "mortgage insurance." However, cheaper alternatives are available.

There are two clear advantages to term insurance. First, it provides the greatest coverage for the least cost. Second, it is the easiest type of coverage to compare.

Like the advantages, the disadvantages of term insurance are seen in relation to whole life. First, unless the insured dies, all of premiums paid are worthless; there is no cash buildup. Second, when the chances of death increase greatly in later years, the cost of term insurance becomes prohibitive. Third, other than the death benefit, there are no tax advantages to term.

These disadvantages can be overcome if you have the discipline to save and invest money each year. Therefore, while term insurance does not provide for any cash buildup as found in whole life, you can make up for that fact by managing your money outside of the term policy. We will talk about ways to invest your money wisely later in the book.

Whole Life Insurance

The name *whole life* means that coverage exists for your entire life, unless you fail to pay the requisite premiums. Whole life policies include what is known as a *cash value*. The cash value of a policy represents the accumulated savings portion of each premium. The policy's cash value may stay at zero for several years or begin to grow during its first year. As a consumer, you should be looking for policies that build up cash as soon as possible. A high percentage of this cash can be borrowed at anytime. The insurance company will charge you a fee to borrow any of the cash value; if the company pays dividends, they may be withdrawn at no cost rather than borrowed.

You are also entitled to any cash value if the policy is cancelled by either you or the insurer. All whole life policies provide a guaranteed cash value; the amount of that cash value depends on the competitiveness of the company as well as how long the policy has been owned. Whole life insurance comes in one of six forms: traditional, interest-sensitive, single-premium, limited payment, variable, and endowment.

Traditional whole life insurance. This type of insurance has been around for over a hundred years. It is the best known type of life insurance. When you buy traditional whole life, your premium and death benefit stay level. If you die before you reach age 100, then your beneficiary receives the death benefit (the face amount of the policy minus any outstanding loan balances) plus accumulated dividends, if any. If you should live to age 100, the insurance company will pay you the same dollar amount.

This type of coverage includes a cash value, an amount you can borrow from the insurer at anytime. The longer you own the policy, the greater the cash value. If you are looking for a very conservative tax-deferred growth vehicle, coupled with life insurance, this is a good option. It will be worth your time to check out several companies first. The variances in the cost of the insurance and the rate of growth on the cash value are surprising. Penalties and loan provisions are also important considerations, not to mention the safety of the insurer.

Interest-sensitive (universal life insurance). When universal life insurance was introduced approximately 15 years ago, it was heralded as a breakthrough, a new type of life insurance. The reality is that universal life is a form of whole life. The investment portion of each premium goes into a side fund comprising very conservative money market type instruments (bank CDs, short-term bonds, etc.). During the early 1980s, this turned out to be a great option because of high returns on interest-sensitive investments. However, as rates dropped and investors realized that universal life policies were expensive to administer, and such hidden costs were being passed on to them, the appeal of this product diminished rapidly.

Today, the insurance industry's costs of administering universal life have declined, but so have interest rates. People who purchase this type of coverage are also acquiring an interest-sensitive investment that goes up and down, just like money market accounts and CD rates. Thus, universal life would be a good choice if you did not want to have the cash value of your life insurance locked in to a specific rate. However, be aware that in periods when interest rates are low, the return on the investment portion of the policy will also be low.

One could say that universal life insurance is like combining insurance and a money market account—with two big differences. First, with universal life insurance the percentage of each of your premiums that goes into the money market portion is growing tax deferred (the remaining percentage is being used to buy life insurance). Second, there is a great deal of flexibility as to how and when you pay your premiums. This means that if you do not have enough money one year to pay the costs of your insurance policy, part of the accumulated cash value can be used to pay the premium. On the other hand, if you ever have extra money to invest, universal life allows you to increase your coverage and/or cash value.

Single-premium whole life insurance. Single-premium means that you are paying for insurance with one payment, one premium. This appeals to those people who do not like paying bills or premiums year after year. Once the premium is paid you no longer have to worry about coverage in the future. The death benefit is known up front. In time, the death benefit can increase if the cash value exceeds the face amount of the policy. It takes a number of years for the cash value to exceed the face amount with any type of whole life policy. Under all types of insurance, when the cash value becomes greater than the original face value, this higher figure becomes the new death benefit.

Until Congress changed the rules, single-premium whole life insurance used to be a great way to go. Imagine buying inexpensive insurance and getting a very good rate of return on a safe investment. During the early 1980s, people were getting the equivalent of a 10 percent return on their entire premium, even though not all of the money was going toward the investment side. What made this an even better deal was that these earnings could be taken out at anytime, income tax free. People were buying this type of coverage because they could not get a high rate of return, both free of taxes and free of any fluctuation of principal, anywhere else.

During the mid-1980s, Congress realized that a great number of people were abusing the law and quickly changed the rules and regulations regarding tax-free withdrawals from life insurance. Today, single-premium is alive and well, but new policy owners are no longer able to borrow the cash value out of their policy tax free. All cash values continue to grow and compound tax deferred, just like any other type of whole life product, but withdrawals (loans) are now fully taxed for single-premium owners.

Due to other available options, single-premium is not recommended for most people for two reasons. First, there are no tax advantages to withdrawals. Second, any other form of life insurance would turn out to have been cheaper if the insured dies within the first several years of owning the policy. This is because an annual premium mode means that fewer dollars are committed for the same amount of coverage paid for by a much higher, single premium.

Limited-payment whole life insurance. Limited-payment means that premiums are spread over a set number of years, usually 10 or less. Total premiums are less than traditional coverage where annual payments are made since the insurer has use of your money sooner. As in any type of life insurance, the beneficiary(s) is entitled to the full death benefit no matter how many premiums have been paid, assuming the policy is still in force.

What makes limited-payment and traditional whole life potentially so attractive is if the policies qualify under the *seven-pay test.* This simply means that annual premiums have been paid in roughly even amounts for anywhere from four to seven years. If the premium payment schedule passes the test, then the cash value of the policy can be withdrawn without any income tax consequences. You could say this is a way to get tax-free income or growth along with life insurance.

As with single-premium, better alternatives to limited-payment are available in most situations. This is because the insurance company is getting to use your money faster than it would if annual payments were made under traditional whole life or term. Nevertheless, limited-payment becomes very attractive if you satisfy the seven-pay test and view this type of insurance as protection *and* an investment.

If the limited-payment whole life policy satisfies the seven-pay test for IRS purposes and you view it as a deferred investment program, then this may be for you. The investor/insured could end up having his or her cake and eating it too—life insurance coverage and a means of receiving tax-free income for life (or a lump-sum of money also free of income taxes). Tax-advantaged income is more fully discussed in Chapter Nine, Postretirement Investing.

Variable life insurance. Whenever you see the word *variable* to describe a life insurance policy, it means that there are different investment options to choose from within the cash value portion of the policy. Since you decide which portfolio to go into, you assume all of the risk and all of the reward. You can choose a stock, bond, government security, and/or money market account. As in other forms of whole life insurance, a portion of each premium pays for the mortality and administrative expenses, and the balance goes into the forced savings plan.

Unlike traditional policies, variable life insurance allows you to decide how the cash value portion is to be invested. As in a mutual fund family, you are free to move monies among the different portfolios (i.e., money market, government bond, growth, international, etc.). Often, the investment side is managed by a mutual fund company while protection (e.g., the death benefit, guarantees, etc.) is provided by the insurance company.

When looking at variable life, remember that: (1) the premiums are usually fixed and will not normally vary, (2) there is no minimum interest rate guarantee on the cash value side of the policy; (3) the amount of the death benefit will vary according to the success or failure of the investments; and (4) in no event can the death benefit ever go lower than the initial face value of the insurance.

You should strongly consider variable life insurance if you are looking for all of the following: (1) life insurance coverage for you or someone else, (2) the potential of dramatically outperforming the rate of return found in a traditional policy, (3) tax-deferred growth, (4) no tax consequences if money is shifted between portfolios, and (5) the ability to take money out when needed (tax free if the seven-pay test is satisfied).

Term versus Whole Life

One method for comparing the long-term economic value of purchasing whole life with that of buying term is to subtract the term insurance premium from the whole life premium and invest the difference. For comparison purposes, the invested difference should earn a conservative rate of return, close to what you can currently get in a money market fund or a medium-term bond fund. This value then could be compared to the projected cash value of the whole life policy at various time intervals. When making these calculations, keep in mind that the invested difference on the term side must be reduced by your tax bracket, state and federal combined.

If life insurance is needed for at least 20 years, then whole life is usually the best way to go. It may even be more appealing for shorter periods of time. You will be able to determine this by making the comparison described above. Life insurance purchased for estate planning needs should be whole life since the proceeds will be needed at the insured's death. Term insurance becomes too expensive if the insured lives to life expectancy or beyond. For example, a $600,000 term policy for a 75-year-old male would have an annual premium of $25,000, the figure jumps to over $35,000 at age 80. Whole life coverage over an extended period of time would result in an annual premium that would never increase, and the annual cost would be a fraction of the $25,000 to $35,000 figure for term insurance.

Second-to-Die Life Insurance

During the last couple of years, the insurance industry has begun promoting a form of life insurance that pays off when the second of two people dies. Referred to as last-to-die, survivorship, or second-to-die, these policies are popular with married couples who have a combined net worth of over $1.2 million ($600,000 without proper tax counsel) and have children whom they want to inherit their estate intact.

Uncle Sam allows you to bequeath or gift up to $600,000 without any gift or estate tax liability. There is no dollar limit on transfers between spouses during lifetime or on the death of either the husband or the wife. This is known as the *unlimited marital deduction*. (If the surviving spouse is a non-U.S. citizen, the marital deduction is lost and only $600,000 can be passed free of estate taxes.) These figures apply to all forms of life insurance, including second-to-die, as well as personal effects, securities, and real estate.

A married couple can combine their $600,000 exclusions and gift or will up to $1.2 million without any tax ramifications. Amounts in excess of the exclusion, $600,000 if single or $1,200,000 if married and filing a joint return, are subject to estate and gift taxes. The tax on the excess amount starts at 37 percent and goes up to 60 percent. As you can see by the example below, this is the most compelling reason for second-to-die policies—to make sure your estate passes intact to your loved ones.

To give you an idea of how devastating estate taxes are, consider a $10 million portfolio that yields an annual income of $1 million before taxes, $630,000 after paying income taxes (a 37 percent state and federal combined tax bracket is assumed throughout this example). Mom and dad eventually die, and their estate becomes subject to an estate tax of almost $5 million. The remaining $5 million estate produces $500,000 per year for the children on a pretax basis, $310,500 after taxes. Years later the children die, and the grandchildren end up inheriting $2.5 million after paying estate taxes. This $2.5 million estate that the grandchildren have inherited produces $250,000 of annual income, $157,500 after taxes.

From this example you can see how a couple who spent their entire lives paying income taxes and accumulating an estate for their children and grandchildren eventually lost 75 percent of their estate to taxes. Could the situation have been worse? Surprisingly, the answer is yes. If mom and dad had an estate that was not liquid and marketable, the children would have had to sell assets in perhaps troubled times (bad real estate market, right after a stock market crash, etc.) since the government wants its share of the estate within nine months of death. The only other alternative for the children is to borrow money from a lender and pay interest on the loan.

Mom and dad could have passed the $10 million to their children and grandchildren if their estate could have produced a $34 million profit (from this figure you would subtract $12,580,000 in income taxes and then pay over $11 million in estate taxes to net $10 million).

Enter last-to-die life insurance. If mom and dad had bought a million dollar second-to-die policy (which would have a death benefit of several million dollars), the entire $10 million would be in the hands of their children. If, in turn, the children also purchased this same type of insurance, the grandchildren would now be sitting with $10 million instead of $2.5 million. Life insurance does not eliminate estate taxes; it merely provides a source of ready cash to pay them. Surprisingly, the cost of coverage that can save an estate millions of dollars is relatively cheap. The alternatives are simple to understand: your kids will pay the entire amount in the future, or you can pay it for them now at a 90 percent discount.

What makes second-to-die so appealing for a married couple with a large net worth is the fact that the insurance premiums are much less than if either spouse were to go out and buy traditional life insurance on one life. The premiums are cheaper because the insurer does not have to pay until the second spouse dies. Second-to-die policies are priced based on the spouse with the longest life expectancy, and then set back three years. For example, if spouses were both 65 years old, the joint life survivor (second-to-die) policy would be priced based on a 62-year-old female. Statistically, women live longer than men. Furthermore, in most marriages the woman is younger than the man. In the eyes of the insurance industry, the woman represents a better risk; combining the lives of a woman and a man make the risk even more attractive.

Second-to-die policies usually require premium payments until the second death; however, they can be structured as a single or limited premium. Whether these policies are better than equivalent single life policies on each spouse depends on the length of time until the first death and how much time elapses between the first and second deaths. As a broad generality, if you assume that the surviving spouse will live for at least 10 more years, single life policies probably make more sense.

Since there is no way of knowing how long each spouse will live, couples interested in protecting an estate that has a net value of over $1.2 million should look at a combination approach. As an example, if your estate needed $2 million of coverage, the spouses could buy $1 million of a second-to-die policy and also purchase a $500,000 single policy on each of their lives. Premiums for such coverage would be approximately 20 percent less than comparable coverage with a single, second-to-die policy.

LIFE EXPECTANCY TABLE

Your age, current health, and lifestyle are the three things that determine how much your insurance premiums will be. As you can see from Exhibit 2-1, the life expectancies of a man and woman at age 40 are 34.7 and 40.4 years, respectively. These same people at age 65 have revised life expectancies of 14.6 and 18.7 years, respectively. In fact, even these numbers are a little pessimistic. They are based on a sampling of Americans across the country as of 1985 and include smokers as well as nonsmokers. Thus, depending on your particular lifestyle, you have a good chance of greatly outliving your life expectancy, particularly in light of medical developments over the past several years.

CANCELING A POLICY: TAX CONSEQUENCES

No tax consequences result when you cancel a term policy, but there may be a taxable event if you drop your whole life insurance policy. If you cancel a policy and the cash value and/or any outstanding loan balance exceeds the sum of your premium payments (what is referred to as the *basis*), then the excess amount is taxable in the calendar year of cancellation. All of the money you receive is treated like ordinary income for tax purposes. This entire figure is added to your other sources of taxable income for that year to determine your tax liability.

Cancellation also triggers income taxes if you have an outstanding loan against your whole life policy. Thus, if you had borrowed $10,000 a year from your policy for each of the past 20 years and for some reason decided to then cancel the policy, you would have to show $200,000 worth of additional income on your tax return for the year (minus the sum of your premium payments)—

EXHIBIT 2–1
Life Expectancy in the United States by Sex

Age in 1985	Both Sexes	Male	Female
35	42	39	45
36	41	38	44
37	40	38	43
38	40	37	42
39	39	36	41
40	38	35	40
41	37	34	40
42	36	33	38
43	35	32	38
44	34	31	37
45	33	30	36
46	32	29	35
47	31	28	34
48	30	28	33
49	30	27	32
50	29	26	31
51	28	25	30
52	27	24	29
53	26	23	28
54	25	22	28
55	24	22	27
56	24	21	26
57	23	20	25
58	22	20	24
59	21	19	23
60	20	18	23
61	20	17	22
62	19	17	21
63	18	16	20
64	18	15	19
65	17	15	19

Source: U.S. National Center for Health Statistics, *Vital Statistics of the United States, 1985.*

despite the fact that you had taken the money out years ago and spent it.

As you can see, cancellation is something you should avoid if a cash value or outstanding loan is involved. If you no longer like the company you are dealing with, transfer your business to another insurer. This is what is known as a *1035 tax-free exchange.* It means that no tax event is triggered since the investment portion of the life insurance policy is being moved over to another company. If you do not want to continue paying premiums, you could purchase a paid-up life insurance policy from your existing carrier. This may result in lower coverage, but it will also avoid a taxable event.

Keep in mind that cancellation and death are two different things. The IRS does not consider death a voluntary event and, therefore, does not punish you or your estate. Presuming the policy is in force, death of the insured wipes out any and all potential income tax events, whether there are outstanding loans or simply cash value.

Now that you have learned about the pros and cons of life insurance, both term and whole life, let us conclude our discussion of life insurance by looking at some of the different riders (options) that can be added to your protection.

POLICY RIDERS

When you buy term or whole life insurance, you can usually add to your protection by purchasing what are known as *riders.* These options become part of your policy. There are two types of riders. One type adds or extends your coverage; the other type protects the policy itself. Extended policy riders include family, accidental death, cost of living, guaranteed insurability, term insurance, and nondeath benefit payments. Riders that protect the policy include waiver of premium, automatic premium loan, and spendthrift. Each of these riders is discussed below.

Family

Family riders provide life insurance for your spouse and/or children. Usually coverage is limited to $10,000 for the spouse and up to $10,000 for each child. The costs are about $300 annually for the spouse and up to $80 per year for each child. A family rider allows you to purchase life insurance on other family members for less cost than taking out separate, nonrelated policies. A family rider is recommended if you are insuring your spouse or if your children are supporting you. Do not buy this rider for your children simply because it is inexpensive or because you have invested a lot of money in them. The chances of your children dying before you die are very slim.

Accidental Death

Also known as *double indemnity*, the accidental death rider increases the death benefit if the insured dies as a result of an accident. The accidental death rider is not recommended. Far more people die of natural causes than from accidents. You are better off increasing your existing coverage.

Cost of Living

A cost-of-living rider indexes your policy to protect its real value. The death benefit increases each year to offset the effects of inflation, as measured by the consumer price index (CPI). This rider is worth considering, particularly if you plan to hold onto your life insurance for five years or longer.

If you purchase $100,000 worth of term or whole life coverage today, its real value will drop to $50,000 in 12 years, assuming an annual inflation rate of 6 percent. A cost-of-living rider would gradually increase the coverage from $100,000 to $200,000 over this same 12-year period.

A cost-of-living rider is particularly helpful if you have a large estate and want the death benefit used to pay estate taxes. The necessary coverage will surely increase in the coming years because of the increased value of your estate, either due to your efforts or to inflation.

Guaranteed Insurability

If you feel that you may not be in good health in later years and may possibly want to increase your coverage sometime in the future, then the guaranteed insurability rider is what you want. It means that you can buy additional whole life coverage based on your age, not your health.

Usually, this rider is available for purchase only when you are young, and there are time limits in which you must purchase the additional coverage; this option usually ends when the insured reaches age 40. It is available only with whole life insurance policies.

For a healthy person, this rider is not generally recommended for three reasons: (1) as you get older, your need for life insurance should decrease, not increase; (2) once this option is purchased, it must be exercised within a set period, otherwise it is lost; and (3) most people are able to buy additional coverage through their existing carrier or with a new company without paying for a special rider.

Term Insurance Rider

A term rider provides extra protection for the least cost, since none of the premium is being diverted to the cash value side of a whole life policy. When the insured later achieves a better financial condition, the term policy can be converted into additional whole life coverage. A term insurance rider is recommended if you need a bigger bang for your insurance buck but still want whole life cash value benefits.

Nondeath Benefit Payments

A nondeath benefit payment rider provides the insured with benefits if an illness or severe injury occurs, such as loss of an eye or limb. The amount of the benefit depends on the body part lost or the duration of the illness. Included under this rider are strokes, heart attacks, and long-term nursing care. Nondeath benefit payment riders are not recommended because of their cost, the amount of the benefit to be received, and the unlikelihood of the illness or injury.

Waiver of Premium

If you become disabled for the period defined in the rider, the insurance company will pay your life insurance premiums for you. This allows you to continue to provide protection for your loved ones in the event you are temporarily or permanently unable to.

Although popular, the waiver-of-premium rider is not recommended for several reasons. First, if you have whole life, the rider *may* end up paying only for your insurance with nothing going toward the cash value. However, most of these riders do provide insurance (to pay the premiums) and cash value benefits. Second, the definition of disability may be narrowly interpreted, and you may find that it does not apply to your situation. Third, there is often a substantial waiting period before the rider becomes effective. A six-month waiting period, retroactive, is commonly used. Fourth, many of these riders cease paying premiums once you reach age 65, even if there is still a disability.

Automatic Premium Loan

This rider protects you in the event you forget to pay one of your whole life premiums. The insurer uses existing dividends or the cash value in your policy to pay the premium. Unlike other riders, this one is free; but you must check off the appropriate box on the application.

Spendthrift

A spendthrift rider protects you from a creditor attaching the cash value in your policy. This rider is available only for whole life insurance. If you think your creditors might take you to court, you may want to consider this optional coverage.

CHECKLIST OF THINGS TO DO

1. Determine if you need life insurance. A single person with no dependents does not need life insurance. Married couples or people living together can also avoid purchasing life insurance if the standard of living would not decrease as a result of the death of either partner. On the other hand, coverage should strongly be considered for anyone raising a family. If you need this type of insurance, the National Insurance Consumer Organization (NICO) recommends coverage that equals at least seven times the annual

income of the person being insured (this figure would be reduced by any other policies you had at work or privately owned).

2. If you are the homemaker, do not rule out life insurance. Ask yourself who would take care of the home (children, cleaning, cooking, etc.); this may be the equivalent of a $20–30,000 job. If your services could be replaced for, say, $25,000 a year, then you should look at a policy with a death benefit in the range of $300,000.

3. If you already own life insurance, contact other companies and get some comparison quotes; you will be surprised to see the range in premiums. If your policy includes any riders, review them in light of the information given about the different types of riders in the latter part of this chapter.

4. You can contact several sources that will give you price quotes on life insurance: (a) Insurance Information, Inc., of Hyannis, Massachusetts (800–472–5800)—for $50 you will get the names of five insurers that offer some of the cheapest term policies; (b) Selectquote of San Francisco (800–343–1985) will send you a comparison list of several companies showing the cost over the next 5, 10, 15, and 20 years—the service is free; (c) InsuranceQuote of Chandler, Arizona (800–972–1104), will send you a free list of policy prices; (d) TermQuote of Dayton, Ohio (800–444–TERM), will send you a list of information on six companies for free. Each of these services will also send you brief descriptions of each policy recommended.

5. If the standard or quality of living of your loved ones would not decline if you die and you have life insurance, contact your agent or broker about dropping your policy(s). A word of warning: The person who sold you the policy receives renewal commissions every year you pay your premium. It is not likely that your broker or agent will share your beliefs that coverage is no longer needed. Be prepared for a fight. This is not something that should be automatic, however. The policy you have may be mature enough wherein its cash value is now growing at a competitive rate. Or, your estate may not be liquid enough to pay any estate tax liability without the forced sale of a business, real estate, or volatile stock.

6. Avoid any insurance endorsed or promoted by a celebrity. This type of coverage is usually very expensive for what you get, and there are often several exceptions. Speaking of things to stay away from, drop any mortgage-life insurance you might have. This

type of term coverage is some of the most expensive insurance you can get.

7. If you think you are the *beneficiary* of a policy that cannot be found, send a self-addressed, stamped envelope to the American Council of Life Insurance, Missing Policy Service, 1001 Pennsylvania Ave., N.W. Washington, DC, 20004, with a request for a policy-search questionnaire.

Chapter Three

Health and Disability Insurance

Disability Insurance.
Health Insurance
Medicare
Medicaid
Long-Term Health Care Insurance

I do not know anyone who does not have automobile insurance. Most people I know also have fire insurance on their home. Granted, a house and car are two of the most valuable assets we acquire during our lifetime, but both can be replaced. Many people who have car and homeowner's insurance do not have adequate health or disability insurance. It almost seems as though people value their possessions more than themselves. To put it into proper perspective, ask yourself who is going to fix you up if you get broken or damaged?

Life, disability, and health insurance are things you need to be informed about: They are an essential part of retirement planning. Lack of or inadequate coverage in one or more of these areas can ruin what otherwise would have been an enjoyable retirement.

To give you an idea as to what can happen to you if you do not have adequate protection in this area, look at the "Net Worth Worksheet" in Chapter One, Setting Goals. Look at one of the final lines, the one called "Total value of assets." If you become disabled and do not have adequate disability insurance, you can start *subtracting* a couple of thousand dollars *each month* from this figure. How long will such erosion last? If your disability is "average," continue reducing your net worth for several years.

Insurance is simply a vehicle that transfers the risk of loss from you (the insured) to someone else (the insurance company). Like auto insurance, the premiums you pay may seem like a waste of money, but such protection is certainly welcome when the unexpected accident occurs. Never lose sight of the fact that insurance is a necessary evil; lack of or improper coverage may be the only thing that stands between you and a great retirement.

DISABILITY INSURANCE

Life insurance is the most complex form of coverage since it offers so many options, methods of purchase, duration of coverage, and means of creating cash values. Disability insurance is much easier to understand and more important to have.

If one or more people are dependent on you financially, life insurance may be a virtual necessity. Sometimes, an individual or couple may be unable to purchase both life and disability coverage. The example described in the next few paragraphs illustrates how important disability insurance is.

You are willing to spend only a certain amount of income or savings for insurance. If your budget is limited and you had to choose between buying life insurance or disability coverage, which would you choose? Well, the answer is simple: first buy disability.

Disability insurance should be your first choice for two reasons. First, if you become disabled you are still a consumer and will have housing, clothing, food, therapy, and medical expenses. The disability also may require extensive changes within your home: widening doorways, adding ramps, changing countertop levels, and so on. If you are unable to work, who is going to support you and your family? Over 40 percent of all mortgage foreclosures are the result of disability. Second, the chances of disability, even at age 65, are much greater than the chances of dying. The insurance industry chart in Exhibit 3–1 shows the chances of death versus disability at different ages. As you can see, the chances of long-term

EXHIBIT 3–1
Death versus Disability (select ages)

Age	Probability of > 90-Day Disability per 1,000 Lives	Probability of Death per 1,000 Lives	Probability of Disability as a Multiple of Probability of Death
22	7	0.9	7.5
32	8	1.2	6.6
42	13	3	4.3
52	23	8	2.8
62	45	21	2.2

disability for a male age 52 are almost three times greater than the probability of death.

At every age between 20 and 65, you are more likely to become disabled than die. There is an 11 percent chance that a 40-year-old male will die before reaching age 65; his odds of becoming disabled before 65 are 20 percent. The average duration of a disability that lasts over nine months is more than two years.

Insurance statistics concerning the length of disability and chances of recovery are also revealing. If the disability commences at age 57 and lasts for one year, there is a 73 percent chance that the disability will continue for an additional two years and a 55 percent chance that it will continue for an additional five years. The probability of being disabled for three months or more between the ages of 35 and 65 is about 33 percent. The average length of those disabilities will be over five years, and 30 percent of these will never recover. Although disability, unlike death, is not a certainty, it is far more likely for persons under age 60 than death.

Few People Covered

Three out of four Americans are not covered by disability insurance. Most people *believe* that their odds of becoming disabled are remote or that if a disability occurs, their employer's policy will provide the needed coverage. According to the Life Insurance Marketing and Research Association, fewer than 20 percent of upper-

EXHIBIT 3–2
Assets and Cost of Insurance Coverage

Your home is worth $ _____	Your homeowner's insurance premium is $ _____
Your cars are worth $ _____	Your auto insurance premiums total $ _____
Your total earnings from now until retirement are $ _____	Amount spent each year to protect your annual earnings $ _____

middle income people have individual disability policies, yet over 90 percent of this same group have individual life insurance coverage.

The majority of us probably feel that if disability were to occur, we could rely on social security, invade our savings or, if married, rely on our spouse's income. Unfortunately, none of these things is very likely or dependable. First, close to two thirds of social security claims for disability are denied. If you do collect, the maximum benefit is $1,500 a month. California, Hawaii, New Jersey, New York, and Rhode Island provide benefits to their residents, but the coverage is normally limited to six months of benefits—benefits tied to that state's maximum unemployment payment. Second, invading your savings may be only temporary relief. If you save 7 percent of your income each year, six months of disability could wipe our nearly five years of investing. One year of disability will erase over 15 years of savings for most couples. Third, a working spouse is probably already strained taking care of the house, raising children, and earning an income. You will be lucky if this "extra" income is enough to provide you with nursing and rehabilitation care; there is little likelihood that it will offset your loss of salary.

What Things Are You Protecting Now?

Fill out the table in Exhibit 3–2, and then see if your priorities are really in the right order. Do not think that your company has sufficient coverage. Less than 20 percent of the working population has long-term disability protection through their employer.

There are five things to look at when purchasing disability insurance: (1) definition of disability, (2) elimination period, (3) length of protection, (4) amount of monthly benefits, and (5) cost. Each of these five areas is discussed below.

Defining Disability

Disability policies are written in one of two ways: *own occupation* or *any occupation*. *Own occupation*, sometimes referred to as *own occ*, means that you are protected if you cannot perform the job you have been trained for. As an example, if a right-handed surgeon was unable to use her right hand, she would receive full benefits. This, despite the fact that she might be able to be retrained to use her left hand or take on an administrative or teaching position within the hospital or university. *Any occupation*, sometimes referred to as *any occ*, means that coverage can be denied or reduced if you are disabled but could perform some other kind of work. Even though own occ is more expensive, do not consider any other type of coverage.

Group policies often define disability as "any occupation." Since you probably do not want to perform just any job, purchase supplemental coverage unless your company has "own occupation" coverage and it fulfills the criteria listed below.

Elimination Period

Elimination period, also known as the waiting period, determines how long the disability must last before coverage begins. The most common elimination periods are one, three, or six months. The longer the time until coverage begins, the less expensive the premiums will be. A six-month elimination period may be 35 percent cheaper than a one-month waiting period.

The decision as to what elimination period to choose depends on other sources of family income and the value of your savings. If your nest egg is large enough to support you and your family for several months, choose the longest elimination period possible, thereby decreasing insurance costs. On the other hand, if you have no savings, a short waiting period should be chosen. The typical group policy provided by employers has a 180-day waiting period before benefits begin. If you can survive for this long, fine; otherwise look into additional coverage.

Length of Protection

Disability protection can be purchased for any length of time, ranging from a couple of years to death. Some people want coverage only for a few years because they cannot afford long-term protection. Others may choose short-term benefits because a positive financial event looms in the near future (spouse will be going back to work, college costs will end soon, home mortgage will soon be paid off, inheritance is expected from a relative in poor health, and so on). The majority of people who buy disability insurance seek coverage until age 65. At this point, government assistance programs such as medicare or medicaid would step in. Some people feel that public help will not be enough or may not be there when needed and therefore choose to buy coverage for life.

Amount of Monthly Benefits

If one becomes disabled, the amount of coverage depends on earned income. Up to 70 percent of salary, commission, and bonuses can be paid for by disability insurance. Unlike life insurance, there is a cap on the amount of the monthly benefits. If, as an example, you were earning $50,000 a year, your maximum coverage would be $35,000 annually, regardless of the number of policies you had in force.

If you have a group policy, find out what is covered. Some policies do not include certain forms of income such as bonuses, deferred compensation, 401(k), or IRA contributions. Company coverage normally is limited to 60 percent of salary or wages. Benefits paid from group policies are normally fully taxable, and therefore your true benefit may be much less than expected. For example, a 60 percent benefit that is taxed 33 percent (state and federal brackets combined) leaves you with only 40 percent of your income. This could be reduced even further since employer policy benefits are offset by any benefits received from social security. Individual policies, on the other hand, provide benefits that are normally tax-free and can be structured so that there is no social security offset. These are two more reasons to look into additional coverage.

If a disability occurs and one insurer discovers that you have multiple policies, each company would reduce its monthly payment to you even though you had been paying each of them their required premiums. The reductions would be prorated among the insurers paying out the benefits. You are still entitled to coverage, but such coverage cannot cumulatively exceed 70 percent of your earned income. Such limitation is done in the public's interest. It would not be right for someone to earn more money disabled than in the workplace.

The benefits you receive are free from income taxes unless the premiums were paid by your employer *and* such expenses were deducted by the company. The IRS will let you have it either way, but not both. If the boss wants to deduct the premiums he is paying on your behalf, that is fine; if there are disability benefits later paid out, they would be fully taxable to you. If you pay your own premiums, then they would not be deductible in most cases, and, as such, the benefits would be received tax-free as long as they lasted.

Most group policies are not indexed for inflation. Check to see if your monthly disability benefit will increase with time.

Disability Policies: Individual versus Group

The worksheet in Exhibit 3–3 will help you compare your company's disability policy with one that you might currently have or are looking into.

Price

Once you have determined the type, elimination period, desired duration of benefits, and amount of coverage, you are ready to shop price. Normally, it is better to deal with someone who represents several disability carriers. Assuming all things are equal, choose the least expensive policy from a financially sound insurance company.

HEALTH INSURANCE

With proper financial planning, you are almost assured of a comfortable retirement. In such a case, only two things could then

EXHIBIT 3-3
Comparisons of Individual and Group Disability Coverage

	Individual	Group
Benefits Payable When Unable to Perform		
Own occupation	Yes	
Due to partial disability	Yes	
Maximum Monthly Benefit		
Max percent of salary and wages	70–75%	
Max percent of commissions, bonuses	70–75%	
Max percent of deferred compensation (IRA, 401k)	100%	
Monthly dollar limit	Up to $25,000	
Net Benefits		
Are benefits taxable?	No	Yes
Are benefits reduced by social security, employer or state disability payments?	No	Yes
Elimination Period		
Days disabled before benefits begin	As low as 30 days	
Duration of Benefits When Unable to Perform		
Own occupation	Up to age 65	
Any occupation	Beyond 65	
Inflation Protection		
Will disability benefits rise with the cost of living?	Yes (optional)	
Continuity of Coverage		
Will coverage cease if you leave employer?	No	Usually
Can policy be cancelled?	No	Yes
Can coverage be unfavorably altered?	No	Yes
Can policy premiums increase?	No	Yes

destroy your future: lack of, or insufficient, disability or health insurance coverage. Close to 40 million people have no health insurance. In the real world, this means that these people are not adequately protected. Make sure you are covered. Health insurance coverage comes in several forms: individual policies, group coverage, and government benefits.

Government Benefits

State and federally funded programs are covered in detail in a future chapter, but a quick review of government benefits and limitations may be helpful here. Medicare partially pays medical bills for people who are 65 or older. On average, medicare pays only about 50 percent of heath care costs for the elderly, down from 80 percent in 1965. Medicaid does not have an age limit, but it is only for the poor. Benefits are also offered by the Veterans Administration. You may be entitled to compensation from one or more of these agencies.

Individual Policies

Individual policies can be purchased from an insurance provider, such as Blue Cross or Blue Shield, or through agents and brokers. Buying individual or family policies can be expensive. Premiums can be significantly reduced by opting for a large deductible. If you have a net worth of over $50,000, look at the premium savings with a $2,500 or $5,000 deductible. Your concern here is to make sure that you are protected against catastrophic losses. Your portfolio might never recover from a $50,000 or $300,000 medical bill.

The biggest problem with individual policies is that the applicant may not be able to obtain coverage if he or she has a significant existing health problem. If a policy can be obtained, it may contain so many exclusions that the actual coverage is minimal.

Group Policies

A group is defined as an organization of people who share something in common. The group may be composed of employees from the same company, a union, religious order, fraternal society, or any other identifiable collection of people. Group health insurance offers two big benefits: cost and coverage. Since the insurer is dealing with a large number of people, the cost per person is often less than that of individual or family policies. With groups of 10 or more, coverage is enhanced since most forms of group policies cover preexisting conditions. Medical examinations usually are not required with group policies, and the benefits are often greater than those found under individual or family policies.

If you are thinking of changing jobs before retirement, look into the benefits offered by the prospective new employer. If you have any health problems, find out if the new coverage has a waiting period for pre-existing conditions. Also find out how the new employer's coverage stacks up against your existing company's. Health insurance and retirement benefits are two of the most important perks of a job; make sure you are fully informed before you make the transition.

Recent court decisions are telling employers that once they start providing retiree health insurance to an individual they must continue it and cannot significantly cut it back; there is also a new requirement from the Financial Accounting Standards Board that such liabilities (providing health coverage to retirees) be calculated and reported. Employers now realize that their health insurance liability is real. The labor department has estimated that the liability is at least $125 billion with annual growth of $5 billion. Others have placed the amount as high as $2 trillion for just the 500 largest corporations.

Coverage between Jobs

If you are covered by an employer's or union's group policy and you lose coverage for any reason (e.g., termination, death of your spouse, children reaching adulthood or divorce), you are entitled to continued coverage for a certain period of time. You are entitled to coverage for up to three years from the date of the employee's death. Premiums must still be paid by the survivors. The same thing is true for employee spouses who are not eligible for medicare. Employee coverage normally ends when the worker reaches age 65, but coverage can continue for up to three years for a younger spouse and children.

Converting Group Coverage to an Individual Policy

If you convert from group to individual coverage, you pay the full premium yourself. The converted coverage is usually more expensive and covers less than continued group coverage but costs about the same as comparable health insurance purchased individually. An advantage of converting an existing policy is that converted policies usually do not exclude coverage for pre-existing conditions—health conditions you had prior to purchasing the policy. Moreover, you do not have to take a medical examination or submit a medical history, as you might be required to do if you applied for individual health insurance coverage on your own.

Group plans underwritten by commercial insurers usually include a conversion privilege for persons who leave their jobs prior to age 65. These converted coverages often cannot be renewed past age 65. If you are retiring before age 65 and are considering the purchase of individual health insurance, be sure to find out whether a policy can be renewed past age 65 and, if so, what kinds of benefits are provided. Usually, benefits are modified when you reach age 65 and become eligible for medicare.

MEDICARE

Over the next five years, the elderly's use of medical services will increase 50 percent faster than the total population. Currently the over 65 population consumes one third of total medical care services. The United States has been more successful than any nation in history in building an economic security structure for its people. The medicare system provides cash income, savings, and insurance against such risks as unemployment, poor health, disability, or death. Social security began paying benefits in 1939, medicare in 1965.

Medicare is a federal health insurance program for persons 65 or older, and you are eligible for coverage whether you are still working or retired. It also covers people of any age who have permanent kidney failure and certain disabilities. The program is overseen by the Health Care Financing Administration of the U.S. Department of Health and Human Services. This administration sets the standards that hospitals, skilled nursing facilities, home health agencies, and hospices must meet to be certified as qualified providers. Social security offices across the country can take applications for medicare and also provide general information about the program.

When Medicare Is Available

You apply for medicare automatically when you apply for social security benefits. If you plan to retire after age 65, apply for medicare separately. Your spouse also qualifies for medicare at age 65 (even if you are not yet 65) if you are entitled to monthly social security benefits. If you do not want to delay coverage or possibly increase the costs to you, enroll in medicare no sooner than three months before and no later than four months after you become eligible.

The medicare program has two parts. Part A is hospital insurance (HI), part B is supplementary medical insurance (SMI). HI (part A) covers institutional care, including care in the following: inpatient hospital, skilled nursing home, home health, and, under certain circumstances, hospice. Part A is financed mostly by social security taxes. SMI (part B) deals primarily with doctors' fees (regardless of where the services are rendered), most outpatient hospital services, physical therapy, ambulance trips, medical equipment, prostheses, and a number of other services not covered under part A. SMI is financed from monthly premiums paid by those who enroll in the program, as well as payments from the federal government and certain related services. The government's share of the costs far exceeds that paid by the enrollees.

When you enroll in part A of medicare, you also automatically enroll in part B, unless you tell the Social Security Administration that you do not want it. A 65-year-old individual enrolled in part B in 1991, paid premiums of $29.90 per month during 1991. These premiums, which pay only about a fourth of the cost of part B, are ordinarily deducted from your social security checks. If you enroll late or drop out and enroll again, you may have to pay higher premiums. You will pay 10 percent more for each 12 full months that you did not participate when you were eligible. Monthly premiums are adjusted every January.

If you are not eligible for part A, you can still obtain the hospital insurance plan if you are 65 or older, enrolled in part B, and pay premiums of $177 a month.

EXHIBIT 3-4
Summary of Part A Benefits

First 60 days you pay a $628 deductible	Days 61–90 you pay $157 a day	Days 91–150 you pay $314 a day (this is your one-time lifetime exclusion)	Days 151 and beyond you pay all costs

Benefits under Hospital Insurance (Part A)

Part A covers persons 65 or older and persons who have received disability benefits from social security for at least two years. The hospital insurance will cover the cost of inpatient hospital care for up to 90 days in each benefit period. The patient pays a $628 deductible for the first 60 days. If hospital care goes beyond 60 days, the patient must pay $157 a day from day 61 to day 90. There are also 60 additional lifetime reserve days that will cost you $314 per day. These additional 60 days take effect from day 91 of hospitalization through day 150. These 60 days can be used only once during your lifetime, unlike your first 90 days of coverage, which are renewed after you have been out of the hospital for at least 60 days. See Exhibit 3–4 for a summary of benefits.

As an example, let us suppose that you were hospitalized for 160 days and the cost was $500 per day. The first 60 days would cost you $628. The next 30 days would come to $4,710 ($157 × 30). If you then decided to use all of your lifetime reserve days, the next 60 days would be covered at a cost of $18,840 (60 days × $314 per day). The final 10 days would be your full responsibility and would cost you $5,000 more ($500 a day charged by the hospital times 10 days). Your total expense would come to $29,178. Without medicare coverage, your bill would have been $80,000 (160-day stay × $500 per day). Despite the tremendous financial help medicare provides, you may want to consider purchasing a supplemental policy from a private insurer (discussed at the end of this chapter).

Skilled nursing facility. Part A also covers skilled nursing care after your hospitalization for up to 100 days in each benefit period. For medicare purposes, a skilled nursing facility is defined as a nursing home, a wing or ward of a hospital or a part of an old-age home that has: (1) 24-hour nursing service, (2) doctor supervision for each patient, (3) certification by the state, (4) at least one registered nurse employed full time, and (5) the primary goal of providing skilled nursing care or rehabilitation for injured, disabled, or sick people.

Medicare covers up to 100 days of skilled nursing care in each benefit period. There are no limits to the number of benefit periods you can have. The first 20 days of such posthospital care are free. The next 80 days will cost you $78.50 per day. After 100 days of coverage, the patient must pay the full cost of the skilled nursing care facility.

Whether or not you decide to buy additional forms of coverage from an insurance company, consider strongly the protection afforded by part B. The cost of this extra coverage is nominal, and its protection covers several areas not addressed by part A. As an example, the basic hospital insurance plan (part A) does not pay for the services of a doctor, surgeon, pathologist, radiologist, private duty nurse, or psychiatrist.

Benefits under Supplementary Medical Insurance (Part B)

Unlike part A, which is compulsory, part B is voluntary; it is offered to almost everyone age 65 or older. The patient pays the first $100 of the covered services in each calendar year (the annual deductible). The plan then pays 80 percent of the approved charges for the following services:

Doctor and surgeon services, whether furnished in a hospital, clinic, office, home, or elsewhere.

Home health care visits, if not covered under your hospital insurance.

X rays and other diagnostic tests.

Outpatient physical therapy and speech pathology.

Radium and radioactive isotope therapy.

Surgical dressings and rental of durable medical equipment.

Ambulance transportation.

Services and supplies relating to a doctor's services, including drugs that cannot be self-administered.

Dentist bills for jaw or facial bone surgery.

Comprehensive outpatient rehabilitation facility services; therapy and supplies are included.

The cost of pap smears for early detection of cervical cancer.

Partial hospitalization services incident to a doctor's services.

You do not have to pay the $100 deductible or the 20 percent coinsurance if: (1) a second opinion is required by medicare, (2) you need home health care services, or (3) you need outpatient diagnostic laboratory tests.

What Is Not Covered by Medicare

Medicare does not cover things that are not "reasonable and necessary" for the diagnosis or treatment of an illness or injury. Furthermore, it does not cover "custodial care." Custodial care includes help in walking, getting in and out of a bed, bathing, dressing, eating, and taking medicine. Therefore, if someone is in a hospital or skilled nursing facility mainly for custodial purposes, he would not be covered. If you are placed in a facility where the kind of care needed could be provided elsewhere, your stay would not be considered "reasonable," and you would not be covered by medicare. The same is true if you stay at a hospital or nursing care facility longer than necessary. Last, you are not covered for doctor's visits that are considered "excess."

Medigap Insurance

Since there are so many exclusions under medicare, you may wish to purchase insurance from the private sector to fill in the gaps. The purpose of this additional coverage, known as medigap or medicare supplemental insurance, is to cover deductibles, copayments, excess charges and exclusions not paid by medicare.

Individual medicare supplements, or *medigaps*, may be purchased from various insurance companies. Medigap policies typically pay many of the medicare deductibles and coinsurance charges for services covered by medicare and pay for additional days of hospital coverage. A good medigap plan will pay the part A hospital deductible, coinsurance charges for hospital stays up to 90 days (and 60 lifetime reserve days), coinsurance charges for skilled nursing home stays up to 100 days, 90 percent or more of the cost of 365 additional days in the hospital, and the 20 percent coinsurance portion of the medicare-defined "reasonable" medical charges. Some plans also pay part or all of the part B deductible or pay for additional skilled nursing-home services.

Several hundred insurers provide this type of coverage. Before purchasing a medigap policy, take the following steps:

Review several policies offered by different companies with different agents.

Look for the words "medicare supplement" on the policy; this means that the policy meets the minimum federal and state standards for doctor and hospital care.

Do not buy more than one policy; if it is good it should cover most, if not all, of your needs.

Think about what benefits you may need in the future; then look at what services are not covered by the policy you are considering.

Federal law requires all insurers to give you a 30-day "free look." If, after receiving the policy there is something about it you do not like, you have up to 30 days to return it for a full refund.

MEDICAID

Medicaid is funded by state and federal governments. It pays for extended nursing home care. You must be 65 or older, blind, or physically or mentally disabled. Medicaid is a means-tested program. Individuals applying for medical assistance must document their income and resources. States, which manage the medicaid program under general guidance from the federal government, determine whether individuals are poor enough to qualify for assistance. Many elderly today have income in excess of the qualifying standards (described on p. 52). Thus, when confronting the catastrophic costs of a nursing home placement, they either must spend down their resources to meet the income test, or divest their assets and become prematurely impoverished.

LONG-TERM HEALTH CARE INSURANCE

Long-term care provides nursing and at-home care. According to the Health Association of America (HIAA), by the year 2000, more than 8 million Americans age 65 and older will probably need some form of long-term care due to disability or chronic illness. It is estimated that two of five people who are at least age 65 will enter a nursing home. Half of these people will end up staying six months or less, half for a little less than three years, and a small number longer than five years. Long-term health care costs run anywhere from $30,000 to $40,000 per year. On average, medicare pays for 2 percent of the nursing home care for the nation.

Nursing home care is the third largest segment in the health care industry following hospital and physician services. Service capacity has tripled in less than 20 years. One of every 10 dollars of personal health care expenditures flows to nursing homes.

Contrasted with the acute care sector, the nursing home sector is an economic giant. Nursing homes outnumber hospitals three to one. There are more nursing home beds than hospital beds. Nearly twice as many patient days are delivered in the long-term care setting as in the acute setting—and it is care delivered at one eighth of the cost! While hospitals struggle to operate two-thirds full, nursing homes' occupancy rates average nearly 95 percent.

Medicare covers 100 days of skilled nursing care. Some people are then forced to spend down their personal assets until they qualify for medicaid. Only after most of your assets are spent and gone will your stay in a nursing home be covered by the government. Medicaid ends up paying for 40 percent of the nation's nursing home care. According to the United States Health Cooperative, men over 65 have a 30 percent chance of entering a nursing home sometime in their future. Women over age 65 have a 54 percent chance. The average stay in a nursing home is over one year. Eleven percent of nursing home residents stay over three years. On a positive note, 31 percent of nursing home stays last from one to three months.

Despite these mostly dismal figures, only an estimated 3 percent of persons age 50 and over own a private long-term care insurance plan. Yet, at least 40 percent of all seniors can afford such coverage. This is largely because most of us cannot bring ourselves to believe that some day we may be a patient in a nursing home. People buy this type of insurance for one or more of the following reasons:

- To protect family assets in the event of a long-term confinement.
- To make sure that their children or other loved ones are not saddled with the burden.
- To be able to afford high quality care rather than spending down their net worth and ending up in a medicaid facility that will probably not be of the same quality.
- To preserve the lifestyle of the healthy spouse.

You should look into long-term coverage if you are 65 or older if you wish to preserve your estate or want to determine the quality of nursing care you might later receive. When reviewing these policies, ask the following questions:

- What is exactly covered?
- Must certain conditions such as prior hospitalization exist before you are eligible?
- Is the policy guaranteed as to renewability?
- What are the policy's time and dollar limits per stay?
- What does the policy pay now and five years from now?
- What pre-existing limitations are there?

Using Your Life Insurance to Pay for Coverage

Many life insurance policies will pay you a percentage of the death benefit during your lifetime, provided you are either receiving long-term care or are diagnosed as having a terminal illness. Two types of riders might be helpful: a long-term care rider and the living benefit rider.

The *long-term care rider* provides money while the insured is receiving long-term care. Benefits are paid monthly, and they are based on a percentage of the face amount of the policy up to a monthly maximum. Insurance companies pay anywhere from 50 to 100 percent of the death benefit for long-term care. The *living benefit rider* pays a percentage of the death benefit if the insured is terminally ill or contracts a named catastrophic illness.

Determining if You Need Long-Term Coverage

Whether nursing home insurance makes sense for you depends mostly on your age, health, and financial condition. In general, such coverage may not be a good deal for people in their 50s and early 60s, despite the low premiums at those ages, because the risk of having to check into a nursing home is small. The chances of needing nursing home care increases dramatically with age. The odds are only 1 in 100 that you will have to enter a nursing home between the ages of 65 and 74, but they rise to 7 in 100 if you are between 74 and 84, and to 23 in 100 after age 85.

Long-term care is defined as up to lifetime coverage in either a nursing home or in the home of the insured. A survey conducted by the Government Accounting Office disclosed that policy costs range from as low as $200 a year to as high as $7,000, depending on age, health condition, and coverage. If you wait until you're 70 or older to buy coverage, you can plan on paying at least $1,000 a year; in most cases, a person nearing 80 should not have to pay more than about $3,000 for a policy with good coverage. Average annual cost of long-term health care insurance: age 50—$350 per year; age 65—$1,000 per year; age 80—$3,000 per year.

A top-of-the-line policy will pay benefits for an unlimited number of days for each nursing home stay and unlimited days for your cumulative stays. Less expensive policies limit the number of days per stay and the total number of days allowed cumulatively for all stays. To receive benefits for a repeat stay, you must in some cases have been out of a nursing home for at least 180 days.

CHECKLIST OF THINGS TO DO

1. If you are working, get disability insurance. If you are covered by a company plan, chances are that your coverage is only moderate; look into supplemental coverage.

2. Contact your company's benefits coordinator for a description of your health coverage. If you are not covered, telephone Blue Cross or Blue Shield for individual policy quotes. Make sure coverage includes major medical. Concentrate on those policies that are either conditionally renewable, guaranteed renewable, or noncancellable. If supplemental health care coverage is needed, review your spouse's work coverage to make sure that there will not be an overlap in benefits.

3. If you or your parents are in their late 60s, consider long-term health care insurance. Postponement of this type of coverage is recommended for as long as possible because of the numerous areas not covered by most insurers. For information and a list of companies that offer long-term health care insurance, write for a free copy of *The Consumer's Guide to Long-Term Care Insurance*, Health Insurance Association of America, P.O. Box 41455, Washington, DC, 20018. You may also telephone them at 1–800–423–8000.

4. Keep in mind that one in four people 65 years and older will enter a nursing home before their death. For more information on long-term care insurance: American Association of Homes for the Aging (202–296–5960); Division of National Cost Estimate (301–965–8243); National Center for Health Statistics (301–436–8830); and *Before You Buy: A Guide to Long-Term Care Insurance*, single copies available free from the AARP, 1909 K Street, N.W., Washington, DC, 20049.

5. When you are shopping for health insurance, follow these tips:

Buy group coverage whenever possible—it is almost always cheaper and can end up covering someone who could not get individual coverage due to some preexisting condition.

If you are in good health, take an exam—companies that refuse health risks can offer cheaper rates than those that are not as discriminating.

Opt for a big deductible—a $2,500 deductible may cost you 30 to 50 percent less than a $100 deductible policy.

Make sure the policy is "guaranteed renewable"—you want to make sure that coverage cannot be cancelled and will last until medicare kicks in at age 65.

6. When a medical or health need arises, do the following to reduce your costs and/or ensure better quality:

Telephone doctors and medical facilities recommended to you and ask what they charge for routine exams, their daily room rates, and so on.

Ask your doctor what hospitals he or she likes and then find out what their charges are.

Get advice from your doctor or nurse by telephone whenever possible.

If you are on medicare, look for a doctor who "accepts assignment"—this will save you from paying any excess charges.

If surgery is needed, make sure everyone on the team also accepts assignment if medicare is being used.

If a specialist is needed, make sure he or she is "board certified"—this means that the doctor has met certain standards as set forth by the AMA.

Get itemized bills so that you do not end up paying for something you never received.

Do not opt for hospital procedures that can be done less expensively in a clinic.

Compare drug prices at several pharmacies—prices can vary by quite a bit.

7. Even though you may be covered for disability by a company or union plan, worker's compensation, social security, and/or veteran's insurance, chances are that such coverage is not enough. Since you will probably need additional coverage, look for private policies that include the following language or benefits:

Benefits that last until age 65 (or earlier if you plan on retiring before age 65).

A noncancellable policy.

The greatest coverage possible (this is usually up to 75 percent of your salary up to certain limits).

A policy that defines disability as "own occ" (your specific occupation).

A "residual benefits" clause (which means you can still receive some benefits if you end up going back to work part time.

A 90-day elimination period (180 days is even better)—if you can live off your savings or investments for the first 90–180 days of disability, your premiums may be slashed by up to 35 percent.

A nonsmoker discount if you do not smoke.

8. When shopping for disability insurance, make sure you check out annually renewable disability income policies (ARDI)—premium costs increase each year but initial costs may be 25 to 50 percent less than what you would pay for traditional disability coverage.

Chapter Four

Social Security

Complaining about income taxes is almost universal. Nobody likes to pay them, and most people think they pay too much. I rarely hear people complain about paying social security taxes. Yet, for most Americans, social security taxes are greater than income taxes. One would think that people would want to know how the system works. After all, when it comes to government programs, this is one of the few that seems to work.

Best known as a source of retirement income, social security also functions as a multipurpose insurance policy. If you die, your family will receive monthly checks. If you are seriously disabled, social security will replace part of your monthly income. At age 65, you are covered for health and medical expenses. As you can see from the Chapter One pie chart (Exhibit 1-6), "Sources of Retirement Income," this government-sponsored program will play an integral role in your retirement. To get all of these benefits, just make sure that you have paid social security taxes for a long enough time.

The social security system provides four types of benefits: medical insurance (also known as medicare), disability payments if you are unable to work for a prolonged period of time, survivor's benefits for family members, and retirement benefits. Social security was enacted into law with the passage of the Social Security Act of 1935.

Social security and medicare will pay out over $400 billion in benefits this year. Most of these benefits will be tax free. If you are not one of the 140 million people paying into the system, then you are probably one of the 40 million receiving benefits. Over $450 billion in social security taxes was collected from workers last year. To put this figure in perspective, almost the same amount was collected in individual income taxes, and approximately $150 billion was raised by corporate income taxes.

The social security system is not just for the retired. Close to half of all benefits paid out go to disabled workers, families of employees who have retired, become disabled or died, and to those people eligible for medicare. It is important that you know how the system works since there is a strong likelihood that you are now paying for benefits you will be receiving in the future. Some people are paying as much as $8,170 (15.3 percent of $53,400) into social security each year. Most families pay more social security and medicare taxes than federal income taxes.

Based on current maximum rates, the amount of money set aside for workers, their contributions plus those made by their employers, over a 40-year period would be close to $325,000 per employee. Based on current life expectancies, the expected payout for an employee with a nonworking spouse is a little less than $400,000.

When calculating your retirement income, do not forget the obvious—social security. On average, it constitutes almost 30 percent of one's income in later years. Almost everyone is eligible for these benefits, yet few know how to determine their benefits, the different eligibility dates, or how to make sure that they have been credited with all of their contributions.

COMPUTING YOUR CONTRIBUTION

The social security system is funded by employer and employee contributions. For 1991 and beyond, your company will pay 7.65 percent of your earnings; as an employee you are required to match this amount. Both percentage figures apply to your gross earned income up to $53,400. No employer or employee contributions are made for any earned income above this figure. All salaries, wages, tips, bonuses, and commissions you receive are taxed for social security and credited to your earnings record. The first six months of sick pay are also taxed. The social security tax is withheld from every paycheck until the maximum taxable amount for the year is reached.

If you are self-employed, you will pay social security taxes of 15.3 percent on the first $53,400 of your earned income and nothing thereafter. By being your own boss, you can deduct one half of your social security liability from your income tax liability.

Capital gains, interest, dividends, rents, and royalties are not subject to social security tax. Payments from almost all employee benefit plans are also excluded from social security taxes.

Taxes after Retirement

Although social security benefits are tax free for most people, those with incomes above a certain level may have up to half of their social security benefits taxed. The threshold income levels are $25,000 for single persons, $32,000 for married couples filing joint returns, and zero for married couples filing separate returns if they live together at any time during the year. Income from all sources, including interest from tax-free bonds, plus half of social security benefits are used to compute the threshold amount.

As an example, let us suppose that you are married, file a joint return, and have the following sources of income:

$10,000 from stock dividends.

$ 6,000 interest from government bonds.

$15,000 interest from tax-free municipal bonds.

$ 2,000 capital gains profit from the sale of a mutual fund.

$ 9,000 in annual benefits from social security.

To find out if up to one half of your social security benefits are taxable, add up all of these sources of income, but include only one half of the money received from social security. Thus, the total in this example would be: $10,000 + $6,000 + $15,000 + $2,000 +

$4,500 ($\frac{1}{2}$ of your social security benefits) = $37,500. As a married couple, you can now subtract $32,000. The resulting figure, $5,500, or $4,500 ($\frac{1}{2}$ of your social security benefits), whichever is less, would be taxable. Since $4,500 is less than $5,500, you would now have to pay federal income taxes on $4,500; your exact tax liability would depend on your tax bracket.

WHO GETS BENEFITS AND WHEN

You are entitled to full benefits if you retired at age 65. This is what is known as the "normal retirement age." You also qualify for reduced benefits if you retire at age 62. These ages are being changed, whether or not the changes affect you depends on when you were born. If you were born before 1938, you are not affected by the changes. If you were born between 1938 and 1942, you will have to wait an extra two months for each year after 1937 to collect full benefits. If you were born between 1943 and 1954, you will have to wait until you reach age 66 to collect full benefits. Finally, if you were born in 1960 or later, you will have to be 67 before you reach the "normal retirement age." See Exhibit 4-1 for situations in which you and/or your spouse and children may receive social security benefits.

After you have applied for benefits, your first check should arrive within 33 days after you retire. Thereafter, your check should arrive on the third day of the month. The Social Security Administration prefers to deposit your benefits into a checking or savings account, but you can ask to have checks mailed to you. Most payments are increased each January to reflect changes in the cost of living.

How to Qualify for Benefits

To qualify for retirement benefits, you must be fully insured; that is, you must have the required number of quarters of coverage (QCs) under social security. Most workers need 40 QCs to qualify for retirement benefits; this works out to about 10 years of work. Workers born before 1929 need fewer QCs. One QC is credited for every $520 in earnings per quarter.

EXHIBIT 4–1
Availability of Social Security Benefits

Situation	You	Benefits Paid to Your Spouse	Your Child
You retire	Age 62 and over	If age 62 or over At any age, if caring for your child under 16 or disabled	If under 18, or 19 if in high school, or any age if disabled
You become disabled	Any age before normal retirement age	If age 62 or over At any age, if caring for your child under 16, or disabled	If under 18, or 19 if in high school, or any age if disabled
You die	At any age	If age 60 or over At any age, if caring for your child under 16 or disabled	If under 18, or 19 if in high school, or any age if disabled

Early Retirement

You can retire as early as age 62 if you are fully insured, but you will have a smaller monthly benefit for the rest of your life. It will be smaller for two reasons. First, you will probably have lower average earnings since income usually increases the longer you stay on the job. Second, you will receive more monthly benefit checks since they will begin sooner.

Late Retirement

If you wait until after your normal retirement age to claim social security, it will be increased by a percentage factor. If you were born between 1917–24, the increase is 3 percent for each year that you delay receiving your benefits, up to age 70. For people born in 1925–26, who reached age 65 in 1990–91, the increase is 3.5 percent per year. If you were born after 1926, the percentage increase is larger, rising gradually to 8 percent per year of delay for those born after 1942.

EXHIBIT 4–2
Benefits Chart

Benefits Paid to	Percent of Your Benefits
Your spouse, if age 65 or greater	50%
Your spouse, any age, with eligible child under age 16 or disabled	50
Each of your eligible children	50
Your spouse, if age 62	37.5

Earnings after the normal retirement age may increase your monthly benefits and those of other family members who receive benefits based on your earnings.

FAMILY BENEFITS

When you retire and become entitled to social security benefits, other members of your family may also be entitled to monthly benefits based on your earnings record. These benefits are in addition to your own benefits. Their benefits are based on a percentage of what you get. Exhibit 4–2 shows you which family members receive benefits when you retire. The actual amount these family members receive depends on when you retire; the dollar amount would be higher if you quit working after the normal retirement age, somewhat less if you retired early. The 37.5 percent figure that applies to your spouse if he or she is age 62 will be reduced gradually starting in the year 2000.

Maximum Family Benefits

The total amount that all members of one family may receive is limited. The range is between $600 and $2,180 per month. The specific figure depends on when you retire, the amount of your average indexed monthly earnings (based on your lifetime earnings history), and whether you are disabled. Generally, the amount payable to a divorced spouse is not included in figuring the maximum family benefit.

The average monthly benefit for a survivor's family is $1,300; $1,100 for a disabled worker and family. The table below shows the absolute maximum benefit one could expect if death or disability occurred in 1991 (the figures are adjusted each year for inflation). The numbers assume the worker was subjected to the maximum 1991 social security payroll tax of $53,400.

Year of Birth	Survivors	Disability
1966	$2,180	$1,800
1956	$2,110	$1,770
1946	$1,980	$1,660
1936	$1,840	$1,560
1926	$1,820	$1,530

BENEFITS REDUCTION IF YOU WORK AFTER RETIREMENT

People under age 70 who continue to work while receiving social security retirement benefits are subject to an earnings test. If the recipient is under age 65, the 1993 annual exemption is $7,680. For recipients age 65 through 69, the exempt amount is $10,560. If you exceed this amount, part or all of your social security retirement benefits are taken away. For those under age 65, $1 is lost for every $2 of earnings above $7,680; for those 65 through 69, $1 is lost for every $3 of earnings over $10,560. There is no reduction in benefits, no matter how much you earn, if you are age 70 or older.

Beginning in the second calendar year of benefits, the earnings test is on a monthly basis. Thus, workers under 65 are subject to reduced benefits for any month in which they earn more than $640; for recipients between ages 65 and 69, the limit is $880 monthly.

The following example will give you a good idea as to how benefits are determined. It covers a number of the areas described so far.

HOW SOCIAL SECURITY BENEFITS WORK: AN EXAMPLE

Jill and Dean were born in 1930 and 1929, respectively. Both of them worked a number of years, but Jill stopped working long before she reached age 62. She is now 63, her husband is 64 and she wants to start receiving her benefits.

Jill can receive benefits because she is at least 62 and she has her own earnings record. Her benefit will be reduced even though she worked the requisite number of quarters because she has elected to receive benefits before her 65th birthday. The figure she receives will go up each year based on cost-of-living increases. When her husband retires, she *may* end up receiving a larger monthly benefit based partly on *his* earnings record.

Dean has a choice. He can retire at age 62 or later. The earlier he elects, the smaller his benefit will be. His wife's benefit may or may not increase, depending on the benefit Dean receives. Whatever he elects, Dean's benefit will stay the same for the rest of his life, adjusted for any cost-of-living increases. If Dean claims his benefit at age 62 but continues to work and earns more than the earnings limitation, his benefit would be further reduced. Jill's benefit could also be reduced if she were relying on the percentage she was receiving from Dean's benefit. Her benefit would never be reduced below what she was entitled to under *her work record*.

When Dean reaches age 65, his benefit will be increased to recognize those months when benefits were withheld or reduced because of his work from age 62 to 65. The additional years of earnings after age 62 may also raise his average indexed monthly earnings. Jill's benefits may also end up being increased at this point.

Jill can collect benefits based on Dean's work record whenever he retires. If Dean waited until age 65 to retire, she would get one half of his benefits on top of whatever her husband receives (this figure would drop to 37.5 percent if she was age 62). She is entitled to this even if she never worked. In this hypothetical case, we are assuming that she did work and because of this, she has the option of receiving up to one half of Dean's benefits or what she is entitled to based on her work record, whichever is greater. All benefits received are adjusted each year to reflect the effects of inflation.

CHECKING ON YOUR EARNINGS RECORD

The Social Security Administration, which is headquartered in Baltimore, Maryland, maintains records of your earnings. It gets these earnings reports from your employer(s). If you are self-employed, the information is received from the IRS.

Once every few years you should verify that your reported earnings are correct. You can contact your local social security office and ask for the form "Request for Earnings and Benefit Estimate Statement." You should hear from social security within three weeks after sending in the completed form. The statement you get back will show a history of your social security earnings, how much you have paid into the system, an estimate of your future social security benefits, and will also provide you with some general information as to how the social security system works. If you have trouble reaching your local social security office, telephone 1–800–234–5772 to request the necessary form.

WHAT YOU CAN EXPECT FROM SOCIAL SECURITY

To use the table in Exhibit 4–3, find your age and the figure closest to your earnings last year. These figures will give you an estimate of your retirement benefits at various ages. This is the same table that was used in Chapter One, Setting Goals.

Disability Benefits

If you are under the social security system and are severely disabled, you are entitled to disability benefits. The benefit is not reduced because your disability began before your "normal retirement age." Exhibit 4–4 shows the approximate monthly benefit you are entitled to. The figures shown assume that you worked steadily and received pay raises until you became disabled.

Defining disability. In this context, "severe disability" means that you are so severely impaired, mentally or physically, that you cannot perform any substantial work. The impairment must be expected to last at least 12 months or be expected to result in premature death. This determination must be based on medical evidence and is ordinarily made by a government agency in your state.

Waiting period for disability benefits. To qualify for benefits, you must have been disabled for at least five months continu-

EXHIBIT 4–3
Projected Social Security Benefits

To use the table, find your age and the figure closest to your earnings last year. These figures will give you an estimate of your retirement benefits at various ages.

Retired Worker's Earnings Last Year

Worker's age in 1992	Worker's Family	$25,000	$30,000	$35,000	$40,000	$50,000	$55,000 or more[1]
25	Retired worker only	$1,201	$1,364	$1,450	$1,535	$1,706	$1,801
	Worker and spouse[2]	1,801	2,046	2,174	2,302	2,559	2,701
35	Retired worker only	1,111	1,263	1,342	1,421	1,580	1,662
	Worker and spouse[2]	1,666	1,894	2,013	2,131	2,370	2,493
45	Retired worker only	1,019	1,159	1,231	1,302	1,436	1,491
	Worker and spouse[2]	1,528	1,738	1,846	1,953	2,154	2,236
50	Retired worker only	971	1,106	1,166	1,226	1,334	1,375
	Worker and spouse[2]	1,457	1,658	1,749	1,839	2,000	2,062
55	Retired worker only	924	1,052	1,101	1,150	1,231	1,258
	Worker and spouse[2]	1,386	1,578	1,652	1,725	1,846	1,887
60	Retired worker only	893	1,015	1,054	1,094	1,156	1,173
	Worker and spouse[2]	1,340	1,522	1,581	1,641	1,734	1,760
65	Retired worker only	863	977	1,008	1,038	1,081	1,088
	Worker and spouse[2]	1,294	1,465	1,511	1,557	1,621	1,632

[1]Earnings equal to or greater than the social security wage base from age 22 through the year before retirement.

[2]Spouse is the same age as the worker. Spouse may qualify for a higher retirement benefit based on his or her own work record.

Source: Social Security Administration. Approximate monthly retirement benefits assume worker retires at age 65 with steady lifetime earnings. The accuracy of these estimates depends on the pattern of the worker's actual past earnings and earnings in the future.

ously. For example, if you become disabled on June 5, you could not receive benefits for those five months beginning July 1. If you were still disabled on December 1, your first benefit would be paid on December 3. The only way the waiting period can be eliminated is if you had previously received disability benefits and the disability ended less than five years before the present disability began.

Family benefits if you become disabled.   If you become disabled, your family members can receive benefits under the same rules

EXHIBIT 4–4
Monthly Benefits at Disability

Your Age in 1990	Person Receiving Benefits	Your Present Annual Earnings				
		$12,000	$20,000	$30,000	$40,000	$51,300 and Up
64	You	$480	$670	$870	$ 920	$ 960
	Child or children and spouse	240	340	440	460	480
60	You	490	690	890	940	970
	Child or children and spouse	250	340	440	470	490
55	You	490	690	900	950	990
	Child or children and spouse	250	340	450	480	500
50	You	490	690	900	970	1,020
	Child or children and spouse	250	340	450	490	510
45	You	490	690	910	990	1,050
	Child or children and spouse	250	340	450	500	520
40	You	490	690	910	1,010	1,080
	Child or children and spouse	250	340	450	500	540

that would apply if you retired. The maximum family benefit (the total of what the disabled spouse and his or her family receive) is lower for disability benefits than for retirement or survivor benefits.

Survivor Benefits

If you are part of the social security system, then chances are that your family would be entitled to some type of monthly benefit if you were to die. These benefits, shown as approximate figures in Exhibit 4–5, are adjusted every January to reflect changes in the cost of living.

EXHIBIT 4–5
Monthly Benefits if You Die in 1992

Your Age in 1990	Person Receiving Benefits	Your Present Annual Earnings				
		$12,000	$20,000	$30,000	$40,000	$51,300 and Up
65	Spouse, age 65	$490	$ 680	$ 890	$ 940	$ 980
	Spouse, age 60	350	490	630	670	700
	Child; spouse caring for child	370	510	670	700	730
	Maximum family benefit	790	1,260	1,550	1,640	1,710
60	Spouse, age 65	490	690	890	940	970
	Spouse, age 60	350	490	640	670	690
	Child; spouse caring for child	370	510	670	700	730
	Maximum family benefit	790	1,270	1,550	1,640	1,700
55	Spouse, age 65	490	690	900	950	990
	Spouse, age 60	350	490	640	680	710
	Child; spouse caring for child	370	510	670	710	740
	Maximum family benefit	790	1,270	1,570	1,660	1,730
50	Spouse, age 65	490	690	900	970	1,020
	Spouse, age 60	350	490	650	690	730
	Child; spouse caring for child	370	520	680	750	790
	Maximum family benefit	790	1,270	1,580	1,700	1,780
45	Spouse, age 65	490	690	910	1,000	1,060
	Spouse, age 60	350	490	650	710	760
	Child; spouse caring for child	370	520	680	750	790
	Maximum family benefit	790	1,270	1,590	1,740	1,850
40	Spouse, age 65	490	690	910	1,020	1,100
	Spouse, age 60	350	490	650	730	790
	Child; spouse caring for child	370	520	680	760	830
	Maximum family benefit	790	1,270	1,590	1,790	2,000

THE FUTURE OF SOCIAL SECURITY

The increase in social security taxes created a surplus in the social security retirement and disability trust that had reached $58 billion in 1989. It is projected to hit $11.8 trillion by 2030, exactly when the baby boomers are expected to begin to withdraw their benefits. Resources will be depleted by 2046. If the Treasury Department continues to be the planet's most reliable debtor, the trust fund should be secure. However, the most pessimistic assumptions call for the Disability Insurance Fund to face trouble in about 10 years. Any longer-term problems are about 50 years off, giving plenty of time to make any needed adjustments.

The American Association of Retired Persons (AARP) tells its members that they can expect a stable social security for at least another 35 years—after that, they say, it is anybody's guess. For updated information, you may call the Social Security General Accounting Office at 202–275–6241 or call Social Security Information at 1–800–562–6350 or 1–800–234–5772.

CHECKLIST OF THINGS TO DO

1. Telephone (1–800–248–3248) Commerce Clearing House and request the following publications: *1993 Social Security Benefits* (48 pages) and *On Your Retirement: Tax and Benefit Considerations* (128 pages).

2. Contact Social Security (1–800–234–5772) and request the following free publications: *Understanding Social Security, Retirement, Your Social Security Taxes: What They're Paying for and Where the Money Goes, How Your Retirement Benefit Is Figured,* and *The Retirement Earnings Test.*

3. Telephone 1–800–772–1213 to determine your social security retirement benefits. The Social Security Administration says that the benefits it provides will cover about 27 percent of the income needed for retirement. A pension plan will take care of another 18 percent. That leaves 55 percent that will be needed to make up the difference from personal savings, investments, and earnings.

Chapter Five

Qualified Retirement Plans

The Cost of Procrastination
How Retirement Plans Work
IRAs
Corporate Retirement Plans
401(k) Plans
Keoghs
403(b) Plans
Which Plan You Should Have
If You Are Retiring within Two Years
Determining if You Can Retire Early
Taking Charge of a Premature Retirement Distribution

We have all read the stories or seen the cartoons about the tortoise and the hare or the chipmunk who stores food for the winter. The ending is always the same. We know that the tortoise is going to win and the hard-working chipmunk will survive another cold winter. Sure, what the tortoise and the squirrel do is boring, but it always works. I don't know about you, but I don't want my friends thinking that some critter was smarter than I was. Retirement is something you are going to have to face one day. It is just like winter or entering a race—seasons change and there is a finish line. You cannot tell nature to skip the next winter, and you cannot have the race stopped just because you were not prepared. Similarly, you cannot skip retirement or pretend it does not exist.

THE COST OF PROCRASTINATION

As noted throughout our discussion of retirement planning, the cost of procrastination is tremendous. Exhibit 5-1 shows two investors, investor A and investor B. Both invest in an IRA account, a type of retirement plan, that grows at 10.5 percent compounded annually. The difference is that investor A begins making contributions immediately; investor B waits nine years until he starts making contributions. Even though investor B makes contributions for 20 years, he is unable to catch up with investor A, who made a total of only eight investments. Surprisingly, investor B will never be able to catch up, even if he could make contributions for 30 or 40 years.

Now that you know the price of procrastination, make sure you do not have to pay it. Do not continue to postpone setting up or funding your retirement account(s) until "the right time." Set up or enroll in a retirement plan as soon as possible.

HOW RETIREMENT PLANS WORK

One of the best ways to prepare for your leisure years is to set up and contribute to a retirement plan. Several different types of retirement plans exist, but most share these common features: (1) contributions are made with pretax dollars and are therefore tax deductible; (2) money grows and compounds tax deferred in the account until withdrawn; (3) you pay taxes on the money as it comes out; and (4) with few exceptions, there are penalties on withdrawals made before a certain age, usually 59½.

All qualified retirement plans require that you have *earned income*. Earned income includes salary, tips, bonuses, commissions, and alimony. If your sole source of income is from rental properties, dividends, interest, capital gains or royalties, then you have what is known as *unearned income*. Unearned income cannot be used in computing whether or not you can contribute to a retirement plan or the amount of such contributions. If your only current source of income is unearned, you may keep any and all existing retirement accounts, but you cannot add to them again until you have earned income. Let us proceed with the assumption that you are working and have *earned* income.

EXHIBIT 5–1
A Comparison of Two Retirement Investment Programs

	Investor A		Investor B	
Year	IRA Contribution	Value at Year End	IRA Contribution	Value at Year End
1	$2,000	$ 2,210	$ 0	$ 0
2	2,000	4,651	0	0
3	2,000	7,347	0	0
4	2,000	10,325	0	0
5	2,000	13,616	0	0
6	2,000	17,251	0	0
7	2,000	21,267	0	0
8	2,000	25,703	0	0
9	0	28,394	2,000	2,210
10	0	31,368	2,000	4,651
11	0	34,652	2,000	7,347
12	0	38,281	2,000	10,325
13	0	42,289	2,000	13,616
14	0	46,717	2,000	17,251
15	0	51,609	2,000	21,267
16	0	57,014	2,000	25,703
17	0	62,984	2,000	30,604
18	0	69,579	2,000	36,019
19	0	76,865	2,000	42,000
20	0	84,914	2,000	48,607
21	0	93,805	2,000	55,906
22	0	103,627	2,000	63,970
23	0	114,475	2,000	72,878
24	0	126,446	2,000	82,718
25	0	139,708	2,000	93,589
26	0	154,338	2,000	105,599
27	0	170,449	2,000	118,866
28	0	188,352	2,000	133,522
29	0	208,075	2,000	149,713
30	0	229,864	2,000	167,599
Subtract IRA contributions		(16,000)		(44,000)
Net gain		$213,864		$123,599

Most investments are available options within your retirement plan. Generally, your investment choices are limited only by the financial institution where your retirement plan is set up or the options provided by your company-sponsored plan. The only investments that cannot be part of a retirement plan are:

- Tangibles (gemstones, gold, silver, and other metals).
- Collectibles (rare coins, rare stamps, baseball cards, etc.) with the exception of the American Eagle coins minted by the U.S. Treasury.
- Commodities (except within a limited partnership).
- The selling of put or call options (selling call options on stocks you own, what is known as "covered call writing," is allowed).
- What is referred to as *self-dealings* (e.g., general partnership interests, real estate, or business interests you have direct control over).

The amount of control you have over your retirement accounts depend on whether you are self-employed or participating in an employer's plan. The types of plans available to individuals or the self-employed may include IRAs, SEP-IRAs, Keoghs, and SAR-SEPS. Plans available to employees in larger companies may include defined contribution plans, defined-benefit plans, IRAs, and 401(k)s. Each of these plans offers unique features and advantages, and sometimes complicated restrictions. The plans are outlined below. However, it is worth your time to ask your financial adviser and employee benefits manager for details of all the options available to you. As complicated as they may seem, formal retirement plans are excellent tools for setting aside tax-deferred savings for retirement.

To appreciate the benefits of tax-deferred growth, look at Exhibit 5-2. It compares two identical investments; one is a tax-deferred plan, in this case an IRA, and one is a fully taxable investment account. The longer the time period and the greater the assumed rate of interest, the larger the gap between a regular account and a tax-deferred account.

IRAs

Individual Retirement Accounts, better known as IRAs, are the simplest form of retirement plans. IRAs, as the name indicates, are

EXHIBIT 5–2
How the Power of Tax-Deferred Compounding Can Help Your
*Retirement Savings Grow**

		$2,000 Invested Annually for		
Annual Rate of Return (%)	Value of	10 Years	20 Years	30 Years
8%	IRA	$28,980	$ 91,520	$226,560
	Taxable investment	27,400	75,400	157,600
10%	IRA	31,880	114,560	328,980
	Taxable investment	29,700	88,000	206,600
12%	IRA	35,100	144,100	482,660
	Taxable investment	32,200	105,200	270,400

*This table assumes that earnings on the taxable investment are reduced by 28 percent tax.

set up and funded by individuals under 70½ years of age. If you are 70½ or older, you may keep your IRA but cannot make any additional contributions to it. Like all retirement plans, money in an IRA grows and compounds tax deferred. The unique feature of IRAs is that contributions of up to $2,000 may be deductible, depending on your income level and if you participate in another qualified retirement plan.

IRAs can be set up through a bank, brokerage firm, insurance company, mutual fund, or with a financial planner. You can determine how and in which instruments your IRA is invested; however, the type of institution you choose may dictate how the IRA is invested. For example, buying the IRA through a bank may limit you just to cash equivalent investments; setting up the IRA through a mutual fund will allow you to invest in a fund family. If you set up your IRA before April 15, the tax-deductible benefit will count toward your last year's tax return. For example, if you set up the IRA on April 13, 1993, you can qualify to deduct your contribution from your 1992 taxes.

Numerous contingencies, however, determine whether the annual contribution to the IRA is tax deductible. First, if you are covered by another qualified retirement plan such as through your

EXHIBIT 5–3
Retirement Contribution Deduction Schedule

*Find Your Adjusted
Gross Income Below
(Total income –
Certain deductions)*

Joint Return	Single Return	Are You or Your Spouse Covered by an Employer Retirement Plan?	Your IRA Contribution Is	Your IRA Earnings Are Tax Deferred
		Not covered	Fully deductible	Yes
≥ $40,000	≥ $25,000	Covered	Fully deductible	Yes
$40,000–	$25,000–	Not covered	Fully deductible	Yes
$50,000	$35,000	Covered	Partially deductible	Yes
		Not covered	Fully deductible	Yes
≥ $50,000	≥ $35,000	Covered	Not deductible	Yes

employer, you may not be able to deduct the full amount of your contribution. Second, the amount of the deduction depends on your or your family's income level; the higher your income, the less you can deduct. Exhibit 5–3 summarizes the deduction schedule.

Money taken out of an IRA before age 59½ is subject to a 10 percent penalty. IRS penalties are not deductible. Furthermore, all distributions are taxable in the year in which they were received by you. Let us suppose a 45-year-old man had $40,000 in his IRA and decided he needed some money. If he liquidates $9,000 he will be hit with a $900 penalty (10 percent of the amount withdrawn). He would also have to add the $9,000 withdrawn to his other sources of taxable income for income tax purposes. The money would have to be reported in the year in which it was received. The entire $9,000 would be shown as income for the year; the $900 penalty could not be used as any kind of offset.

There are four ways to avoid the pre-59½ IRS penalty: (1) death, (2) disability, (3) lifetime annuitization, and (4) a domestic relations court order. The IRS does not consider death or disability a voluntary event and therefore waives the penalty. This means that if disabled, you or your heirs could receive money from an IRA and only have to pay ordinary income taxes on the money withdrawn.

The third method, lifetime annuitization, means that you can take out a set amount each year for your remaining life expectancy. Thus, a 40-year-old male with a life expectancy of 39 years could take out $\frac{1}{39}$th of his IRA each year. If more than $\frac{1}{39}$th was taken out before age 59½, there would be a penalty.

If you are not satisfied with the performance of your IRA, you may want to consider a rollover or transfer. These are two ways to move part or all of your account to another institution and/or investment vehicle. An IRA *rollover* means that the institution at which you have an IRA has sent you a check for part or all of the proceeds. You have up to 60 days to reinvest this money in another IRA or face the tax consequences on that portion of the money that is not placed in a new IRA (the 10 percent penalty would also apply if you were under 59½). If you reinvest within 60 days, there is no tax or penalty. Rollovers can be done once per calendar year per account. During the 60-day period, you are free to do whatever you like with the money. If you had three different IRA accounts you could end up having three different 60-day "loans" each year. There is close to $20 billion worth of IRA rollover activity each year.

Transfers are different from rollovers. A transfer means that part or all of your money has gone to another institution and no check was received by you. Since you never see the money with a transfer, the IRS allows an unlimited number of transfers per year for each IRA account. If you are interested only in moving your IRA from one institution to another, you would use the transfer.

CORPORATE RETIREMENT PLANS

Corporate retirement plans, if available to you, should be an important part of your overall retirement planning. Created in the late 1800s, pensions were designed to help employees cover the cost of living after retirement. Today, employer pensions won't cover all your postretirement, but can make a significant contribution to your retirement income.

Corporate plans are offered in one of two forms: defined-contribution plans or defined-benefit plans. *Defined-benefit plans* are the traditional and most common pension plans designed to pay a fixed amount of money to the vested employee upon retirement.

The amount of money depends on the number of years of service and the income level and is paid entirely by the employer. The company pension portfolio is managed by the company investment officer or an outside money manager, and therefore the employees rarely influence how the money is invested. A defined-benefit plan has two advantages. First, contributions and benefits are tax deferred until retirement. Second, the employee knows exactly how much money will be paid upon retirement.

The *defined-contribution plan* is based on variable contributions by the employer to the plan, and therefore the amount paid upon retirement will vary depending upon the accumulated contributions. There are two basic types of defined-contribution plans: the profit-sharing plan and the money-purchase pension plan. In the *profit-sharing plan*, the contribution is the lesser of 15 percent of compensation or $30,000. The *money purchase plan* sets a schedule for employer contributions, based typically as a percentage of the employee's salary. The limit per calendar year is 25 percent of compensation or $30,000, whichever is less. A profit-sharing plan offers more flexibility than a money-purchase plan since contributions do not have to be made each year. If a contribution is made, it can range between 0 and 15 percent of the employee's compensation. Under a money-purchase plan, once a percentage figure has been chosen (0–25 percent), it must be adhered to each year, even if there is no "profit." The contributions are accumulated in the employee's accounts, and upon retirement the employee can withdraw as much as can be "purchased" with the money in the account.

Another type of defined-contribution plan growing in popularity is the *401(k)* plan. In the 401(k) plan, employees can contribute to their own accounts on a tax-deferred basis, and their contributions will be matched to some degree by the company. Because employees can contribute to these plans, the employee has a say in how the money is invested; this distinguishes the 401(k) from the other plans (see next page).

Compared to defined-benefit plans, which pay out a guaranteed amount upon retirement, the defined-contribution plans sound a little risky to the employee; we would all like to know exactly what we will have upon retirement. However, while defined-contribution plans do not pay a fixed amount, the plan may pay out more than the defined-benefit plan depending on factors like corporate growth, investment performance, and so on. The employee may end up better off because the possible payouts may be greater than through the defined-benefit plan. In addition, in some defined-contribution plans, the employee may also contribute and have a voice in how the money is invested (e.g., in company stock or outside investments). Younger employees, who have a longer time horizon to watch their retirement accounts grow, may prefer the defined-contribution plans. Employees with a shorter time horizon before retirement may want to be sure of a fixed benefit amount through a defined-benefit plan. Unfortunately, employees don't have a choice and can only participate in the plan that the company offers.

More and more companies are moving toward the defined-contribution plan. The corporate environment has changed drastically since pensions were first created in the late 19th century. At that time, employees were expected to live only until 55. Now life expectancies have increased and so have salaries and the cost of living. In many companies, the projected liability of retiree payouts exceeds the current funding capabilities. Companies therefore may be forced to adopt other retirement plans that would reduce the employers' liability and still provide adequate retirement benefits. As more companies restructure their benefit plans, it is very important that employees understand their retirement benefits and be aware of the investment options to supplement that retirement income.

Employees also are entitled to receive, upon request, an annual accounting of their personal benefits. In addition, people can obtain from their employer or the labor department a copy of the full annual report that the plan filed with the federal government. The full report includes a breakdown of the plan's portfolio by types of investments.

If your employer cannot give you information about your pension, contact: U.S. Department of Labor, Pension and Welfare Benefit Program, Office of Communications, 200 Constitution Avenue, NW, Washington, DC 20216. For information on whether your pension plan is insured by PBGC or is about to terminate, contact: Pension Benefit Guaranty Corporation, 2020 K Street NW, Washington, DC 20006.

401(k) PLANS

The 401(k) plans offer a new approach to traditional profit-sharing programs. Close to 25 percent of the U.S. work force is covered by a 401(k), and 95 percent of all Fortune 500 companies offer 401(k)s. The name of these defined-contribution plans comes from Section 401(k) in the IRS tax code.

You as the employee can choose whether or not to participate in the 401(k) plan. If you choose to participate, you determine the percentage of your pretax income to invest. Some plans also allow you to invest aftertax money as additional savings. 401(k) plans are structured so both you and your employer can make contributions. If you are the only one making contributions, the annual maximum is close to $9,000. This figure may be adjusted each year for inflation. In no event can the total contribution exceed more than 15 percent of your salary. The total contributions between your employer and you cannot exceed $30,000 or 25 percent of your salary, whichever is less.

Your 401(k) account is payable upon retirement, death, or termination of employment. If your employment is terminated, you will receive the amount you contributed plus any employer contributions which have vested. As with an IRA, if the distribution is made before you are 59½, you will pay a 10 percent early distribution penalty unless the amount is transferred or rolled over into another retirement plan. Some plans may allow an employee to temporarily withdraw money for emergencies or in order to buy a home without having to pay the penalty.

A nice feature of most 401(k) plans is that employees may choose how their retirement accounts are invested. Most 401(k) plans offer a wide variety of investment choices ranging from very conservative to speculative. An employee may also have the option of investing in the company's stock portfolios. 401(k) plans also allow the employee to change the investments or allocations. We will discuss later in the book the factors such as risk aversion, long-term goals, and so on, which influence your investment decisions. Keep in mind that retirement plans are intended to be long-term investments; therefore choose investments in your 401(k) plan that will maximize your long-term return.

SEP-IRAs

This type of retirement plan allows employers to contribute up to 15 percent of an employee's gross salary or $30,000, whichever is less, into an IRA. There are no annual reporting requirements with this type of plan; initial set-up cost is $10 to $30 per employee. Employees are responsible for directing their own investments.

Contributions are flexible. Owners can vary the amount each year, or even skip years, as long as they contribute the same percentage for themselves as they do for all eligible employees. If a contribution is being made, all employees age 21 and older who have earned at least $385 per year, and who have worked three of the last five years, must be covered. Employees cannot borrow from their SEP-IRA, as they can from a profit-sharing or 401(k) plan.

Perhaps the greatest benefit of a SEP has to do with deadlines. Unlike Keogh or corporate retirement plans, SEPs can be set up after December 31st. As long as contributions are made by April 15th, a deduction may be taken for the previous year.

SAR-SEPs

Salary Reduction Simplified Employee Pension Plans (SAR-SEPs) are often called the "small-business owner's 401(k)," offering an employer with 25 or fewer employees an opportunity to provide an employee-funded retirement plan. Employee salary deferrals reduce the worker's current taxable income and may be as much as the lesser of $8,994 or 15 percent of gross salary, adjusted upward each year for inflation.

Many small-business owners are unaware of the SEP-IRA and SAR-SEP. In fact, only one employer in five provides a retirement plan. Yet, retirement planning is a very important issue to employees. In a recent survey, 7 of 10 employees revealed they would prefer to contribute part of their salaries to retirement plans rather than receive the dollars as part of their pay. SAR-SEPs are easily established and require no annual tax reporting.

KEOGHS

If you are self-employed or work for someone who is not incorporated, you may opt for a Keogh. If you are an employee, you can choose only one of these retirement plans if your employer has set up a Keogh and you fulfill the eligibility requirements described below. These qualified retirement plans are offered in one of three forms: defined contribution, hybrid, and defined benefit.

There are two types of defined-contribution plans: profit-sharing and money-purchase. A defined-contribution plan means that the amount set aside each year for retirement is a percentage of your income. If you use a *profit-sharing* plan the limit is 15 percent of your self-employment income; with a *money-purchase* plan you may contribute up to 25 percent of your self-employment income or $30,000, whichever is less. These percentage figures are a little lower if you are an employer instead of an employee.

The hybrid Keogh, also known as a combination plan, is a cross between a money-purchase *and* a profit-sharing plan. And because a hybrid plan lets you maximize your contributions while still leaving you a certain degree of flexibility, it offers some advantages. Here is how it works, *if you wish to maximize your contribution:* Your money-purchase plan is fixed at 10 percent of net income (this figure cannot later change unless the plan document is amended by the employer) and your contribution to the profit-sharing plan is not fixed at any percentage of income. By having these dual plans, you must contribute at least 10 percent of your net self-employment income, but you can also contribute anywhere from 0 to 15 percent into your profit-sharing plan. You have complete flexibility in the 10–25 percent range.

The other type of Keogh plan, defined benefit, allows you, and/ or your employer, to contribute whatever is necessary to achieve a target benefit at retirement. Your contributions are not limited, but your annual future retirement benefit is.

Keoghs must be established by December 31 if you wish to deduct that year's contribution. The actual contribution does not have to be made until you file your tax return, which could be up to April 15 or later. Extensions for tax returns also extend your time to make Keogh contributions.

As with IRAs, you can transfer your Keogh to another Keogh or IRA account. The assets of one Keogh account are transferred from one institution (custodian) to another. People transfer Keogh accounts for one or more of the following reasons: (1) poor performance, (2) the hope or guarantee of getting better results in a different investment vehicle, (3) convenience (consolidating multiple Keogh accounts), (4) lower custodial fees, and (5) termination of employment.

If you are an employer, the only advantage of a Keogh over an IRA is the size of the annual contribution; employees have the additional benefit of being able to borrow from their retirement account. If you want to sock away as much money as possible and take a tax deduction at the same time, set up a Keogh. Also consider having an IRA, whether it is deductible or not. The tax-deferral of retirement plans such as IRAs and Keoghs can be tremendous.

403(b) PLANS

These retirement plans can be used only by teachers and other employees of a school district, hospitals, and nonprofit organizations. The maximum annual contribution is the lesser of 20 percent of one's gross salary or $9,500. These yearly limits are supposed to be increased each year to reflect CPI adjustments, but changes appear to occur about once every two years.

One of the attractive features of 403(b) plans is that money can be withdrawn before retirement for "financial hardship." This definition allows penalty-free use of your money for the purchase of a home. These withdrawals are limited to 100 percent of the employee's contributions (employers rarely contribute to these plans). Interest, dividends, and growth resulting from these contributions cannot be taken out before retirement without penalty. All withdrawals, either before or after retirement, are fully taxable; it is just the IRS 10 percent penalty that may be waived.

WHICH PLAN YOU SHOULD HAVE

You should participate in each and every retirement plan you can either set up on your own or that is offered to you if you are not self-employed. If you work for the XYZ corporation during the week and also have a part-time job as a professional photographer, sign up for whatever your company is offering and also set up your own Keogh. Whether you have a second job or work by yourself, you should also have an IRA, even if it is not deductible.

What makes retirement plans so great is the fact that your contributions are tax deductible and earnings are tax-deferred. Your nest egg will grow much faster and larger if it is not hindered by current taxes. The number of plans you avail yourself of and the total amount of your contributions should be limited only by how much money you need for current expenses. All investments, whether part of a qualified retirement plan or not, require sacrifice today in order to end up with a benefit tomorrow.

The other reason retirement plans are pushed so heavily by financial planning and investment books is that most Americans do not retire with enough resources. According to a recent study by the Department of Health and Human Services, for every 100 people starting their careers, the following situation exists at age 65:

23 are dead.
13 have annual incomes under $4,000.
55 have annual incomes between $4,000 and $26,000.
3 have annual incomes over $26,000.

These figures are quite depressing, especially when it is discovered that the median income for the 55 percent who have annual incomes between $4,000 and $26,000 is only $6,100 per year.

IF YOU ARE RETIRING WITHIN TWO YEARS

If you will be retiring in the next couple of years, find out your exact retirement date, the payout options available to you, whether you should consider a lump-sum payment, and also look into an annuity payout schedule (see below).

Knowing your exact retirement date is important. By having your employee benefits coordinator calculate your benefits based on different retirement dates, you may discover that by working just a couple of more months you can add a full year of service for benefit purposes.

Employees are often given the choice of receiving a lump-sum payment or an annuity. Your decision should be based on your income from other sources, the health of you and your spouse, and whether you want the responsibility of managing a large sum of money.

Annuities are offered by the insurance industry. They provide the worker with an alternative that is both safe and provides a set, guaranteed payment each month. Annuities provide the worker with an income stream that he or she cannot outlive. Payments continue as long as the retired employee is alive. Often, retiring employees are offered a payment schedule that continues for a single life (until the employee dies) or joint life (until the employee and his or her spouse are both deceased).

The most common type of annuity payout schedule used for retirement plans is the joint and survivor variety. These annuities pay a monthly check for the rest of your life; upon death, your surviving spouse receives a percentage of the income you were receiving. If your spouse consents, you can select a single life annuity. These annuities stop paying benefits at your death, but the monthly income is much higher. A single annuity may be a good choice if your spouse has his or her own pension or receives a good deal of income from other sources or if your spouse is not expected to outlive you. There are certainly a great number of advantages to an annuity:

- Monthly checks.
- Guaranteed safety.
- Income as long as you live.
- The option of having the payments continue until both the worker and his or her spouse are deceased.
- Peace of mind.

As in any other type of retirement option, there are also disadvantages to an annuity. First, if the insurer runs into severe financial difficulty, the "guarantee" may disappear. Fortunately, almost every state has a guaranty fund that should be able to partially or fully protect you in such an event. Second, other than choosing a single-life or joint-life payout, there are no investment options. Third, your monthly payments will not keep pace with inflation. These payout options do not contain any type of adjustment for inflation.

DETERMINING IF YOU CAN RETIRE EARLY

To know if your retirement nest egg can generate enough income for you to call it quits, find your approximate savings in Exhibit

EXHIBIT 5–4
Retirement Income Levels at Various Ages and Savings Amounts

	Annual Income if You Are Retiring At:			
Savings	*Age 50*	*Age 55*	*Age 62*	*Age 65*
$ 100,000	$14,400	$14,500	$14,600	$14,800
200,000	18,400	18,800	19,200	19,400
300,000	22,300	23,100	24,000	24,200
400,000	26,300	27,400	28,600	29,100
500,000	30,300	31,700	33,300	34,100
600,000	34,300	36,000	38,000	39,000
700,000	38,300	40,300	42,700	44,000
800,000	42,300	44,600	47,400	48,900
900,000	46,200	48,900	52,000	53,800
1,000,000	50,200	53,200	56,700	58,700

5–4 and read right to locate the number below your age. That number is the annual income (including social security when it kicks in at age 62) that you would receive in 1990 dollars for the rest of your life. Of course, you will be able to get by with less if you get a pension. By most experts' accounts, you will do fine on 80 percent of your preretirement income and perhaps on far less, if mortgages and college bills are behind you. The exhibit assumes inflation of 5 percent a year, a life expectancy of 92, and that the money is invested at 7½ percent. Note how little you lose by retiring at age 50 instead of 55.

If these dollar figures appear to be too large, keep in mind that they include social security benefits and the gradual erosion of your savings (principal). If these numbers seem to be too low to you, remember that they take into account the effects of inflation; phrased another way, the annual income streams shown reflect a constant purchasing power—inflation-adjusted dollars.

TAKING CHARGE OF A PREMATURE RETIREMENT DISTRIBUTION

Switching jobs, getting laid off, or working for a company that merges with another means a lot of changes. But one you may not expect is having to take charge of your retirement money. Retirement-plan distributions can be triggered by a variety of events. It is not uncommon to find yourself years away from retirement and suddenly having to decide what to do with a chunk of money that may range from a few hundred dollars to over a half million.

The problem is that unless such distributions are rolled over into another qualified plan, such as an IRA, within 60 days from when the check is received by you, you will be subject to penalties and taxes that can total up to 40 percent of the lump sum (make sure it is a transfer instead of a rollover in order to avoid the 20 percent withholding tax). If you feel rushed or pressured into an investment decision in such a situation, roll the money into another retirement plan and initially opt for a conservative holding such as a money market account. You can then gradually move into other investments that you might find more appealing, such as growth funds, individual stocks, bonds, global bond funds, real estate, or foreign securities.

This is a good time to go back and make sure you used the correct numbers when you filled out the "Retirement Accounts and Deferred Income" section of Exhibit 1-1 in Chapter One. If you made a mistake in this section, make sure you also change the corresponding summary number in the "Summary of Assets" part of the net worth worksheet.

Speaking of investing, the next chapter gives you an overview of how the major categories of investments have performed in the past, how they have been affected by inflation, taxes, and other forms of risk. Most people think that the only type of risk is losing part or all of one's principal. As you will see, there are several other types of risk that you might unknowingly be subjected to. The chapter ends with some useful strategies as to how risk can be minimized or avoided.

CHECKLIST OF THINGS TO DO

1. Set up an IRA; if you already have one, make sure you contribute the maximum amount allowed each year (review compound table).

2. Participate in other retirement plans available to you. Talk to your company's benefits coordinator and find out what your

retirement plan is invested in; if you are a participant in a defined-benefit plan, make sure that it is properly funded.

3. If you are self-employed or work for a company that is not incorporated, look into Keogh accounts. They allow you greater tax deductible contributions than IRAs (you can also have an IRA at the same time). See if you can set up both a defined-benefit pension plan and a profit-sharing plan. Such a combination or hybrid plan allows you flexibility as to how much is contributed each year while still allowing you to make the maximum contribution each year if you so desire.

4. Employees of a school district, hospital, or charitable group should look into a 403(b) plan (also known as a tax-sheltered annuity). In many respects, these work just like other retirement plans—you get a deduction and your investments grow and compound tax deferred. For $10 you can get a copy of the *Annuity Shopper* (write to U.S. Annuities, 98 Hoffman Rd., Englishtown, NJ, 07726), which gives information on several of the top-yielding annuities. You can also telephone them at 800–872–6684. Another good source is *Best's Retirement Income Guide* (A.M. Best Customer Service, Oldwick, NJ, 08858). For $53 a year, Best will show you current interest rates, expenses, and surrender values for a large number of companies.

5. Contact the IRS and request the following publications: *Self-Employment Retirement Plans* (publication no. 560) and *Individual Retirement Accounts* (publication no. 590). These free publications will provide you with detailed information about the range of retirement plans, some of which are probably available to you.

6. Upon retirement, if you are given a choice of receiving your pension as a monthly income or as a lump sum, take the lump sum and have it transferred directly into an IRA. IRA rollover accounts through brokerage firms and mutual fund groups give you tremendous investment flexibility. More important, you should be able to end up with a monthly income stream that is greater than what your company is offering.

Chapter Six

Introduction to Investing

Only Two Types of Investments
Generic Historical Studies
The Impact of Inflation
Tax Considerations
Types of Risk
Minimizing Your Portfolio's Risk

The preceding chapter pointed out the different retirement plans that are either offered through your job or can be set up by you independently. People often ask if an IRA or participation in a company-sponsored retirement plan is a good investment. The answer is that it depends. Retirement accounts per se are not good or bad; it is the *investment* within the retirement plan that determines if participation is a good or bad idea. The fact that contributions are usually tax deductible is a major benefit of a retirement plan, but if the investment loses money most of the time, either due to the effects of inflation or because of bad performance, then such programs should be reexamined and a new investment strategy utilized. In any case, you often may have to develop an investment strategy to complement the financial plans in order to meet your financial goals.

This chapter begins by discussing, in very general terms, how the two major categories of investments and the most popular types of investments, which all fall within these two classifications, have fared over every five-year period over the past half century. You will then learn how inflation and income taxes affect these investments, which investments are tax-free and which are tax-deferred, and find out whether or not you should invest in tax-free investments.

ONLY TWO TYPES OF INVESTMENTS

Surprisingly, all investments can be categorized as being either debt or equity instruments. *Debt* instruments are those investments in which we have loaned our money to someone else, usually a bank, corporation, government, or municipality. These instruments include savings accounts, CDs, all types of bonds and bond funds, money market accounts, and trust deeds. *Equity* instruments are things in which we have an ownership interest: stocks, mutual funds that invest in stocks, preferred stocks, real estate, certain types of real estate investment trusts, and tangibles (gold, silver, other metals, and collectibles such as rare coins and stamps). Historically, equity vehicles have outperformed debt instruments; the longer the time period, the greater likelihood there is of this happening. This is particularly true if you exclude most collectibles and metals.

Debt instruments are also referred to as *fixed-rate investments* since they usually offer a set rate of return. A fixed rate of return would be great if you and I lived in a world of fixed *expenses*. Unfortunately, no such place exists on earth. This does not mean that equities are always better than debt instruments; certainly there are some instances over the past half century when debt has outperformed equity. These occasions become fewer and fewer when you look at longer periods, such as 5-, 10- and 20-year blocks of time.

GENERIC HISTORICAL STUDIES

Exhibits 6–1 through 6–6 show the difference in investment performance over the past half century, in five-year intervals, from the very end of 1942 through the end of 1992. The six bar charts include performance figures for the following: (1) Treasury bills, (2) long-term government bonds, (3) long-term corporate bonds, (4) intermediate-term government bonds, (5) common stocks, as mea-

EXHIBIT 6–1
United States Treasury Bills, 1942–1992

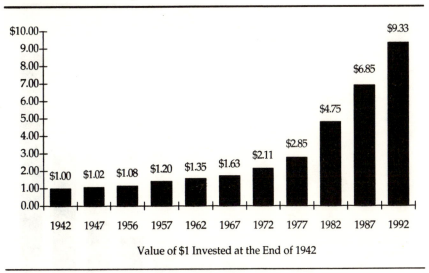

Value of $1 Invested at the End of 1942

sured by the Standard & Poor's 500, and (6) small capital stocks, defined as those representing the bottom 20 percent of the NYSE, as measured by market capitalization. A seventh chart summarizes these seven different indices and measures average annual returns for the same 50 years, 1942–1992.

Over the past 50 years, U.S. Treasury bills (Exhibit 6–1) fared better than inflation on an *annual* basis about 60 percent of the time, on a pretax basis. Over any given 5- or 10-year period, T-bills outperformed inflation 64 percent of the time; for any 20-year period the number jumps to 88 percent. The figure is close to zero percent of the time if income taxes are included for any given 1-, 5-, 10-, or 20-year period.

Long-term government bonds (Exhibit 6–2) have not done as well over the past 50 years as T-bills when viewed in certain ways. In any given year, these bonds fared better than inflation only half of the time on a total return basis. Over any given 5- or 10-year period, government bonds outperformed inflation only 42 percent of the time; for any 20-year period the number climbs to 48 percent. These figures become very small during most of these measurements if income taxes are subtracted.

EXHIBIT 6–2
Long-Term Government Bonds, 1942–1992

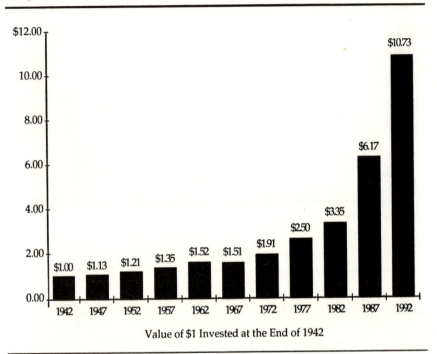

Value of $1 Invested at the End of 1942

Over the past 50 years, long-term corporate bonds (Exhibit 6–3) have fared better than inflation only half of the time on a total return basis. Over any given 5- or 10-year period, corporate bonds have outperformed inflation 48 percent and 50 percent of the time, respectively; for any 20-year period the number climbs to 64 percent.

Intermediate-term government bonds (Exhibit 6–4) over the past 50 years have done better than their long-term counterparts. This is because all the figures shown in these charts are total return numbers and take into account the value of the underlying principal (the investment) *at the end of each year*. If just current yield figures were shown, long-term instruments would almost always look better.

In any given year over the past half century, intermediate-term bonds have fared better than inflation half the time on a total return

EXHIBIT 6-3
Long-Term Corporate Bonds, 1942–1992

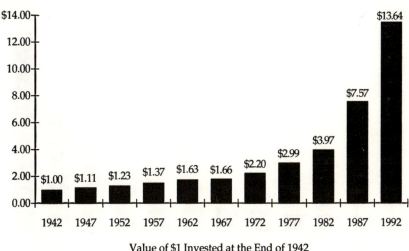

Value of $1 Invested at the End of 1942

basis. Over any given 5-year period, the number climbs to 62 percent; the figure increases to 68% for 10-year periods and jumps to 84 percent of the time for any 20-year period. The figures become nominal during most of these measurements if income taxes are included for any single, 5-, 10-, or 20-year period.

The financial assets of U.S. households total some $13 trillion, of which $2.5 trillion, or 19 percent is in stocks. This $13 trillion is double the combined assets of private and public pension plans, insurance companies, mutual funds, security brokers, and foreign investors. However, large as it is, this 19 percent in equities is down from over 35 percent in the late 1960s.

Over the past 50 years, U.S. common stocks (Exhibit 6-5) have fared better than inflation 68 percent of the time. Over any given five years, the figure jumps to 84 percent of the time and 86 percent for 10-year periods. During any 20 years in a row, common stocks have outpaced inflation 100 percent of the time, almost always by wide margins.

Small stocks (Exhibit 6-6), as measured by the bottom quintile (market price multiplied by the number of outstanding shares) of

EXHIBIT 6–4
Intermediate-Term Government Bonds, 1942–1992

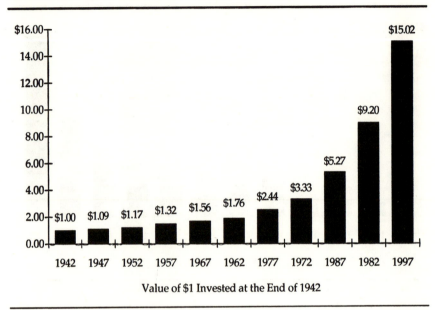

Value of $1 Invested at the End of 1942

EXHIBIT 6–5
Common Stocks, 1942–1992

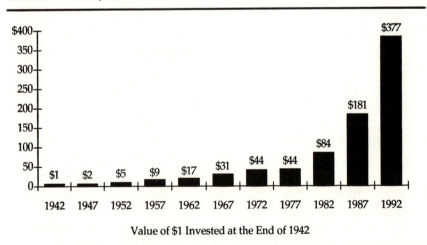

Value of $1 Invested at the End of 1942

EXHIBIT 6–6
Small Stocks, 1942–1992

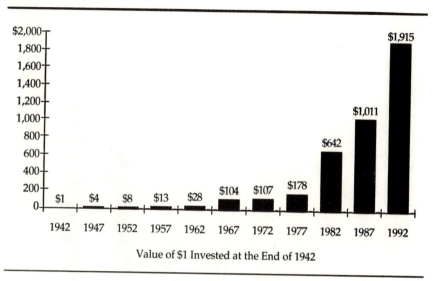

Value of $1 Invested at the End of 1942

equities listed on the NYSE, have fared better than inflation 68 percent of the time over the past 50 years. Over any given five years, the figure jumps to 88 percent of the time and 92 percent for 10-year periods. During any 20 years in a row (e.g., 1953–1972), small stocks have outpaced inflation 100 percent of the time, usually by wide margins.

As you can see, debt instruments have not fared particularly well when measured against the rate of inflation over the past 50 years (Exhibit 6–7). Returns on bonds of all kinds, as well as T-bills, have either underperformed the consumer price index or have generally matched it. For most taxpayers, returns on debt instruments are often negative, once the effects of income taxes and inflation are factored in.

THE IMPACT OF INFLATION

The Preface pointed out some of the evils of inflation. Let us now look at the impact of inflation and taxes together. We begin by reviewing inflation from a different perspective.

EXHIBIT 6–7
Average Annual Compound Rate of Return, 1942–1992

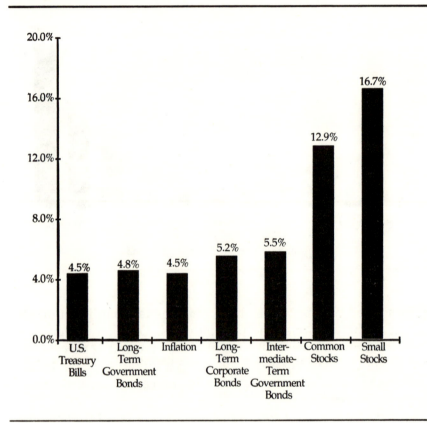

During any given year, the effect of inflation on our spending habits or standard of living is not normally noticeable, except perhaps when it comes to the purchase of a big-ticket item such as an automobile. However, the cumulative effects of inflation are quite a different matter. Consider Exhibit 6–8. People continue to be concerned about the rising cost of living. It is easy to see why. The 15-year graph in Exhibit 6–8 shows that the purchasing power of the dollar on January 1, 1978 has fallen to only 41 cents. What you bought for a dollar in 1978 costs over $2.28 today.

Assuming a 6 percent annual rate of inflation over the next dozen years, you would need exactly twice as much money to equal your

EXHIBIT 6–8
Purchasing Power of the U.S. Dollar

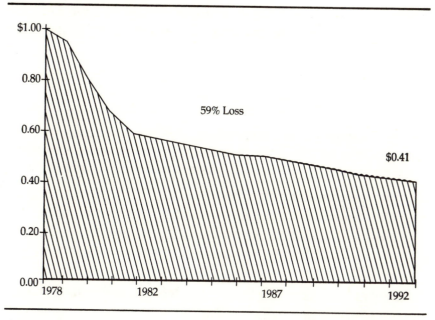

current standard of living. That is, if you had an asset base worth, say, $200,000 that provided $16,000 per year (an 8 percent return), you would need $400,000 in 12 years to have the same purchasing power as you have today. This is because at a 6 percent rate of inflation, the costs of goods and services will be exactly twice as much in a dozen years as they are today. If an 8 percent rate of inflation is projected, then the cost of goods and services doubles every nine years.

You may be thinking that this does not apply to you because you estimate that your life expectancy is, say, less than 12 years. But what will happen if you are wrong? Do you want to depend on your children, relatives, or public assistance to maintain a lifestyle even remotely similar to what you are now enjoying? Even if you are correct and you do not live to see the cumulative effects of inflation, what about your loved ones who survive you? The effects of inflation do not stop simply because you are no longer around.

What is perhaps more startling is the real rate of inflation. Government figures are one thing, but most people experience much higher increases in the prices of the items they buy. In fact, internal bank studies have shown that the true rate of inflation over the past decade has been almost twice the rate reported by the government. This makes it even more important for you to factor in the real "cost" of inflation.

TAX CONSIDERATIONS

Every investment has tax implications. The returns on most investments are fully taxable; however, there are a few that are either tax free or tax deferred. The list of tax-free investments is quite small:

1. Interest from municipal bonds.
2. Withdrawals from certain types of life insurance policies.
3. Income that may be partially or fully sheltered from taxes due to depreciation (real estate, oil, and leasing programs).

The number of investments that are tax deferred is also quite short:

1. Fixed-rate and variable annuities.
2. All investments that are part of a qualified retirement plan (such as investments that are in your IRA, Keogh, pension, and/or profit-sharing plan).
3. *Unrealized* gains (no sale has yet occurred) from any investment (appreciation in your real estate, stocks, bonds, mutual funds, metals, etc.).

To determine whether tax-free instruments should be part of your portfolio, look at Exhibit 6–9. In order to use the table, you first need to determine your tax bracket. This can be done by finding out your taxable income (the first or second column) and seeing what your federal tax bracket is (the third column). By looking in a newspaper or talking to your financial advisor, you can find out what a safe tax-free bond is currently yielding. Look under one of these columns (ranging from 6.0% to 8.0%) and see what the "equivalent taxable yields" are. You can then see which type of investment is better on an after-tax basis.

As an example, suppose you are single and have a taxable income of over $50,000; your federal tax rate (bracket) would be 31

EXHIBIT 6–9
Taxable and Tax-Free Yields

Taxable Income			Tax-Free Yields				
			6.00	*6.50*	*7.00*	*7.50*	*8.00*
Single Return	*Joint Return*	*Federal Tax Rate*	*Equivalent Taxable Yields*				
To $20,350	To $34,000	15%	7.06%	7.65%	8.24%	8.82%	9.41%
$20,350–49,300	$34.00–82.15	28	8.33	9.03	9.72	10.42	11.11
Over $49,300	Over $82.15k	31	8.70	9.42	10.14	10.87	11.59

percent. This means that on all taxable income over $49,300 you are paying 31 percent of every dollar to the federal government (not to mention what you are also paying to your state). If your broker tells you that high quality tax-free bonds are currently yielding 6.5 percent, then you would have to get at least a 9.42 percent taxable return to equal 6.5 percent tax free. If your broker tells you that U.S. government bonds are paying anything less than 9.42 percent, buy the municipal bonds instead. If he or she says that governments are paying 8 percent, then this means your after-tax return will be 5.52 percent (you are only netting 69 percent of 8 percent; the other 31 percent is going to Uncle Sam).

TYPES OF RISK

When we think of risk, the first thing that comes to mind for most people is "what are the chances that I can lose part or all of my principal?" Known as capital or business risk, this is just one type of risk you should be concerned with. Before you invest, look at the different types of risk and see which ones are characteristic of the investment you are considering.

While reading these sections on the different types of risk, you will notice that specific investments are mentioned. These investments will be fully discussed in the following chapter.

Financial Risk

When you invest in something, always know what the likelihood is that you could lose part or all of your money due to the financial troubles of the entity or the nature of the investment itself. If you buy shares or bonds of XYZ Corporation and the company goes bankrupt, you may end up losing most, if not all, of your money. Financial risk is highest with those investments that have a limited life, such as options or commodities.

More traditional investments can also have varying degrees of financial risk. Highly leveraged real estate can result in large losses if the property cannot be carried (low vacancy rate, income being directed to other sources, high overhead, etc.). High yield bonds may provide very attractive *current* returns, but the total return (current yield plus appreciation or minus depreciation) can be minimal or even negative, particularly if the bond issuer goes under. Cheap stocks look appealing because it is easy to dream of the price of a share going from $4 to $14; few people seem to realize that a $4 stock can also drop to $1 or zero just as easily.

Market Risk

You most commonly think of market risk when investing in stocks: the uncertainty of future prices due to changes in the marketplace, investor attitudes, fiscal policy, and factors that may be unique to certain markets. Market risk can be minimized by investing in different types of investments—assets that are not all affected by the same things. As an example, over the past half century, there have been only a few times when stocks and bonds were both down the same year.

Different investments have differing levels of market risk. Common stocks usually have greater market risk than preferred stocks and bonds. Growth funds have more market risk than global funds. A portfolio of aggressive growth stocks fluctuates more than one comprised of high-dividend equities.

Purchasing Power Risk

You and I cannot stop price increases, but we can counter the effects by investing in hedges against inflation. In the past, most types of bonds and liquid accounts have not fared well against inflation. However, real estate and particularly common stocks have dramatically outperformed any increases in the consumer price index.

Interest Rate Risk

Some investments are sensitive to changes in interest rates. Bonds and other marketable debt instruments (second trust deeds, mortgage-backed REITs, leasing programs, etc.) are inversely related to interest rate movements; when rates go up, these instruments always fall in value and vice versa. *Nonmarketable* debt instruments, such as passbook savings accounts, fixed-rate annuities, CDs, and series EE and series HH bonds do not change in value since they are not subject to interest rate risk. Their price does not drop because they have no secondary marketplace; such investments have no appreciation potential or chance of loss.

Equity vehicles are sometimes affected by interest rates. The stock market likes low interest rates but can also do quite well when rates are steadily increasing, as shown by the period 1975 to 1981. Real estate becomes less attractive to prospective buyers when rates go up since this means that new mortgages become less affordable. At other times, interest rates and real estate prices both rise due to a real or perceived fear of continued high levels of inflation.

Political and Social Risk

Depending on where you invest, political and social risk can affect your return. This type of risk is not common but it does exist. Companies that produce high levels of pollutants can be adversely affected by public sentiment and environmental regulations. Investing overseas, particularly in a place such as South Africa, can expose the investor to unexpected risk due to worldwide pressures or changes in public policy.

Currency Rate Risk

Whenever you invest either directly or indirectly overseas, you are subjecting yourself to a currency rate risk or reward. Investments in foreign currency denominations can benefit from a weak U.S. dollar or be harmed by a strong dollar. Gauging the direction of the U.S. dollar, interest rates, or any stock market is extremely difficult, especially when viewed over the short term. Only a handful of international mutual funds practice some type of active currency protection program.

To better understand the effects of a currency's strength or weakness, an example may be helpful. Suppose you liked a British stock that cost two pounds per share (whenever you invest in a foreign asset or security, your dollar is first converted into that country's currency before any purchase can be made). You decided to purchase one share of this stock. At the time of purchase, let us suppose that it took four U.S. dollars to equal two pounds (your $4 was exchanged for two pounds, and one share of this British stock was then bought).

A year later, the stock you bought *appeared* to be a disappointment; it was still trading at two pounds per share. However, during this period the dollar dropped in value. The share of stock was sold for the original purchase price of two pounds. At first you think you have only broken even; but if it now only takes two pounds to equal five U.S. dollars (remember the dollar has weakened in this example so that it takes *more* dollars to equal a pound), then you will end up with five dollars. You started with four dollars and a year later you have five dollars. This translates into a 25 percent annual return. This is an excellent return, particularly in light of the fact that this U.K. stock is still stuck at two pounds per share! You made money in this example because you owned pounds during a period when they appreciated against the dollar.

MINIMIZING YOUR PORTFOLIO'S RISK

If all of the different forms of risk are too overwhelming, consider setting up the conservative portfolio shown below. If such a portfolio (1/3 stocks, 1/3 bonds, and 1/3 cash) appeals to you, make sure that your weightings are based on *all* of your holdings, retirement as well as "regular" accounts. All too often, investors do not consider how their retirement plans are invested when looking at diversifying their portfolio. This usually results in a complete portfolio that

EXHIBIT 6–10
The Benefits of Diversification

Year	Stocks*	Bonds†	60% Stocks 40% Bonds	⅓ Stocks ⅓ Bonds ⅓ Cash‡
1973	−14.7%	−1.1%	−9.2%	−2.9%
1974	−26.5	4.4	−14.1	−4.7
1975	37.2	9.2	26.0	17.4
1976	23.8	16.8	21.0	15.2
1977	−7.2	−0.7	−4.6	−0.9
1978	6.6	−1.2	3.5	4.2
1979	18.4	−1.2	10.6	9.2
1980	32.4	−4.0	17.9	13.2
1981	−4.9	1.9	−2.2	3.9
1982	21.4	40.4	29.0	24.1
1983	22.5	0.7	13.8	10.7
1984	6.3	15.4	9.9	10.5
1985	32.2	31.0	31.7	23.6
1986	18.5	24.4	20.9	16.4
1987	5.2	−2.7	2.1	2.7
1988	16.8	9.7	14.0	10.9
1989	31.5	18.2	26.2	19.4
1990	−3.2	4.0	−0.3	2.9
1991	30.6	19.3	26.1	18.5
1992	7.7	8.1	7.8	6.4
Average compound annual return	11.3	9.0	10.7	9.7

*Stocks: Standard & Poor's 500 Index
†Bonds: Long-term Treasury Bonds
‡Cash: U.S. Treasury bills

is too heavily weighted in one category. The next chapter will show how to improve on the results shown in Exhibit 6–10, no matter which of the four sample portfolios appeals to you.

Exhibit 6–10 shows four different investment portfolios in order of risk, from left to right. The most conservative portfolio, the one with an equal weighting of stocks, bonds, and cash had an average annual compound rate of return over the past 20 years of almost 10 percent. This is particularly impressive when you see that such a portfolio suffered only three negative years, 1973 (off 2.9 percent), 1974 (down 4.7 percent), and 1977 (off 0.9 percent).

Now that you have been introduced to investments, it is time to test yourself as to how much risk you can live with. The next chapter gives you some suggestions as to how a complete portfolio should be structured, including a capsule summary of how several dozen investments work and their expected rates of return in the future. Chapter Seven ends by showing you how you can calculate your *real* return, making compensations for inflation and income taxes.

CHECKLIST OF THINGS TO DO

1. Determine if you are better off with tax-free instruments or paying taxes on higher-yielding taxable securities. Begin thinking about an investment's return on an aftertax, afterinflation basis.

2. Contact the IRS and request the following publications: *Taxable and Nontaxable Income* (publication no. 525) and *Investment Income and Expenses* (publication no. 550). These free publications will aid you in determining the tax consequences of certain types of investments.

3. Telephone *The Wall Street Journal* (1–800–628–9320) and request a copy of their *Video Guide to Money and Markets*. This 30-minute video provides basic information about: stocks, bonds, the Federal Reserve Bank, foreign securities, and commodities. The video will cost you $14.95.

Chapter Seven

Investment Planning

Summary of Investment Options
Diversification: Reduce Risk without Decreasing Returns
Using Equities
Why Bonds Are Appealing
Limited Role for Savings Accounts
Going Global
Determining Your Risk Level: A Test
Mutual Funds
Money Market Funds
International Money Funds
Annuities
Bonds
Balanced Funds
Equity REITs
Leasing
Growth and Income Funds
Specialty Utilities Funds
Blue Chip Stocks
Growth Funds
International Stock Funds
Aggressive Growth Funds
Portfolio Advice
An Alternative Approach
Calculating Returns
Reviewing Your Progress

So far, you have learned why retirement planning is important and how to set your own personal and financial goals, determined your net worth and how much you will need to save each year to retire comfortably (your first two worksheets), learned how inflation and taxes affect an investment's return, and learned about the different forms of risk and at least one way such risks can be managed. Now you are ready to understand diversification a little more, determining your risk level and corresponding investment portfolios, the different types of investments, the benefits of using mutual funds, and how to calculate your progress.

This chapter begins by looking at investments in a little more detail. The first section breaks down the two major categories of investments, equity and debt instruments, into a handful of manageable classifications: U.S. stocks, bonds, money market accounts, and global securities. The section that follows will help you determine your risk level. This simple test gives a strong sense of direction as to what kinds of investments are best for your situation and what amounts should be committed to each area. The test will take only a couple of minutes to complete but will prove to be a tremendous time saver later on. By knowing what general categories to focus on, you won't have to waste time reviewing inappropriate investments.

To make the process of portfolio selection more precise, seven different complete portfolios are listed, followed by detailed information on over two dozen different investments. These descriptions show not only how the investment works, its tax ramifications, how it is purchased, but also what kind of return you can expect and the range of returns—the positive as well as the negative. For you who feel that this is just too much work, the section that follows gives the author's advice as to how a portfolio should be constructed. The chapter ends by showing how to calculate your progress, the easy way to find out how fast your money will double, and how to check on how your broker, financial planner, or registered investment adviser is doing.

SUMMARY OF INVESTMENT OPTIONS

Diversifying your assets across different types of investments can reduce risks while maintaining, or even increasing, your return. It not only opens up your portfolio to additional opportunities, it also decreases the possibility that any event or development will disrupt your entire plan. That is because stocks, bonds, and other financial assets move up and down in different rhythms. A broad slump in U.S. stocks, for instance, could be tempered or offset by gains in bonds or non–U.S. securities.

To be sure, the very nature of diversification means that you are less likely to make that really big killing. It also does not guarantee that your portfolio will not experience interim declines. By taking a crablike stance with your assets, legs spread out so your overall portfolio cannot be tipped over, you increase the likelihood that you will make progress toward your goals.

The appropriate mix for your portfolio will depend on two main factors: your time horizon and your risk tolerance—in other words, how long you have to invest and how much risk you are willing to take. The most important variable is likely to be your time horizon because the very notion of risk changes over time. Over shorter periods price fluctuations are your biggest concern. For that reason, if your financial goals are immediate, you will want to be more conservative in your investment selections. Over longer periods, the main risk will be the loss of your purchasing power to inflation (see the previous chapter for examples of portfolios based on different risk levels). So, even if you are heading into retirement, it makes sense to keep part of your money in longer-term, growth-oriented investments.

DIVERSIFICATION: REDUCE RISK WITHOUT DECREASING RETURNS

Different types of investments tend to perform well in different markets. That is why the returns from various classes of investments tend to vary markedly from year to year. As an example, over the past 65 years, there have been only a half dozen times when stocks and bonds both declined during the same year. It has often been said that stocks perform during good times and bonds do well during periods of panic.

By diversifying your portfolio, you can reduce the likelihood that its value will drop sharply. Case in point: during each major U.S. stock market decline in the past 20 years, other financial assets, such as U.S. bonds and non–U.S. stocks and bonds, have almost always held up better—or even gained ground.

EXHIBIT 7–1
Cumulative Return Figures for the Period 1971–1990

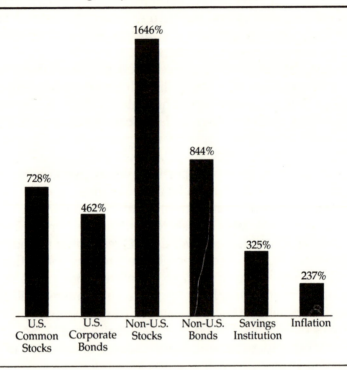

Of course, diversification also exposes your portfolio to additional opportunities. The chart above shows how various financial assets have done over the past 20 years. Included are other pertinent benchmarks, such as the return you would have earned from the average savings institution, as measured by passbook savings accounts, and the effects of inflation. While reviewing this chart, keep in mind that these are all pretax returns. When it comes to investments such as U.S. bonds and savings accounts, the gap between their returns and inflation is much narrower than it appears from the chart.

USING EQUITIES

Over the long haul, stocks may actually be the least risky investment you can make because they are one of the few investments that can help you keep pace with, and hopefully outdistance, inflation.

Of course, stocks can be volatile over short periods, so only longer-term money should be invested in the stock market. But that patience is likely to be well rewarded. Since 1926, when such statistics were first kept, stocks have appreciated an average of 10 percent a year, more than double the return on bonds and more than triple the rate of inflation, according to Ibbotson Associates. Over the past half century, there has not been any 10-year period when investors lost money in stocks.

WHY BONDS ARE APPEALING

Bonds offer something that most stocks do not: high current income. This income is also generally higher than that provided by CDs, money funds, and bank accounts, which explains why tax-exempt, corporate, and government bond funds (each of these are more fully explained below) became so popular during the 1980s as interest rates declined. CDs and bank accounts may offer a guaranteed return of principal and a fixed rate of interest, but no opportunity for your principal to grow.

Many investors have also come to appreciate the stabilizing influence that bond funds can have on a portfolio. Although bond prices do fluctuate, they tend to be less volatile than stock prices; they also respond differently to economic circumstances. The higher income from bonds can help you in different ways. It can be used to meet living costs once you have retired or at other times when your expenses are high relative to your income. When you do not need the income, it can be reinvested to provide for future needs.

LIMITED ROLE FOR SAVINGS ACCOUNTS

Most financial advisers suggest that everyone keep at least three to six months of salary as a cash reserve for emergencies and to take advantage of future investment opportunities. At certain times—in retirement, for instance, or when the economic outlook is uncertain—it may make sense to hold even more.

Money market funds (described in detail later) are a good choice for cash reserves. They are an effective money management tool—offering convenient services such as check writing and exchange privileges to other mutual funds. And, while they are usually not guaranteed, they generally provide higher returns than CDs or bank accounts.

GOING GLOBAL

Chances are that many of the products you use—your car, some of your clothes, even some of the food you eat—were produced outside of the United States. Many investors, recognizing the increasingly global scale of today's economy, are likewise beginning to look past our national boundaries for investment opportunities.

Over the past quarter century, non–U.S. stocks and bonds both have provided returns superior to those of their U.S. counterparts. But there are other, equally important reasons to consider diversifying internationally. First, many of the world's most dynamic companies are located outside the United States. By investing in them, you can participate in their growth. Also, when you put some of your money into global stocks or global bonds, you are reducing the degree to which difficult economic conditions in the United States will affect your entire portfolio. Foreign securities are discussed in detail later.

DETERMINING YOUR RISK LEVEL: A TEST

Never invest in something if you do not feel comfortable with it; no projected returns or assurances from a stockbroker can take the place of a good night's sleep. By first determining your risk level, you can narrow down the list of prospective investments. This not only saves time but also minimizes any confusion. To determine your risk level, score the following seven statements in Exhibit 7–2.

1. Earning a total return that is greater than the rate of inflation is one of my most important objectives.
2. I want investments that provide for the tax deferral of gains, income, and/or interest.

EXHIBIT 7–2
Rating Investment Goals

	Level of Agreement				
Investment objective	*Strong*	*Much*	*Some*	*Little*	*Disagree*
1. High long-term total return	4	3	2	1	0
2. Tax-deferral	4	3	2	1	0
3. Growth more than income	4	3	2	1	0
4. Long- versus short-term horizon	4	3	2	1	0
5. Greater volatility in return for higher returns	4	3	2	1	0
6. Short-term loss in exchange for good returns over 2 years +	4	3	2	1	0
7. Will accept low liquidity	4	3	2	1	0

3. I do not require a high level of current income from my investments.

4. My major investment goals are relatively long term, five years or longer.

5. I am willing to live with sharp up and down swings in value in exchange for a return that is potentially higher than more stable investments such as bank CDs, money market accounts, savings bonds, or Treasury bills.

6. I am willing to risk a short-term loss in return for the chance of making double-digit returns. I understand that during any given year, stocks have about a 75 percent chance of making money and a 25 percent chance of showing a loss.

7. I can accept a low level of liquidity in my investment portfolio.

After you have answered and scored all seven statements, add up your total point score. Next, review Exhibit 7–3 to get a general idea as to how your portfolio (retirement as well as non-retirement accounts) should be structured. While reviewing these mixes, keep in mind that they are only guidelines. Your actual holdings will depend upon a number of other factors such as: (1) whether or not you view your personal residence as an investment, (2) life

EXHIBIT 7-3
Portfolio Mix Table

Total Score	Asset Mix Percentages			
	Money Market	Fixed Income	Stocks	Real Estate + *
28	5%	10%	75%	10%
23–27	10	15	60	15
18–22	10	20	55	15
17–21	10	25	45	20
12–16	15	30	35	20
7–11	20	35	25	20
0–6	20	45	15	20

*"Real estate +" includes all other forms of real estate ownership, as well as participation in nonleveraged (all cash) programs such as leasing and cable television partnerships. Personal residences are not considered an investment within the context of this chapter since most people would not sell their homes if they appreciated greatly or declined in value.

expectancy, (3) inability to sell or reposition existing investments (either due to the triggering of a large gain, lack of liquidity, or sentimental value), or (4) personal bias.

Once you have determined your risk level, look at the levels below to see what kind of investments should be included in your portfolio. If, as an example, your total score was 19, the great majority of your holdings should be those listed under the portfolio described as "total score 17–21." As you look through the sample portfolios in Exhibit 7–4, keep in mind that if your total score is less than seven, there is at least a fair likelihood that you will outlive your resources, particularly if you plan on living more than 15 years. On the other hand, the older you get, the more conservative your portfolio should be, unless your goals are to provide for your spouse and/or children after your death. Many of the investment categories shown below can be purchased individually or within a mutual fund family or variable annuity.

Personal residences are not included in these sample portfolios since most people do not consider their home as an investment in the traditional sense. That is, they are not likely to sell the

EXHIBIT 7–4
Various Portfolio Mixes

Total Score of 0–6 Points (extremely conservative)

15%	Money market account
5	International money market fund
20	High-quality bonds that mature in 10 years or less
10	Long-term bonds that mature in 15 years or more
15	Global bonds (foreign and U.S. securities)
5	Growth and income stocks (high-dividend-paying equities) or growth mutual fund
10	High-quality convertible preferred stocks
10	All-cash (nonleveraged) real estate investment trust (REIT)
10	All-cash (nonleveraged) leasing program

Total Score of 7–11 points (conservative)

10%	Money market account or a fixed-rate annuity
10	International money market fund
5	High-quality bonds that mature in 10 years or less
10	Long-term bonds that mature in 15 years or more
20	Global bonds
10	Growth and income stocks (high-dividend-paying equities)
10	High-quality convertible preferred stocks
5	Blue-chip stocks (companies that have a market value of over $5 billion)
10	All-cash real estate investment trust (REIT)
10	All-cash leasing program

Total Score of 12–16 points (somewhat conservative to moderate)

10%	International money market fund
5	Money market fund or a fixed-rate annuity
20	Long-term bonds that mature in 15 years or more
10	Global bonds
15	Blue-chip stocks (companies that have a market value of over $5 billion)
10	Growth and income stocks (high-dividend paying equities)
10	Foreign stocks of large-capitalized corporations
10	All-cash real estate investment trust (REIT)
10	All-cash leasing program

Total Score of 17–21 points (moderate)

10%	International money market fund
10	High yield (junk) bonds

EXHIBIT 7-4
Various Portfolio Mixes (concluded)

15	Global bonds
10	Blue-chip stocks (companies that have a market value of over $5 billion)
15	Growth and income stocks (high-dividend paying equities)
20	Foreign stocks of large-capitalized corporations
10	All-cash real estate investment trust (REIT)
10	All-cash leasing program

Total Score of 18–22 points (moderate to slightly aggressive)

10%	International money market fund
10	High yield (junk) bonds
15	Global bonds
10	Blue-chip stocks (companies that have a market value of over $5 billion)
10	Growth and income stocks (high-dividend paying equities)
10	Aggressive growth or small company growth stocks
25	Foreign stocks of large-capitalized corporations
10	All-cash real estate investment trust (REIT)
5	All-cash leasing or cable TV program

Total Score of 23–27 points (fairly aggressive)

10%	International money market fund
15	Global bonds or global bond funds
5	Blue-chip stocks (companies that have a market value of over $5 billion) or funds
5	Growth and income stocks (high-dividend paying equities) or funds
15	Aggressive growth or small company growth stocks or funds
35	Foreign stocks of large-capitalized corporations
10	All-cash real estate investment trust (REIT)
5	All-cash leasing program

Total Score of 28 points (aggressive)

5%	International money market fund
10	Global bonds or global bond funds
5	Gold mining (metals) stocks
10	Growth stocks or growth funds
15	Aggressive growth or small company growth stocks or funds
35	Foreign stocks of large-capitalized corporations
10	Foreign stocks of small- and medium-sized companies
10	All-cash leasing program

house no matter how much it climbs in value or plummets in price. Real estate is an important component of most portfolios since personal residences, particularly those with little or no mortgages, are low in volatility and have generally been a good hedge against inflation.

MUTUAL FUNDS

The following pages give specific information on each of the above-listed investments: expected returns, how they work, tax benefits, risks, and where they can be purchased. Several of the investments described are different types of mutual funds. Mutual funds are another way in which the aforementioned investments can be owned. Therefore, mutual funds will first be described.

A mutual fund is an investment company, an entity that makes investments on behalf of individuals and institutions who share common financial goals. The fund pools the money of many people, each with a different amount to invest. Professional money managers then use the pool of money to buy a variety of stocks, bonds, or money market instruments that, in their judgment, will help the fund's shareholders achieve their financial objectives.

Each fund has an investment objective, described in the fund's prospectus, which is important to both the manager and the potential investor. The fund manager uses it as a guide when choosing investments for the fund's portfolio. Prospective investors use the prospectus to determine which funds are suitable for their own needs. There is a wide range of mutual fund investment objectives. Some follow aggressive investment policies involving greater risk in search of higher returns; others seek income from more conservative investments.

When a fund earns money, it distributes the earnings to its shareholders; however, you can elect to have such distributions automatically reinvested so that you end up with more shares. Earnings come from stock dividends, interest paid by bonds or money market instruments, and gains from the sale of securities in the fund's portfolio. Dividends and capital gains produced are paid out in proportion to the number of fund shares owned. Thus,

shareholders who invest a few hundred dollars get the same investment return per dollar as those who invest hundreds of thousands.
Even a single mutual fund can provide broad diversity, of
course, but this is generally in one type of investment. For example,
a growth fund invests in several dozen different common stocks;
a modest portion of the portfolio may be in money market instruments or preferred stocks in order to reduce volatility. A second
example would be a bond fund that invests in a large number of
different bonds with varying maturities; this type of diversification
protects investors against portfolio losses when interest rates climb
or in the unlikely event that one of the bond issuers becomes financially troubled. Investing in more than one fund takes the concept
of diversification a step further to help you benefit from more
opportunities and protect yourself against unforeseen events.

The "expected return" and "range of returns" figures that follow are total return numbers. Both numbers include current income (a cash-on-cash return) plus any expected annual appreciation. Anticipated appreciation is more commonly found in
equity-type investments (e.g., stocks, growth funds, etc.) than in
money market and bond instruments.

MONEY MARKET FUNDS

Money market funds (expected return: 6 percent)

Range of returns: = +3 percent to +10 percent

Money market funds comprise short-term debt instruments such
as U.S. Treasury bills, bank CDs, and commercial paper. These
funds are particularly appealing to people who are either shopping
for other investments or are scared by current events. They were
never intended as long-term investments. Returns from money
market funds have been poor once income taxes and inflation are
factored in.

Money market funds can be acquired from stockbrokers, bankers, or financial planners. Interest from these funds is fully taxable
unless you invest in a tax-free money fund. Investors are attracted
to money market accounts because they provide tremendous
safety. There is no price volatility and virtually no chance of default;

a fund's price always remains constant at one dollar per share. No one has ever lost any money in a money market fund. Since most money market accounts are not insured, there is, theoretically, a chance that losses could occur; however, this has never happened.

If you are looking for a safe haven, consider T-bills, money market accounts, and bank CDs. All of these investments are extremely safe and are an excellent place to park your money for a short term. Do not make T-bills or similar investments part of your long-term portfolio. Their real return is almost always negative.

INTERNATIONAL MONEY FUNDS

International money market funds (expected return: 8 percent)

Range of returns: = +5 percent to +12 percent

International money market funds are composed of high quality, short-term debt instruments issued by governments and corporates from politically and economically secure countries. International investing is attractive for a U.S. investor seeking higher rates of return. Like traditional money market accounts, these funds are not intended as long-term investments. Returns from foreign or international money market funds are fair once income taxes and inflation are factored in.

International money market funds can be obtained from stock-brokers or financial planners. Interest from these funds is fully taxable; interest withheld by foreign governments is fully recouped (foreign taxes paid by the fund can be used as a tax credit by U.S. investors). Investors are attracted to international money market accounts because their safety is almost as great as regular money market funds but the yield is higher. There is very little price-per-share volatility and virtually no chance of default.

ANNUITIES

Fixed-Rate Annuities

Fixed-rate annuity (expected return: 7 percent)

Range of returns = +4 percent to +11 percent

Fixed-rate annuities are issued by insurance companies. The insurer invests your money in short- and medium-term debt instruments. Annuities can be purchased from insurance agents, brokers, and financial planners. Interest earned in an annuity is always tax deferred; you pay taxes only on the interest withdrawn. You do not have to make any withdrawals during your life or the lifetime of your spouse. There are no capital gains in a fixed-rate annuity. Your principal is guaranteed every day; there is no volatility of principal in a fixed-rate annuity (similar in safety to a bank CD).

Variable Annuities

In addition to fixed-rate annuities, there are also *variable* annuities. A variable annuity is like a fixed-rate annuity in all ways except: (1) investment options, (2) performance, (3) guarantees, (4) the ability to make ongoing contributions, and (5) cost.

First, variable annuities allow you, the investor, to choose among one or more different portfolios that are similar to selected funds within a mutual fund family. You can invest part or all of your money in growth, balanced (stocks and bonds), government securities, or money market portfolios. Second, the annual return or growth rate depends on how the portfolio performs; the rate of return is not usually locked in. Third, and important, unlike a fixed-rate annuity, your principal is not guaranteed every day. One month the account may be up 11 percent and then fall 5 percent the very next week or month.

Like mutual funds, variable annuities can be added to at anytime. When you want to add money to a fixed-rate annuity, you must purchase another, separate contract. Fifth, and finally, variable annuities charge an annual administrative fee that ranges from $30 to $50, depending on the issuing company. There is also a yearly mortality charge of approximately 1.2 percent of the account's value, which pays for the guaranteed death benefit. A fixed-rate annuity does not have either one of these charges.

Variable annuities generally outperform fixed-rate annuities, but they can also experience some ups and downs. And, just like mutual funds, the portfolio(s) you select should depend on your risk level and time horizon. Variable annuities are not good or bad. The results of the portfolios you chose will determine your feelings.

BONDS

Intermediate-Term Bonds

Intermediate-term bonds—5- to 10-year maturities
(expected return: 7 percent)
Range of returns: = −3 percent to +21 percent

There are only two differences between intermediate- and long-term bonds: current income and volatility of principal. Intermediate-term bonds, defined here as securities that mature in less than 10 years, have only one third to one half the volatility of long-term obligations. Lower volatility means less upside potential and little downside risk. In return for accepting greater stability, the investor accepts a slightly lower current yield.

Intermediate-term bonds have done better than long-term debentures (bonds) when viewed on a total return basis. This is because, overall, bonds have been in a bear market for the past 50 years (with the exception of the 1980s) and suffered from downward swings in prices more frequently than they have benefited from increases in value due to rates dropping.

Intermediate-term bonds come in three varieties: government, corporate, and municipal. Government bonds are the safest since there is no chance of the U.S. government defaulting; these obligations are free from state and local income taxes. High quality corporate bonds pay about a point more than their government counterparts for two reasons: (1) a slight chance of default and (2) interest from these obligations is fully taxable on a federal, state, and local level. Municipal bonds are usually safer than corporate bonds, but there is still an ever-so-slight chance of default. Interest from municipal bonds is free from federal income taxes and is often free from state and local income taxes as well.

If you are a conservative investor, intermediate-term bonds should be part of your portfolio. Whether you should own government, corporate, or municipal issues depends largely on your tax bracket; the more you pay in income taxes, the greater the reason to first look at municipal, also known as tax-free, bonds. Government and corporate bonds are good candidates for retirement accounts such as IRAs, Keoghs, and pension plans since the interest in such accounts is tax-deferred. There is only one way to make the interest from tax-free bonds taxable: by placing them in a retirement account, since all growth and dividends that come out of these plans are fully taxable.

Intermediate-term bonds provide reliable income that can either be spent or reinvested. Volatility is slight and unimportant if the bonds are held until maturity. Long-term bonds are a favored choice only if you believe interest rates will fall and you are looking for capital gains. Short-, intermediate-, and long-term bonds can either be purchased individually or as part of a mutual fund.

Long-Term Bonds

Long-term bonds—15-year or greater maturities
(expected return: 9 percent)

Range of returns: = −11 percent to +29 percent

Long-term government, corporate, and municipal bonds are appropriate for two types of investors: those who feel interest rates will be falling during the next couple of years or people who do not care about price volatility and are simply looking for the highest possible current return (not total return).

All bonds, short-, intermediate-, and long-term, can be purchased from brokerage firms and financial planners. You can own these types of bonds individually or within a mutual fund. Safety of principal depends on the creditworthiness of the issuer. As an investor, stick to corporate bonds that are rated either BAA, A, AA, or AAA (high yield, also called junk bonds are described later). You want to make sure that the face amount of the bonds is paid off at maturity. Price volatility depends on the maturity of the issue—the greater the maturity, the greater the risk or reward potential.

Since you and most brokers do not closely follow the bond market each day, you should stay away from individual corporate bonds. Invest in a bond fund instead (described below). Managers of these funds study interest rates and credit reports on a daily basis. Credit reports are not important in the case of government bonds since they are backed by the full faith and credit of the U.S. government.

Municipal Bonds

Municipal bonds (expected return: 7 percent)

Range of returns: = −4 percent to +20 percent

As a general category, municipal bonds are safer than any other investment except money market accounts, government obligations, or insured investments. Municipals can be purchased individually or in a unit trust or bond fund. Unit trusts and funds provide the utmost in safety and marketability.

Municipal bonds can be purchased from brokers, financial planners, or directly from a mutual fund or unit trust issuer. Interest from municipal bonds is free from federal income taxes. If you buy bonds issued in your state of residence, interest is also free from state and local income taxes. Some states such as Texas and Florida have no state income tax, thereby allowing their residents a wider selection of pure tax-free issues. Individual bonds pay interest semiannually; unit trusts and funds distribute income on a monthly basis.

Only the interest from municipal bonds is free from income taxes. If you buy a municipal bond, unit trust, or fund for one price and later sell it for a higher price, there will be capital gains taxes. In some cases, sales that result in a loss of principal can be used to offset gains or other forms of taxable income.

In addition to providing tax-free income, municipal bonds are normally quite stable in their price. They exhibit only one half to cne third the volatility of government or corporate bonds with similar maturities. This makes them an ideal choice for the conservative or moderate investor. Due to their limited appreciation potential, aggressive investors will find little use for this investment. This is a great choice for someone who needs current income or wants to be able to reinvest income on a tax-free basis.

Municipal Bond Funds

Municipal Bond Funds (expected return: 7 percent)

Range of returns: = −2 percent to +19 percent

These funds invest in securities issued by municipalities, political subdivisions, and U.S. territories. The type of security issued is either a note or bond, both of which are interest-bearing instruments that are exempt from federal income taxes. There are three different categories of municipal bond funds: national, state-free, and high yield.

National municipal bond funds are composed of debt instruments issued by a wide range of states. These funds are exempt only from federal income taxes. To determine what small percentage is also exempt from state income taxes, consult the fund's prospectus and look for the weighting of U.S. territory issues (e.g., The Virgin Islands, Guam, Puerto Rico), District of Columbia items, and obligations from your state of residence.

State-free, sometimes referred to as *double tax-free*, funds invest only in bonds and notes issued in a particular state. You must be a legal resident of that state to avoid paying state income taxes on the fund's return. As an example, most California residents who are in a high tax bracket will want to consider purchasing a municipal bond fund that has the name "California" in it. Residents of New York who purchase a California tax-free fund will escape federal income taxes but not state and any local taxes.

High yield tax-free funds invest in the same types of issues found in a national municipal bond fund, but with one important difference. By seeking higher returns, high yield funds look for lower-rated issues and bonds that are not rated. A municipality may not obtain a rating for its issue because of the costs involved compared to the relatively small size of the bond or note being floated. Many nonrated issues are very safe. These kinds of municipal bond funds are relatively new but should not be overlooked by the tax-conscious investor. High-yield tax-free funds have demonstrated less volatility and higher return than their other tax-free counterparts.

Prospective investors need to compare tax-free bond yields to aftertax yields on corporate or government bond funds. To determine which of these three fund categories is best for you, use your marginal tax bracket, subtract this amount from one and multiply the resulting figure by the taxable investment. As an example, suppose you were in the 35 percent bracket, state and federal combined. By subtracting this figure from one, you are left with .65. Multiply .65 by the fully taxable yield you could get, let us say 9 percent. Sixty-five percent of 9 percent is 5.85 percent. The 5.85

percent represents what you get on a 9 percent investment *after* you have paid state and federal income taxes on it. This means that if you can get 5.85 percent or higher from a tax-free investment, take it.

A separate description for government bonds is given due to their tremendous popularity. As previously mentioned, these bonds, like corporate and municipal securities, can be purchased individually or in mutual funds.

Long-Term Government Bonds

Long-term bonds—20 years or greater (expected return: 8 percent)

Range of returns: = −13 percent to +31 percent

Government bonds offer reliable income and safety of principal if held until maturity. Long-term government bonds can be volatile since they are subject to interest-rate risk. There is an inverse relationship between interest rates and the price of a bond; when interest rates go up, the price of bonds go down and vice versa. The fact that your principal can go up and down in value is of little concern to investors who plan on holding onto the investment until it matures. The range of returns shown above represents *total* return: current returns plus any appreciation during the year or losses due to interest rate increases.

By using *Treasury Direct*, a program that allows you to buy directly from the government, you can avoid the fees charged by stockholders, bankers, and financial planners. Government bonds pay interest semiannually; interest is subject to federal income taxes but not state or local taxes. If you sell your bonds for more than you paid for them, all of your gain is taxable. Bonds sold for a loss can be used to offset gains from other investments.

You should own some government bonds or a government bond fund if you are a conservative investor in a low tax bracket or plan to purchase them within a retirement plan such as an IRA, Keogh, or pension plan. The biggest mistake most investors make is owning too much in the way of bonds. They normally offer little appreciation potential, are considered only fair hedges against inflation, and are poor hedges against inflation once income taxes are factored in. Nevertheless, they provide the utmost in marketability and a nice current income.

International Bond Fund

International bond fund (expected return: 13 percent)
Range of returns: = −6 percent to +34 percent

Like convertible funds, international bond funds are one of the best-kept secrets. These funds are composed of U.S. and foreign government bonds from only the fiscally strongest countries in the world. International bond funds have outperformed their U.S. counterparts over the past 1, 3, 5, 10, and 20 years. They also possess less risk than a portfolio or fund composed only of bonds issued by one country, such as a government securities fund or corporate bond fund.

Since this is a bond fund, a good portion of your total return will be interest, which is fully taxable. Therefore, these funds should be targeted for your retirement plan. A sizable portion of your IRA, Keogh, pension plan, 403(b), or 401(k) plan could be in an international bond fund. These funds are a good way to reduce your total portfolio's overall level of risk. International, sometimes referred to as foreign or global, bond funds often move in an opposite direction to stocks. This means that when stocks are going down this investment may actually be increasing in value (1990 was a good example of this; the typical stock dropped a few points in value while the average international bond fund was up 13 percent).

Whenever people think about investing in foreign securities, they think of withholding taxes imposed by other countries. This is true but it should not concern you. In almost all cases, taxes withheld by other governments are automatically credited to you on your tax return. Thus, if the ABC international bond fund was to withhold $500 from your account one year, you will now be able to take a $500 tax credit on your tax return for that same year. Since you get a tax credit, the net effect is zero. You are not paying any more or less in taxes.

Most people should own at least one international bond fund. They offer very good returns, provide current income if needed, and are an excellent means to reduce overall portfolio risk. This holds true whether you are a conservative, moderate, or aggressive investor.

Corporate High Yield Bonds

Corporate high yield fund (expected return: 11 percent)

Range of returns: = −7 percent to +25 percent

High yield, also known as *junk* bonds have received negative press in recent years and deservedly so. But there are several different shades or qualities of junk bonds. The upper end of the high yield bond spectrum, those bonds rated B or BB, have actually performed quite well. People are attracted to junk bond funds because of their high current income. By accepting a little less return, investors can get almost the same current income and a lot more safety. The default rate for the higher quality junk issues has been minimal.

You can buy individual junk bonds, but almost everyone would be much wiser to purchase a high yield bond fund. This is a tricky area in the market and should be left to the pros. Any type of bond fund can be purchased through your broker or financial planner or directly from the fund. The current yield on these funds is in the 9–14 percent range. This is quite appealing, but such returns are also fully taxable whether you receive the interest payments or have them automatically reinvested into the fund. These funds have some appreciation potential but normally only during periods when interest rates are falling.

If you do your homework and search for funds that are willing to accept a little less current income in return for quality, then you will have a winner. The research is not complex; you simply want to find out the fund's total return for each of the last 5 to 10 years. These figures will show you how much deterioration of principal has occurred.

BALANCED FUNDS

Balanced fund (expected return: 12 percent)

Range of returns: = −8 percent to +32 percent

Balanced mutual funds invest in common stocks, convertibles, and bonds. The exact mix depends on the manager. These funds offer a compromise for the investor who is uncertain as to whether or not he should be owning equities or debt instruments. Balanced funds are not specifically recommended in the suggested portfolios previously listed. However, they are a good alternative for the investor who wants to minimize the number of mutual funds or other securities being held (e.g., if your recommended portfolio suggested putting 10 percent of your money in bonds and 10 percent in common stocks, you could place 20 percent in a balanced fund instead and achieve similar results).

Due to their composition and tendency to trade in or out of a category with fair frequency, balanced funds are a good choice for the low bracket investor or the qualified retirement plan. Balanced funds rank somewhere between conservative and moderate. They should never be considered aggressive. The safety of this instrument lies in the fact that it is extremely uncommon for stocks and bonds both to be down during the same year. This ends our discussion of debt instruments. The remaining sections describe different types of equities (stocks, partnerships, real estate, etc.).

EQUITY REITS

Equity REITs (expected return: 13 percent)

Range of returns: = −17 percent to +43 percent

If you like the idea of owning real estate and like the freedom of being able to buy and sell securities on a moment's notice, this is for you. When you purchase a real estate investment trust (REIT), you are buying shares. These shares can be bought and sold on different exchanges or over the counter (OTC). Real estate investment trusts come in several different varieties. Some REITs invest in a certain geographic area, others invest in a certain type or mix of real estate. Conservative REITs have little, if any, debt (properties within the program are bought on an all-cash basis); REITs seeking large capital gains are usually highly leveraged and are therefore inherently riskier.

REITs can be purchased from anyone who has a securities license. Income from REITs is usually partially sheltered from income taxes (you are entitled to depreciate the buildings and fixtures since you are one of the REIT owners). Capital gains are deferred until you sell or trade your shares. In some REITs, property appreciation is realized when the real estate is sold.

Unless you own real estate other than your personal residence, equity REITs that purchase properties on an all-cash basis should be part of your portfolio. They are conservative (the range of returns shown above includes highly leveraged programs) and can offer a current income stream similar to bank CDs but with three additional benefits: (1) some tax relief due to depreciation, (2) an income stream that can increase to offset inflation (CPI adjustments in the leases), and (3) growth potential from property appreciation. If you buy the right type of REIT, your risk level is minimal.

LEASING

Leasing (expected return: 11 percent)

Range of returns: = +1 percent to +21 percent

A leasing venture purchases aircraft, cargo containers, medical equipment, railroad flat cars, or computers and leases them to businesses, usually large, well-known firms. The companies lease the equipment because it gives them flexibility and the initial costs are much lower; consequently, their balance sheets look more appealing. The leasors, you, the people who bought the equipment, are receiving quarterly distributions that are partially sheltered since the equipment is being depreciated.

Investors are attracted to leasing programs for two reasons: safety and current income. The tax benefits are a secondary concern. If you invest in leasing, chances are that you will do so as a limited partner. Expect to hold onto this investment for 10 to 15 years (3 to 6 years in the case of high tech assets that quickly become obsolete). Partnership interests are thinly traded, and most programs have no marketability.

Leasing ventures are attractive because their current income can be quite high, ranging anywhere from 10 percent to over 20 percent per year. In a number of programs, however, investors have ended up with large losses or rates of return similar to passbook savings accounts. Your income stream depends on the expected life of the assets. Computers, due to technological breakthroughs, do not have the long-term appeal that airplanes and cargo containers do and therefore must offer a much higher, albeit shorter-term, return.

GROWTH AND INCOME FUNDS

Growth and income fund (expected return: 14 percent)

Range of returns: = −13 percent to +39 percent

If you want a good hedge against inflation but are a little afraid of regular stocks, this is for you. These funds invest in common and preferred stocks but focus on those that pay high dividends. By looking for greater current income, risk is reduced. If the fund is down 8 percent for the year but you received a 5 percent cash dividend, your real loss may be only 3 percent.

Since growth and income funds can yield a fair amount of money in the form of dividends, they are ideal for retirement plans or within other sheltered vehicles. Low bracket investors will find them quite appealing in all cases.

If you could only purchase either a growth or growth and income fund, the choice should be the latter. Growth and income funds are more conservative, provide higher current income, and often outperform pure growth funds.

SPECIALTY UTILITIES FUNDS

Specialty utilities fund (expected return: 13 percent)

Range of returns: = −9 percent to +35 percent

There is only one conservative type of specialty or sector fund, and this is it. Utility funds buy the common and preferred stocks of utility companies. The dividends are high, the total return is fair, and the risk is usually low. These funds get into trouble only when the cost of energy goes up or interest rates rise. Energy and borrowing costs are the two biggest expenses incurred by the utility industry. Utilities are not specifically recommended in the previously described sample portfolios, but could be used as a substitute for that part of a portfolio that is to be invested in "growth and income."

Only a handful of mutual funds specialize in this area. Do not buy individual utility stocks; you never know when the Public Utilities Commission may turn down the company's request for a rate hike or if the utility company is thinking about going nuclear. These funds can be purchased through traditional sources. Since they yield a high dividend, they are best suited for low tax bracket investors or as part of a retirement plan that is sheltered from current taxation.

Utility stocks often act like corporate and government bonds. If you make utility funds part of your portfolio, make sure that you are not too heavily invested in bonds. Like bonds, utilities are very sensitive to interest rate changes. You do not want the majority of your portfolio subject to one type of risk.

BLUE CHIP STOCKS

Blue chip stocks or blue chip equity fund
(expected return: 13 percent)

Range of returns: = −20 percent to +44 percent

These securities represent the most stable part of the Standard & Poor's 500 index, stocks from the largest and most mature corporations in America. When you own common stock, you actually own part of the company, sharing in its fortunes and losses. Historically, stocks have proven to be an excellent investment and offer one of the best possible hedges against inflation.

Look at the bar chart in Exhibit 7–5. Notice how stocks have performed during each of the five-year periods since 1977. In every single instance, the return has been either good or excellent. Indirectly, this chart also points out that holding equities for extended periods of time is a smart investment decision.

Stocks can be purchased through your stockbroker or financial planner; commissions are always negotiable. If you know which securities you want to buy or sell, a discount brokerage firm such as Charles Schwab may be your best bet. Stocks from large companies normally pay dividends every quarter. The receipt or reinvestment

EXHIBIT 7–5
Percent of Compound Annual Rate of Return

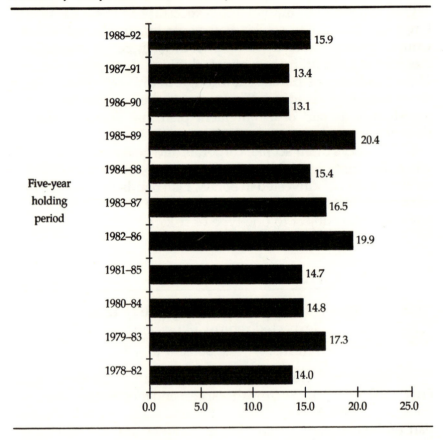

Five-year holding period

Period	Value
1988–92	15.9
1987–91	13.4
1986–90	13.1
1985–89	20.4
1984–88	15.4
1983–87	16.5
1982–86	19.9
1981–85	14.7
1980–84	14.8
1979–83	17.3
1978–82	14.0

of any dividends is a taxable event. Capital gains or losses of principal are recognized when shares are sold. Large stocks can be part of a qualified retirement plan, such as an IRA, Keogh, 403(b) plan, or profit-sharing program.

Consider blue chip stocks for your portfolio if your anticipated holding period is three years or longer and if you select at least a handful of different individual stocks representing several industry groups. Large stocks can provide you with some of your best returns if you have a little patience. Growth and income funds often contain several blue chip stocks. If possible, purchase any high dividend stocks within your retirement plan, thereby deferring taxes from such distributions.

GROWTH FUNDS

Growth funds (expected return: 13 percent)

Range of returns: = −18 percent to +40 percent

These funds generally seek capital appreciation, with current income as a distant secondary concern. Growth funds typically invest in U.S. common stocks, do not deal in speculative issues, and avoid aggressive trading techniques. The goal of most of these funds is long-term growth. The approaches used to attain this appreciation can vary significantly among growth funds.

Over the past 15 years, growth stocks have outperformed corporate and government bonds by almost 90 percent. From 1977 to 1993, common stocks averaged 16 percent compounded per year, versus 10 percent for bonds. A $10,000 investment in stocks grew to over $86,500 over the past 15 years; a similar initial investment in corporate bonds grew to $45,600.

If President George Washington had invested $1 in common stocks with an average return of 12 percent, his investment would be worth over $111 billion today. If George had been a little lucky and averaged 14 percent on his stock portfolio, his portfolio would be large enough to pay our national debt almost three times over!

Looking at a shorter time frame, common stocks have also fared quite well. A dollar invested in stocks in 1942 grew to over $377 by the beginning of 1993. This translates into an average compound return of 12 percent per year. Over the past 50 years, the worst year for common stocks was 1974, when a loss of 26 percent was suffered. One year later, these same stocks posted a gain of 37 percent. The best year so far has been 1958, when growth stocks posted a gain of 43 percent.

Growth funds should be a part of almost everyone's holdings. As is true with any category of mutual funds, whenever larger dollar amounts are involved, more than one fund per category should be used.

INTERNATIONAL STOCK FUNDS

International stock fund (expected return: 17 percent)

Range of returns: = −12 percent to +44 percent

When it comes to foreign or international investing, the majority of U.S. investors have missed the boat. People shy away from foreign securities because they have been told that they are too risky. This can be true if you focus on a particular country. It is complete nonsense if holdings are diversified among several industries and countries (which is what most funds do). International stock funds often outperform growth, growth and income, and aggressive growth funds on a regular basis. These funds also outperform all categories of bond funds with a high degree of frequency.

What is perhaps the most appealing part about international stock funds is that they greatly reduce a portfolio's risk level. This is because U.S. and foreign stocks do not move up and down at the same time or to the same degree. These two investments have what is known as a random correlation. Unpredictable movements mean that your overall portfolio will generally have fewer peaks and valleys in its performance. Equally surprising is the fact that your overall returns will be higher. That's right; you will experience less risk and greater return when you diversify your U.S. holdings into overseas securities.

Unless you are ultraconservative, international stock funds should be part of your game plan. Over time, you will be surprised as to the type of returns you will get and how your portfolio, when viewed as a whole, becomes more predictable and stable.

AGGRESSIVE GROWTH FUNDS

Aggressive growth fund (expected return: 16 percent)

Range of returns: = −24 percent to +56 percent

These funds invest in common stocks of small- and medium-sized U.S. companies. Aggressive growth funds often have excellent long-term results and very volatile short-term swings. They perform best during the later parts of a recession through the initial stages of an economic expansion.

Shares of any mutual fund can be purchased from stockbrokers, financial planners, or the fund directly. Stocks within an aggressive portfolio usually yield small or no dividends, making them an attractive choice for the high bracket investor who is willing to take some risk.

Consider owning one or more aggressive funds for the riskier part of your portfolio. These funds can be exciting and profitable, provided you can live with them for at least five years. Conservative investors should stay away.

PORTFOLIO ADVICE

Look over these different investments and see the range of returns each offers. Many of these figures may look a little scary, but keep in mind that if your portfolio is properly structured, *your* overall volatility can be quite tame. Avoid investments that are appealing because they sound sexy, gimmicky, or tricky. Also, stay away from collectibles and virtually all limited partnerships; their track records are rarely good and they are often promoted by brokers because they pay high commissions to the salesperson.

Place most, if not all, of your holdings into such things as equity funds, tax-free bond funds, government securities, international securities funds, and real estate. The younger you are, the less loaded down with U.S. corporate and government bonds you should be. On the other hand, equities and real estate beat inflation but certainly do not go up every single year. Spread out among several categories.

No one knows what will be the best performing investment next quarter, much less next year or over the current decade. Do not go into an investment because you think you are going to make a killing. Babe Ruth may have hit more home runs that almost any other baseball player, but he also struck out more than anyone else. Stay away from the extremes. If you can hit singles, doubles, and triples, you will be doing much better than 99 percent of all other investors.

AN ALTERNATIVE APPROACH

You may not feel comfortable with the risk-determination test in the previous section. An alternative approach is to determine what kind of return is needed to reach your goals and objectives, as determined in the first two chapters. Thus, you would first ascertain the overall yield or growth rate required of your assets in order to reach a specific dollar goal.

As an example, suppose that you calculated your portfolio would have to grow at a 4 percent real rate (after taxes and inflation). Further assume a 5 percent rate of inflation and a 33 percent tax bracket (state and federal combined). To figure out the minimum level, take the desired real rate (4 percent) and add it to the assumed rate of inflation (5 percent). The resulting figure, 9 percent, is then divided by one minus your combined tax bracket (1 − .33 = .67). The final number (9 percent divided by .67 = 13.42 percent) is the return needed to obtain your goal of a 4 percent real rate of return. The math for this is shown below:

4 percent *real rate of return* needed (your goal).

4 percent plus 5 percent (the rage of inflation) = 9 percent.

9 percent divided by .67 (return after taxes) = 13.42.

13.42 percent is the gross rate of return needed in order to *net* 4 percent (assuming 5 percent inflation and a 33 percent tax bracket).

To better understand this alternate approach, and to check the math, follow these steps:

Take 13.42 percent and multiply it by 67 percent (13.42 percent × 67 percent = 8.99 percent); this is what you keep after paying income taxes.

The projected rate of inflation, 5 percent, is then subtracted from this number (8.99 percent − 5 percent).

The final figure is 4 percent (rounded off).

Continuing the example, if you needed a 13.42 percent rate of return, most of the investments in your retirement portfolio would be found in level 4 (moderate) and above.

CALCULATING RETURNS

To determine how you are doing, you must understand the different ways returns are measured. As you know, the rate of return is the most commonly used method to determine how an investment has performed. Investment returns are often quoted in terms of either simple or compound interest or rate of return.

Simple interest is the basic interest charged on any amount of money loaned. If you loan someone $10,000 at 10 percent simple interest per year, each year you will receive $1,000 back on your money. At the end of five years, you will still have your original $10,000 plus five yearly interest installments of $1,000 each, for a grand total of $15,000.

Compound interest means you are receiving a return on any accumulated interest as well as on principal. Interest accrues periodically; it may accrue daily, weekly, monthly, quarterly, semiannually, or annually. As it accrues, it is added to the principal, and future interest is computed on this total. Thus, you end up receiving interest not only on your principal, but on any and all previous interest as well. Ten thousand dollars loaned out or invested at 10 percent compounded annually yields $16,105 after five years, a bonus of $1,105 over simple interest.

Rule of 72

Unfortunately, one of the problems with compounding is figuring out just how fast your money is growing. You can look it up in tables or compute it with algebra yourself, but mathematical shorthand provides a quicker answer. This short cut is called *the rule of 72*. To determine how long any amount of money invested at a compound interest basis will take to double, simply divide the interest rate into 72. If you're receiving 10 percent interest, for example, your money will double in 7.2 years (72 ÷ 10 = 7.2).

Here are some common interest rate calculations using the rule of 72:

Rule		Interest		Years
72	÷	20	=	3.6
72	÷	15	=	4.8
72	÷	12	=	6.0
72	÷	10	=	7.2
72	÷	7	=	10.3
72	÷	5	=	14.4
72	÷	3	=	24.0

REVIEWING YOUR PROGRESS

No one will watch over your money as carefully as you will. Once or twice a year, sit down with your financial adviser and review your portfolio. If certain investments are not living up to their expectations, they should be scrutinized:

How is this particular investment doing in comparison to its peer group?

- This type of investment may still be sound, but its peer group is just going through a bad quarter or occasional poor year.
- If your investment is doing well compared to its competitors (e.g., the ABC Growth Fund versus all other growth funds), and the category has done well historically, do not rush out and change it.

If there is a portfolio manager, has he or she left?

- With managed investments, such as mutual funds, variable annuities, pooled accounts, and REITs, the performance may be only as good as the decision maker.

Has the nature of the investment changed?

- Until the mid-1980s, high yield (junk) bonds were a very good investment. During the later part of the 80s, these securities became much risker because of how they were used for acquisitions, mergers, and other highly leveraged projects.

Has your risk level changed?

- You may now be more conservative than you were a year ago.
- Your comfort level may now be broader after a few years of investment experience.

Have tax laws changed or are there new opportunities available?

- Recent tax changes may make some of your investments more or less attractive.
- New products that were not previously available are now approved or accepted.

With the ending of this chapter, you are fully armed to begin structuring your own financial plan. The introductory chapters showed you how risk can be transferred by owning insurance and what you can later expect from social security and other public programs. The next few chapters rounded out your knowledge by pointing out the number of investment possibilities. You could say these last few chapters have appealed to your instincts of fear, hope, and greed, pointing out the possibilities and pitfalls. It is now time to start bringing all of this information together.

Before moving on to the next chapter, go back to the "Summary of Assets" section you filled out in the first chapter. See how your assets are broken down by category. This will give you a rough idea of whether you are "top heavy" in any one particular category.

CHECKLIST OF THINGS TO DO

1. Contact several mutual fund groups and request information on those investments that coincide with your risk level. Pay particular attention to how long the current portfolio manager has been calling the shots. Mutual fund groups will send you a prospectus; study this document to find out the fund's expenses. Telephone prospective fund candidates and get a year-by-year reading of their total returns (performance). By studying the track record, you will have a good idea if you can live with the fund's volatility.

2. To check on the financial soundness of a bank or savings and loan association you are doing business with, write to: Conserva-

torship List, Resolution Trust Corporation, 801 17th St. N.W., Washington, DC, 20429, for a free list of companies under government supervision.

3. If you decide that government obligations should be part of your portfolio, send $5 to the Federal Reserve Bank of Richmond (P.O. Box 27622, Richmond, Virginia, 23261) and request a copy of *Buying Treasury Securities at Federal Reserve Banks*. This publication will show you how you can buy U.S. securities without paying a commission or fee to a bank, broker, or financial planner.

4. To find out what U.S. savings bonds are paying, telephone 800–US–BONDS. These government obligations, also known as series EE bonds, grow and compound tax deferred. Under special circumstances, the earnings end up being tax free if they are used for a child's college education and certain qualifications are fulfilled.

5. Avoid limited partnerships that do not have at least a 10-year track record and trade near par value, or higher, in the secondary marketplace. Stay away from collectibles such as rare coins and stamps, diamonds and other gemstones, baseball cards, metals, such as gold and silver coins or bullion, and art for investment purposes.

6. If you own shares or units in a limited partnership and want to find out what it is worth or would like to sell out, write to the Investment Partnerhsip Association, Suite 500, 1100 Connecticut Ave., N.W., Washington, DC, 20036, for a free list of the more than dozen firms that buy and sell these interests.

7. Contact your local bookstore and buy a copy of *The 100 Best Mutual Funds You Can Buy*, published by Bob Adams, Inc., Holbrook, Mass. ($13). If they are out of copies, order the book by referring to its ISBN number: 1-55850-856-2. This book will give you generic information about the different categories of mutual funds, the amount of risk involved, brief interviews with the fund managers, and historical returns.

8. Follow these principals of investing:

Reduce risk of diversifying.

Be patient—the longer your time horizon the more predictable your returns will become and the more equity oriented (stocks, real estate, owning your own business, etc.) you should be.

Use mutual funds and variable annuities instead of buying individual stocks and bonds (less risk, professional management, plus additional services and benefits).

Add money to your investments whenever possible (this is a way of reducing risk by using time diversification).

Reinvest all dividends, interest, and capital gains.

Chapter Eight
Pulling It Together

Financial Planning
A Sample Plan
Your Own Investment Plan

Have you ever put together a jigsaw puzzle? Remember how satisfying it was to put in that last piece? There is a certain sense of accomplishment whenever a job or project is done, particularly if the finished product is something we can be proud of. This is true with all aspects of life.

Throughout our lives we are confronted with sets of instructions, directions, and procedure manuals. We may not like to admit it, but these plans are a necessary part of everyday life. We come across signs, warnings, directions, and advice all the time. Yet, when it comes to retirement planning, there seems to be a void. Perhaps it is because retirement planning is not something people want to talk about or because it seems too far in the future. But, just like everyday life, planning for your future is not something that can be taken lightly. In short, you need a plan, a set of instructions. And that is exactly what this chapter will provide.

This chapter will show you what should go into the construction of a portfolio that will best prepare you for that retirement. You will need to have the net worth statement you filled out in the first chapter handy to complete the second part of this chapter (financial planning).

The first part of the chapter shows you how to develop your own financial plan by walking you through a hypothetical. It is the financial planning process that will have the greatest impact on your retirement well-being. These financial planning sections show you the alternatives you have to choose from if you come up short: save more each year, postpone retirement, become more aggressive, or lower your sights.

The chapter ends with a lengthy financial planning checklist. This is a sort of tickler system that will alert you to those areas that have been raised either directly or indirectly in previous chapters. It also brings up some issues that will be addressed during your retirement years: (1) maximizing your current income and (2) the issues involved in estate planning.

FINANCIAL PLANNING

The importance of financial planning can best be described by analogy. Let us suppose that you are going on a cruise. After boarding the ship, you go the captain and ask him or her, "Captain, how long will it take us to arrive at our destination?" The captain replies, "I don't know." You then ask, "What are we using for fuel?" The captain replies, "I don't have any idea." "Captain," you ask, "what type of navigation system or map are you using?" The captain's response is, "We don't have any system or map to follow." Finally, you ask, "Where are we going?" The response is the same, "I don't know."

After you hear the answers to all of these questions, it is doubtful that you would stay on board. Surely, you think, the captain is either crazy, stupid, or both. Yet, this is exactly how well over 90 percent of all Americans approach their retirement planning. They have no idea where their investments or pension will take them. They do not know how much they will end up with, how long they can count on these sources of income, or the amount of risk they are being exposed to. In short, they have no financial plan.

A financial plan gives us a framework within which to work. With a plan we can map where we are and see where we can expect to end up. A good battle plan also takes into account the enemy. In the case of financial planning, there are three enemies: inflation, taxes, and procrastination. This chapter shows you how to draft your own plan. This does not suggest that you skip seeing an investment adviser. The objectivity and experience a good financial planner can bring to the table has tremendous value. By drafting your own financial plan, you will gain greater knowledge of your assets—information that will make your investment and strategy meetings more meaningful.

This section on financial planning will help you:

- Know what your goals are.
- Be able to translate these goals into dollar objectives.
- Be able to take inventory of what you have.
- Understand how to make projections.
- Learn how to factor in the effects of inflation as well as income taxes.
- Have a process to review your progress on an ongoing basis.

A SAMPLE PLAN

The best way to see how a financial plan is constructed is to study an example. As you read through this example, do not be turned off because this hypothetical illustration does not coincide with your age, current holdings, time horizon, and so on. The important thing here is that you understand how the process works. When you finish reading the example below, you will see how to draft your own tailored plan.

Assume the following investor profile:

Goal: Retire comfortably in 20 years.

Objective: End up with a portfolio that will produce $3,000 a month in income.

Current holdings:

- $50,000 in bank CDs averaging 8 percent.
- $40,000 in tax-free bonds that yield 7 percent.
- $30,000 in a mutual fund that averages 12 percent growth.
- $7,000 can be saved each year and invested in a company retirement plan that averages 14 percent.
- Income and/or growth are to be reinvested in each of these investments.

Investor feels inflation will average 5 percent over the next 20 years.

Investor is in a 35 percent tax bracket (state and federal combined).

Risk level: Moderate.

The investor wants to know what he or she can expect to have at the end of 20 years, when retirement is expected.

The best way to solve this problem is to look at each individual investment and project its future value at the end of 20 years. Our projections will take into account the investor's existing holdings, the amount that can be saved each year, tax bracket, the expected rate of inflation, and the projected rate of return. The value of each asset will then be added up in order to reach a total portfolio value.

$50,000 in Bank CDs

The CD money is expected to grow at an 8 percent compound annual rate over the next 20 years. Before referring to the proper table in the Appendix, we first need to adjust this figure for income taxes and inflation. By following the steps below, you can see what the aftertax, afterinflation rate of return is for this investment.

Expected rate of return	8%
Minus income taxes (35 percent of 8 percent = 2.8 percent)	−3
Equals the aftertax return	5%
Minus the rate of inflation	−5
Equals the *real* rate of return (adjusted for inflation & taxes)	0%

We now know that this particular investment will not grow, once inflation and taxes are factored in. We have now finished with the first investment, let us go on to the second holding.

$40,000 in Municipal Bonds

The tax-free bonds are expected to grow at a 7 percent compound annual rate over the next 20 years. Before referring to the proper table in the Appendix, we first need to adjust this figure for inflation. *No adjustment is needed for income taxes since the interest from this investment is tax free. However, just because something is sheltered from income taxes does not mean that it escapes the effects of inflation.* By following the steps below, you can see what the aftertax, afterinflation rate of return is for this investment.

Expected rate of return	7%
Minus income taxes	−0
(interest from municipal bonds is tax free)	
Equals the aftertax return	7%
Minus the rate of inflation	−5
Equals the *real* rate of return	2%
(adjusted for inflation and taxes)	

We now know that this hypothetical investment will grow at a real rate of 2 percent over the next 20 years, assuming a certain rate of return, income tax bracket, and level of inflation. We still need to determine what the final figure will be. Refer to the Appendix and the page titled "Rate 2%" in the upper left hand corner. Look at Table 1 and match this column with the 20-year row. The figure you will see is 1.49. Multiply this figure by the original lump sum, $40,000. The resulting number, $59,6000, is what $40,000 will grow to over the next 20 years, assuming a real rate of return of 2 percent. We are now finished with the second investment; let us go on to the third holding.

$30,000 in a Mutual Fund

The mutual fund is projected to grow at a 12 percent compound annual rate over the next 20 years. Before referring to the proper table in the Appendix, we need to adjust this figure for income taxes and inflation. By following the steps below, you can see what the real rate of return is for this investment.

Expected rate of return	12%
Minus income taxes	−4
(35 percent of 12 percent = 4.2 percent)	
Equals the aftertax return	8%
Minus the rate of inflation	−5
Equals the *real* rate of return	3%
(adjusted for inflation and taxes)	

We now know that this particular investment will grow at a real rate of 3 percent over the next 20 years. We still need to determine what the final figure will be. Refer to the Appendix and the page titled "Rate 3%" in the upper left hand corner. Look at Table 1 and match this column with the 20-year row. The figure you see is 1.81. Multiply this figure by $30,000. The resulting number, $54,300, is what $30,000 will grow to over the next 20 years, assuming a real rate of return of 3 percent. We have now completed the third item; let us go on to the final investment.

$7,000 that Can Be Saved Each Year

Finally, the investor feels she can save $7,000 each year to be earmarked for a retirement plan. This plan has historically averaged 14 percent compounded annually. Before referring to the proper table in the Appendix, we first need to adjust this figure for inflation. Monies invested in a qualified retirement plan grow and compound tax deferred. By following the steps below, you can see what the afterinflation rate of return is for this investment.

Expected rate of return	14%
Minus income taxes (tax-deferred growth, no current taxation)	−0
Equals the aftertax return	14%
Minus the rate of inflation	−5
Equals the *real* rate of return (adjusted for inflation)	9%

We know that this particular investment will grow at a real rate of 9 percent over the next 20 years. We still need to determine what the final figure will be. Refer to the Appendix and the page titled "Rate 9%" in the upper left hand corner. Look at Table 2 and match this column with the 20-year row. *Do not refer to Table 1.* The figure you will see is 51.16. Multiply this figure by the amount that can be saved each year, $7,000. The resulting number, $358,120, is what $7,000 set aside each year will grow to over the next 20 years, assuming a real rate of return of 9 percent. We are now finished, but before the totals are added, let us see why Table 2 was used here and not Table 1.

Table 1 is used whenever you have a lump-sum figure. In the particular illustration we have just gone through, this would apply to the first three investments. These were pools of money that we were not going to be adding to; they were to grow and compound on their own. Table 2 is used whenever you are making periodic contributions. In our illustration, the fourth investment of $7,000 was going to be added to each year. The annual contribution must be the same for each period in order for this table to be used. The $7,000 annual savings account was growing because of two factors: our annual contributions and the return from the actual investment vehicle.

To finish up the illustration, let us see how we have done. All of the figures listed below represent the real rate of growth.

Original Investment ($)	Grows to ($)
$50,000 in bank CDs	$ 50,000
40,000 in tax-free bonds	59,600
30,000 in a mutual fund	54,300
7,000 saved each year	358,120
Total of all investments	$522,020

As you may recall, the $358,120 that resulted from the $7,000 that was saved each year, was not calculated to figure in the income tax consequences. This was the correct thing to do since money coming out of a retirement plan is taxable only as it is withdrawn.

If the entire $522,420 was invested in 9 percent corporate bonds at retirement, the investor would have an annual income of $46,982 (9 percent of $522,020), well in excess of the $36,000 annual goal sought.

It was assumed that all of the investments, the bank CDs, the tax-free bonds, the mutual fund, and the retirement plan investment were repositioned into 9 percent corporate bonds. Better results could be obtained by broader diversification; corporate bonds are being used merely to illustrate how income could be derived from a portfolio. The repositioning of the $358,120 did not result in a taxable event since it was done within a retirement account. The other investments, which were not sheltered in this manner, did not face a tax event either since their growth was either taxed each year or tax free to begin with.

Now that you have gone through a sample plan, it is time to apply what has been learned to your own particular situation. The next section will show you how to draft your own investment plan, taking into account your goals, objectives, existing holdings, tax bracket, as well as your feelings about inflation.

YOUR OWN INVESTMENT PLAN

An investment plan is comprised of five parts:

1. Goals.
2. Objectives.
3. Strategy.
4. Implementation.
5. Performance.

We will now expand on each one of these five components.

Goals

Each of us has goals we would like to attain. For most people, their chief financial goal is to "retire comfortably." Some individuals and couples have multiple goals such as "send our children through college, travel abroad once every three years, and retirement." Whatever your goals are, you have a good chance of obtaining them all with proper planning.

Step one of your financial plan is to list your goals. On the lines listed below, list, in order of priority, your three most important goals:

1. _____
2. _____
3. _____

Objectives

Once your goals have been listed, we need to see what it will take to achieve them. To do this, you must turn those goals into dollar objectives. As an example, if your major goal was to retire comfortably, that might translate into ending up with a nest egg that will provide $9,000 of income every month. Comfortable retirement for another individual or couple may be $2,000 per month or maybe $800 per month. We all have different dreams and lifestyles. The important thing here is to list those total dollar figures that will ensure that our goals are fulfilled. Before we figure out those dollar figures, a little math review is in order.

Let us suppose that we have decided our chief goal is to retire comfortably. We have further decided that in our particular case, a nice retirement translates into ending up with $9,000 of income per month, after taxes. We now know the end of the equation, but there are still some blanks to fill in. Specifically, we need to know how much principal must be accumulated and what rate of return can be expected from this lump sum.

As of this writing, a conservative investor could purchase high quality municipal bonds that offered a current yield of 7 percent. When you decide to start securing your goals and objectives, municipal, also known as tax-free, bonds might be yielding anywhere from 4 to 11 percent. The precise rate is not important; what is important is that you understand how to solve the problem.

For the sake of illustration, let us assume that tax-free bonds have a current yield of 7 percent. Tax-free bonds are being used in this example because they are a conservative investment that is very popular with retirees; an assumed yield of 7 percent is being used because this is what municipal bonds were averaging at the end of the 1980s and early 1990s. A specific rate of return during retirement is needed to complete the worksheet, even at these initial stages since we need to determine a lump-sum figure for the objective (see below). Now follow the three steps below.

1. Take the desired monthly income figure, $9,000 in this example, and multiply it by the 12 months of the year. The resulting figure, $108,000 ($9,000 × 12), is what you are trying to end up with on an annual basis.

2. To determine how much you must initially invest to have a return of $9,000 per month, we take the annual figure, $108,000 in this example, and divide it by the projected tax-free rate (or whatever investment you wish to use) of

return at retirement. In this case, we are assuming that you can get a 7 percent yield from a municipal bond.

3. The resulting figure, $1,542,857, the result of dividing $108,000 by .07, is the lump-sum figure needed at retirement—the initial investment so to speak.

By investing a lump sum of $1,542,857 into long-term, tax-free municipal bonds yielding 7 percent annually, you will end up with $9,000 per month of income ($1,542,857 times .07 equals $108,000; $108,000 divided by the 12 months of the year equals $9,000 per month).

Our chief goal is to end up with $1,542,857 at retirement. Let us also assume two other goals: sending two children through college and buying a new car every four years. After doing a little bit of research as to the costs of these goals, list the goals and translate them into dollar figures, using today's dollars (adjustments for inflation and income taxes are done in the next section).

Goals	Objectives ($ figure)
1. Retire comfortably.	$1,542,857
2. College educations.	250,000
3. Buy a new car.	20,000

Be sure to list your goals in order of priority. If things do not work out as planned, you want to make sure you end up obtaining at least your top one or two objectives. As you can see, these are all lump-sum figures.

Once our goals have been set and translated into dollar figures, we need to figure out how much money we must save each year to end up with the desired lump-sum figures. Presumably, these annual savings will not be sitting around idle; they will be put into some type of investment. The kinds of investments and their expected rates of return are discussed in the next section.

Strategy

Before figuring out how much must be saved each year to reach the three dollar objectives listed above, take inventory of any existing holdings. For purposes of illustration, assume the following assets are already owned:

$250,000 in high quality corporate bonds yielding 9 percent.

$200,000 in a pension plan that grows at 10 percent.

$ 10,000 that can be saved every year.

Continuing the example, assume 20 years until retirement, a 33 percent tax bracket (state and federal combined), and an inflation rate of 5 percent. College costs will begin in 10 years, and you would like to buy a new car every four years.

Getting back to the example, $250,000 in corporate bonds will grow at 9 percent before taxes, but only at 6 percent once taxes are subtracted. (If you begin with a 9 percent return and a third is taken away in taxes, you end up with 6 percent.) A 6 percent return, reduced by the rate of inflation, 5 percent in our example, ends up with a real rate of return of 1 percent. The *real rate of return* is defined as one's rate of return after taxes and inflation have been factored in.

To see what $250,000 grows to over a 20-year period at 1 percent, look in the Appendix and the page titled ''Rate 1%.'' Refer to Table 1 and follow it down until you get to the 20-year row. The number found by crossing this column with this row is 1.22; multiply this factor by $250,000. The resulting number, $305,000, is what you will end up with at retirement in 20 years.

Our hypothetical investor also has $200,000 in a pension plan that has been averaging 10 percent annually over the past many years. Assuming this rate continues for the next 20 years, let us see what we end up with. A 10 percent return, minus 5 percent for inflation, leaves us with a 5 percent growth rate. Notice two things here. First, income taxes have not been taken out; money in a retirement plan grows and compounds tax deferred. We will deal with income taxes only as withdrawals are made. Second, just because something is sheltered from taxes does not mean that it is also being shielded from inflation. Inflation affects the true rate of return of every investment, whether it is fully taxable, tax deferred, or tax free. There is no hiding from the cumulative effects of inflation.

Going back to to the example, a 5 percent afterinflation rate of return for 20 years results in $200,000 growing to $530,000 (refer to the page in the Appendix titled "Rate 5%" and then follow Table 1 down until you match that column with the row for 20 years; take this factor and multiply it by $200,000).

We have one more source of investment left in our example: the $10,000 that can be saved each year until retirement. Let us assume that the investor will invest this money in tax-free bonds. And, let us suppose that over the next 20 years one can average a 7 percent yield on these municipal bonds. If you start with a 7 percent tax-free yield and subtract income taxes, you still end up with 7 percent (you would be subtracting 0 from 7 percent since there is no income tax due on the interest from municipal bonds). The 7 percent aftertax return is still affected by inflation. Therefore, take 7 percent and subtract the assumed rate of inflation over the next 20 years, 5 percent. This leaves us with a 2 percent real rate of return annually (7 minus 5).

To determine what we will end up with, a different table must be used. Refer to the Appendix again and find the page titled "Rate 2%." Move over to the third column, marked Table 2. This table is used when you have a periodic contribution (the $10,000 that can be saved each year) that can be added to each year. By looking at Table 2 and crossing the 2 percent column (the real rate of return, once taxes and inflation have been subtracted) with the 20-year row (the time frame we are looking at in this particular example), we end up with a factor of 24.30. Take 24.30 and multiply it by $10,000. The resulting number, $243,000, is what $10,000 will grow to in 20 years. This is its real rate of return in our example.

The growth rate, or final value of the original assets, plus annual savings, can now be determined as follows:

Original Investment ($)	Grows to ($)
$250,000	$ 305,000
200,000	530,000
10,000 saved each year	243,000
Total	$1,078,000

As you can see, the hypothetical existing assets and course of action will not satisfy even our retirement goal. The retirement goal alone meant that $1,542,857 needed to be acquired at the end of 20 years. We are close to a half million dollars short of our first goal. A decision needs to be made at this point. Either the amount of monthly income at retirement needs to be reduced, we need to be more aggressive in our investment plan, and/or our final two goals need to be reduced or completely eliminated.

Implementation

As you can see, our hypothetical investor who wants to end up with $1,542,857 in a retirement plan, $250,000 for college education, and $20,000 every four years for a new car will fall short. In order to reach all or most of these goals, something must change. The investor can do one of the following: (1) reposition investments to take advantage of possibly getting higher rates of return and/ or growth, (2) save more money each year, (3) retire later than expected, or (4) lower retirement expectations. Each of these options will be explored below.

Reposition investments. The least painful alternative is to evaluate other investment options that would yield a higher return. By being conscious of your aftertax rate of return and taking on just a little more risk, investors can usually better their positions dramatically. First, the investor should try to shelter as many holdings as possible. Sheltering means that we are moving something that is fully taxable and putting it into an investment that is either tax free or tax deferred. This is not always a desired strategy for one or more of the following reasons:

1. You may be in a low tax bracket already and therefore on an aftertax basis, a tax-free instrument may not produce as high a return as an investment that is fully taxable.
2. You may already have a significant portion of your holdings in municipal bonds and any addition would result in an overweighting.
3. Tax-deferred investments, such as annuities and retirement accounts, cannot be sold before age $59\frac{1}{2}$ without usually incurring a 10 percent penalty.
4. Sheltered vehicles may not provide the investment options or the specific management company you are looking for.

Municipal bonds and tax-free money market funds are the only investments that provide a truly tax-free rate of return. Tax-free bonds typically yield 2 to 4 percent more annually than their tax-free money market counterparts. Thus, the client could shift the $250,000 in high quality corporate bonds yielding 9 percent into 7 percent municipal bonds. This would change the aftertax rate of return from 6 percent (9 percent gross minus one third for income taxes) to 7 percent (municipal bond interest has the same rate of return before and after taxes since their current yield is tax free). The $250,000 would now be worth $372,500 at the end of 20 years (7 percent − 5 percent inflation = 2 percent real rate of return). Refer to the page in the Appendix titled "Rate 2%." Look under Table 1 and match it with the 20-year row; this factor, 1.49, multiplied by $250,000 = $372,500.

Moving on to the second investment, an alternative for the $200,000 in pension plan money would be to go into a global stock mutual fund. This type of fund invests in common stocks around the world. The typical global fund has somewhere between 30 and 60 percent of its assets in U.S. securities; the balance is in foreign stocks. Global funds have historically averaged 15–20 percent annually. According to a Stanford University study, global funds have 51 percent less volatility and have experienced greater returns than U.S. stocks.

If the $200,000 pension plan averaged 15 percent annually instead of 10 percent, the account would be worth $1,346,000 at the end of 20 years (15 percent minus 5 percent for inflation minus 0 for taxes equals 10 percent). Look at the Appendix page titles "Rate 10%" and cross Table 1 with the 20-year row. The resulting factor, 6.73, is then multiplied by $200,000.

Finally, the $10,000 that can be saved every year could be invested in a balanced mutual fund. By choosing a balanced portfolio composed of stocks and bonds, and assuming an average annual rate of return of 12 percent, the $10,000 of savings each year would grow to $268,700 at the end of 20 years (12 percent minus 4 percent for taxes and minus 5 percent for inflation equals 3 percent). Look at the Appendix page titled "Rate 3%." Then go over to Table 2, since annual contributions can be made, and cross the 3% column with the 20-year row. The resulting factor, 26.87, is then multiplied by $10,000.

Our new figures look quite different:

Original Investment ($)	Grows to ($)	Repositioned Grows to ($)
$250,000 (repositioned into municipal bonds)	$ 305,000	$ 372,500
200,000 (repositioned into global funds)	530,000	1,346,000
10,000 each year (repositioned into balanced funds)	243,000	268,700
Total	$1,078,000	$1,987,700

As you can see, we have almost satisfied the retirement goal of $1,542,857 just with the $200,000 in the pension plan. At this point you may be thinking that since this is the best-performing segment of our hypothetical portfolio, why not invest everything in global funds? The reasons you should not do this are: (1) even the reduced volatility, versus just using U.S. stocks, may still be too high for a conservative investor, and (2) there is no guarantee global funds or any type of stock-oriented investment will average 10, 12, or 15 percent during the next 10 or 20 years. What will happen is that a diversified portfolio will include some surprises (better than projected returns) and some disappointments (less than expected growth); blended together, the overall return then becomes more predictable since the poor performers will be canceled out by the better-than-expected investments. We can now go back and see if the second and third goals can be reached from this repositioning.

The second goal was to end up with a college education of $250,000 in 10 years. The $250,000 that was originally in corporate bonds will certainly meet this goal, even without any real growth. Finally, the $10,000 that can be saved can now be earmarked for the third goal, a $20,000 new car every four years. By investing $10,000 every year into a balanced fund that has a real rate of return of 3 percent means that it will grow to $41,800 every four years (see Appendix page titled "Rate 3"; go to Table 2 and match it with the four-year row to end up with the factor 4.18).

Since $41,800 is a little more than twice what is needed for the new car, only $5,000 would have to be committed to the automobile account this year. The remaining $5,000 could be committed for a longer period to add to the retirement plan. Thus, $5,000 growing at a real rate of 3 percent for 20 years equals $134,350.

Our original retirement objective was to obtain $1,542,857 at the end of 20 years. The repositioned pension money will grow to $1,346,000, add this to $134,350 and you end up with $1,480,350. This new figure, coupled with any excess amount earned in the college account, will more than equal the $1,542,857 objective.

We were fortunate in this example. All of the goals were reached by only having to reposition assets. But suppose that either this was not enough or that any repositioning would have been beyond the risk tolerance level of the investor; what then? There are only three alternatives: save more each year, postpone retirement, or lower expectations.

Save more each year. Some or all of the repositioning suggestions described above may not appeal to the investor because of either preconceived notions about stocks and bonds or an ultra conservative investment outlook. It is very difficult for most people to invest in stocks or stock-oriented mutual funds when the stock market has just experienced a crash or correction. Bonds are difficult to get enthusiastic about if you owned them during the mid-1970s and saw their value on paper erode to 50 percent of face value in less then six years (by the way, they fully recovered this paper loss by the mid to late 1980s). If this is the case, an alternative would be to save more than $10,000 each year. A larger annual savings would result in a larger final number at retirement.

This alternative may simply not be possible. It may be that the hypothetical investor cannot save anything, much less $10,000 annually. A great number of families either live beyond their means or lack the discipline to save. If this is the case, this alternative can quickly be eliminated.

Postpone retirement. By postponing retirement, the existing portfolio will have more time to grow and compound. A $100,000 investment that is sheltered from income taxes and experiences a real growth rate of 8 percent (after adjusting for inflation), will grow to $200,000 in nine years. The same investment will be worth approximately $300,000 if it is allowed to grow for an additional four years.

Lower expectations. The final alternative is for the investor to decrease his or her expectations. Perhaps the kids will have to pay part of their education costs. Or maybe a new car can be purchased only every six years instead of every four.

The reader can juggle the numbers, time horizons, and rates of return and end up with a wide range of possibilities. Once a course of action is decided on, it is important to implement the plan. Many people think that by doing nothing they are somehow protected from all forms of risk. This is simply not true. Your money is doing something right now; it is invested in something. Whatever it is invested in, it is being subjected to one or more forms of risk. There is no risk-free rate of return in the real world. Conservative investments such as Treasury bills, bank CDs, and money market accounts are subjected to income taxes and the cumulative effects of inflation. High yielding corporate bonds possess the risk of default. Stocks and real estate are subject to market conditions and sometimes wide fluctuations in value.

It is infinitely better to have an investment plan that you follow through on than to maintain the status quo or go off in a bunch of different directions. An investment plan will give you something to strive for, a measurable goal that can be visualized. Investing with no sense of direction means that you will either be chasing the stock of the month or will become stagnant by sticking to investments that offer poor returns. It has often been said that "those who fail to plan will end up planning to fail."

Performance and Review

No matter how conservative, moderate, or aggressive part or all of your portfolio is, it is important that your progress be reviewed. Once or twice a year, sit down with your investment adviser and see how each investment is performing (see Chapter Eleven, Choosing a Professional). A sample checklist that you might wish to use is shown in Exhibit 8–1. Fundamentally sound investments should not be moved around just because they have experienced a bad quarter or year.

EXHIBIT 8–1
Investment Review Checklist

Name of Investment	Expected Return/Yield	Actual Return	Review Necessary?	Outcome of Review
1. _____	_____%	_____%	__Yes __No	__Keep __Change
2. _____	_____%	_____%	__Yes __No	__Keep __Change
3. _____	_____%	_____%	__Yes __No	__Keep __Change

If you were to move your money every time a loss was suffered, you would soon end up either broke due to commissions and poor market timing or strictly confined to secure investments such as CDs, money market funds, or T-bills. Remember, these "safe" investments have performed very poorly against inflation on an aftertax basis over the past 10, 20, 30, 40, etc. years.

After reviewing the portfolio over a period of two or three years, the investor may wish to become more aggressive or conservative. This change of heart may be due to age, new goals and objectives, unforeseen circumstances, or risk level. Actually experiencing the ups and downs of investments can change one's tolerance for risk. It is like other things we go through in life; the experience provides us with familiarity and understanding. This translates into either accepting greater volatility or the realization that enough is enough and it is now time to accept one's losses and try something different. Whatever the reason, most investments can be repositioned easily.

After a few annual reviews, you may be pleasantly surprised to learn that returns have been better than expected. This means that the final dollar figures may be much higher. You may end up with enough principal at retirement to increase your monthly income by a couple of thousand dollars. It can also mean that perhaps the overall risk level can now be reduced or that retirement can occur faster than expected. Reducing your risk level could mean that growth mutual funds can be exchanged for balanced funds or that high yield bonds can be exchanged for U.S. government obligations. A faster retirement means that you may be able to stop working at age 62 instead of 65 or 70. On the other hand, less than expected returns may signal a needed change or an increase in annual savings.

The major reason you should be doing a review is to make sure that you are not surprised after too much time has passed. Goals and dreams can be attained even if mistakes are made along the way. Successful investment planning partially means that mistakes are minimized and better-performing alternatives are substituted.

The financial planning checklist in Exhibit 8–2 will aid you in remembering the major points and concepts highlighted through the book. All of your answers that are "no/not sure" should first be looked up in the index at the end of the book to see if the topic is covered. If it is, review the appropriate sections. Next, make a note to yourself so that you are sure to follow up and complete the task.

This chapter has shown you how to define goals and objectives, determine rates of return and growth on an aftertax, afterinflation basis, and provided a method that you can use to measure your investment progress. The different steps of drafting your own financial plan also highlighted some of the aspects of risk and pointed out the importance of periodic reviews.

The next chapter provides some ways to increase your current income. All too often financial publications give the reader a very limited approach to this topic, ideas that have proven to be repetitive and needlessly to subject one to a reduced standard of living the longer one's life. As you will soon see, you can maximize your current income while maintaining your risk comfort level and still offset the long-term effects of inflation, whether you are in a low or high tax bracket.

CHECKLIST OF THINGS TO DO

1. Try to draft your own financial plan using the sample format shown in this chapter. Work on your goals and objectives by getting opinions from your spouse; look at the planning process as a team effort, each of you has certain strengths and weaknesses. Go to the Appendix and become familiar with the use of the four tables—the guts of any financial or retirement planning calculations. Even if you are not successful in writing your own plan, you

EXHIBIT 8–2
Financial Planning Checklist

	Yes	No/Not Sure

Planning and Record Keeping

1. Have you established realistic short-term financial goals?
2. Have you established realistic long-term financial goals?
3. Have you developed a satisfactory record-keeping system that is simple enough to use yet comprehensive enough to be useful?
4. Do you use a safe-deposit box for storage of valuable papers and possessions?
5. Do you maintain an up-to-date inventory of the contents of the safe-deposit box?
6. Have you prepared a comprehensive and up-to-date inventory of household furnishings and possessions?
7. Do you prepare a personal balance sheet periodically?
8. Have you prepared a household budget, listing expected income and expenses?
9. Do you have sufficient cash reserves to avoid being financially strapped periodically because of unexpected expenses or large annual bills?

Insurance

1. Have you obtained sufficient life insurance to prevent your dependents from suffering financial hardship in the event of death?
2. Has your spouse obtained sufficient life insurance to meet the financial needs of dependents in the event of death?
3. Have you determined the most appropriate form of life insurance to meet those needs?
4. Does the entire family have comprehensive and continuous health insurance coverage?
5. Have any elderly members of the family acquired medicare gap insurance and considered acquiring long-term care insurance?
6. Do you have adequate long-term disability insurance coverage (equivalent to at least 60 percent of salary)?
7. Does your spouse have adequate long-term disability insurance coverage?

EXHIBIT 8–2
Financial Planning Checklist (Continued)

	Yes	No/Not Sure
8. Do both spouses' disability policies provide benefits as long as they are prevented from gainful employment in their "usual and customary" occupation?	____	____
9. Do your disability policies cover both illness and accident?	____	____
10. Do you have adequate homeowner's or renter's insurance?	____	____
11. Does your homeowner's or renter's policy provide replacement cost coverage for the home?	____	____
12. Does your homeowner's or renter's policy provide replacement cost coverage for the contents of the home?	____	____
13. Have you obtained additional insurance protection for jewelry, silverware, safe-deposit box contents, or other valuables?	____	____
14. Do you have adequate personal liability (umbrella) insurance coverage?	____	____
15. If your profession warrants it, do you have adequate professional liability insurance coverage?	____	____
16. Does your spouse have adequate professional liability insurance coverage, if applicable?	____	____

Borrowing and Credit

	Yes	No/Not Sure
1. Have you established your credit through borrowing for worthwhile purposes?	____	____
2. If you have a home equity loan, are you paying off the principal on a regular basis?	____	____
3. Are you confident that you will have sufficient resources to fund your children's education?	____	____
4. Are you aware of your personal credit rating as reported by the national credit bureaus?	____	____
5. If you have an automobile loan, will it be paid off well in advance of your acquiring another automobile?	____	____

Savings and Investments

	Yes	No/Not Sure
1. Do you save through payroll withholding or other regular savings programs?	____	____
2. Have you established an emergency fund of liquid savings equal to at least three months' salary?	____	____
3. Is more than two thirds of your total portfolio invested in the stock market?	____	____

EXHIBIT 8–2
Financial Planning Checklist (Continued)

	Yes	No/Not Sure
4. Is more than two thirds of your total portfolio invested in savings instruments (e.g., savings accounts, certificates of deposit, bonds, government securities)?	____	____
5. Do you have appropriate investment objectives?	____	____
6. Are your investments appropriate for your age, wealth, and family status as well as for your investment objectives?	____	____
7. Do you review the investment portfolio regularly?	____	____
8. Are your investments appropriate in terms of risk?	____	____
9. Do you participate in your employer's stock purchase and/or thrift plans?	____	____
10. Is your investment portfolio appropriately diversified?	____	____
11. If you expect to receive a substantial inheritance, have you considered how to invest and manage it?	____	____

Real Estate

	Yes	No/Not Sure
1. If you don't own a home or condominium, do you plan to buy one in the future?	____	____
2. If you are contemplating future real estate investments, either directly owned or through limited partnerships, do you understand the risks associated with them?	____	____
3. Are your real estate investments appropriate to your financial circumstances?	____	____

Tax Planning

	Yes	No/Not Sure
1. Are you well informed about tax-saving techniques and current tax law?	____	____
2. Do you keep a notebook handy to record miscellaneous tax-deductible expenses?	____	____
3. Do you maintain adequate tax records?	____	____
4. Are you familiar with tax-advantaged investments?	____	____

Retirement Planning

	Yes	No/Not Sure
1. Do your make regular contributions to an Individual Retirement Account?	____	____
2. If your have any income from self-employment, do you contribute to a Keogh plan or simplified employee pension (SEP)?	____	____
3. Are you currently enrolled in a company pension plan?	____	____

EXHIBIT 8–2
Financial Planning Checklist (Continued)

	Yes	No/Not Sure
4. Do you participate in an employer-sponsored salary reduction [401 (k)] plan?	____	____
5. If you are contemplating early retirement, are you preparing for the increased financial requirements of such an action?	____	____
6. Will your estimated retirement income be sufficient to meet your retirement expenses?	____	____
7. Are you taking action now to ensure financial security by retirement age?	____	____
8. If you are nearing retirement age, have you evaluated your investment portfolio mix in light of retirement income needs?	____	____
9. If you are nearing retirement age, have you decided where to live during retirement?	____	____
10. If you are nearing retirement age, have you discussed expected pension benefits with a company representative?	____	____
11. Have you requested from the Social Security Administration a record of your earnings and an estimate of your retirement benefits?	____	____

Estate Planning

	Yes	No/Not Sure
1. Do you have a valid will?	____	____
2. Do you review your will periodically to ensure that it still conforms to your wishes?	____	____
3. Does your spouse also have a valid and current will?	____	____
4. Have you prepared a letter of instructions?	____	____
5. Has your spouse prepared a letter of instructions?	____	____
6. Have you discussed both the location and the contents of the will and letter of instructions with your family?	____	____
7. Have you appointed a financial guardian for any dependent children?	____	____
8. Have your appointed a personal guardian for any dependent children?	____	____
9. Have you established an adult guardianship arrangement (durable power of attorney, living trust) in the event that either spouse becomes disabled or mentally incapacitated?	____	____

EXHIBIT 8–2
Financial Planning Checklist (concluded)

	Yes	No/Not Sure
10. Is the manner in which you own property (single ownership, joint ownership) consistent with effective estate planning?	____	____
11. Have you evaluated the estate planning and estate tax implications of owning business or real estate interests in more than one state?	____	____
12. Have you evaluated the impact of possible long-term uninsured hospitalization during retirement?	____	____

will learn from the experience. This will better equip you when you see a financial planner or investment adviser.

2. If you are going to trade individual stocks and want to do your own research, send $29.95 to Mercer, Inc., 80 Fifth Ave., Suite 800, New York, NY, 10011 and ask for a copy of Mark Coler's *Discount Brokerage Survey, Investor's Edition*. This book includes a list of 30 of the cheapest firms for 25 different securities trades. It also includes the names and addresses of 85 discount brokerage firms and 115 banks that offer similar services.

3. If you are planning to use a full-service brokerage firm and want to learn about your broker (employment history for the past 10 years, bankruptcies, unsatisfied judgments, securities violations, and arbitration awards of $5,000 or more), call the North American Securities Administrators Association (202–737–0900). The information is free.

4. When you open an account at a brokerage firm, do not sign any discretionary trading papers (this allows the broker to trade in your account without first telling you). If you are opening a joint account with another adult, keep in mind that either person can trade in the account as well as liquidate all holdings.

5. No matter who you deal with (stockbroker, financial planner, investment advisor, discount service at a bank, etc.), follow these steps to protect yourself:

- Read every word of any agreement or new account form before signing.
- Confirm every buy or sell verbally and in writing.
- Review your monthly or quarterly statements.
- Contact the firm as soon as you discover any mistake.
- Keep written notes of every conversation.
- Keep copies of all correspondence received and sent.

6. The cost of buying individual stocks can be significantly reduced (sometimes to zero) in the case of more than 1,000 U.S. companies that allow you to buy additional shares of their stock without going through a brokerage firm. To learn more about these plans, send $28.95 to Evergreen Enterprises, P.O. Box 763, Laurel, MD, 20725, and request a copy of the *Directory of Companies Offering Dividend Reinvestment Plans*.

7. Meet with your financial adviser to evaluate where you are today and where you want to be at retirement (see Chapter Eleven if you want to learn how to select an adviser). Implement the changes that coincide with your goals, time horizon, and tolerance for risk. Mark your calendar for a meeting in six months from now with your broker(s) and adviser to see how the plan is performing.

8. If you come into what you consider a lot of money, such as from an inheritance or a lump-sum distribution, put it into a money market fund immediately. Then, take your time, learn about the different current investment options, making sure it coincides with your overall game plan.

Chapter Nine

Postretirement Investing

Ways to Obtain Current Income
Maximizing Current Income
An Actual Systematic Withdrawal Plan
Current Income for High Bracket Taxpayers
Variable Annuities
How Long Your Money Will Last

Although we seldom think about it, after a sporting event each team goes on to the next event. This may mean taking a bus or train or getting ready for the next season, but something happens. The game we just witnessed or read about may be over, but today's winner can be tomorrow's loser, or vice versa. We don't think about these things because we really don't care. We are not part of the team.

Retirement is like a game or season. No matter how well we played (or how much money we saved), there is always next season. If we don't end up playing next year (perhaps due to death or incapacity), we still hope that our team does well. When it comes to investing, each new year or season brings with it several choices. Instead of learning new offensive or defensive moves, strategy is determined by a simple calculator and the then current investment opportunities. We may be on the sidelines, but this does not mean that we are not still active and want to see certain things done.

So far, we have accomplished a great deal. We have completed a series of worksheets, learned about investments, types of risk, inflation, taxes, insurance, and social security. We have seen ways to protect ourselves against company programs that may either be insufficient or unsafe. Most important, we have learned how to prepare a financial plan, the road map for a successful retirement. We have learned to look out for those "red flags," signs that certain questions must be answered before monies are invested or papers are signed. The puzzle is almost completed. Only a few questions remain to be answered.

As we approach retirement, we must have ways to manage our money to pay expenses and offset the effects of inflation and taxes on our principal. Furthermore, the older we get, the more interested we are in increasing our current income. The problem most people have is that they do not know all of the available options.

This chapter presents several different ways to increase current income during retirement—methods you may not previously have thought of. The beauty of some of these alternatives is that, in some ways, they are safer than what the popular press promotes: bank CDs, government bonds, and money market accounts. Safety can be defined in different contexts, including purchasing power, lost opportunity cost, and aftertax returns—three areas often not addressed. The chapter also looks at different ways to minimize taxable income.

The chapter begins with a method of obtaining current income while still providing a hedge against inflation. This is of utmost importance. You are going to be living a long time and want to make sure your assets will provide the standard of living you are accustomed to for the remainder of your life and your spouse's. The plan of getting attractive monthly checks is then looked at from a different perspective: the investor who is already paying a lot in taxes. Ideas described here could benefit you by tens of thousands of dollars. The chapter ends by showing a chart that indicates how long your principal will last if it is determined that an invasion is necessary.

Before reading on, go back to Chapter One and review how you answered the tough questions asked at the beginning of that chapter. By reviewing your responses, you will have a better idea of the level of income you will need and which strategy(s) you should follow in *this* chapter.

WAYS TO OBTAIN CURRENT INCOME

Many people receive money from social security each month. A high percentage of these people also receive some type of monthly retirement benefit from their former employer. Outside of these two sources, the great majority of us will have to rely on income from our investments.

What we invest in should depend on our risk level, time horizon, existing portfolio, and tax bracket. Most people entering retirement are not willing to, and probably should not, be looking at any high risk investments. These individuals and couples should be looking at sources of current income that are considered moderate to conservative. The investments you should be looking at depend on your risk comfort level, real rate (rate of return minus taxes and/ or inflation) of return needed, and short- as well as long-term objectives. To determine your level of risk, review the risk test you took in an earlier chapter.

If you expect to live only a couple of years, then equity vehicles such as common stocks, mutual funds that invest in stocks, business interests, real estate, and all types of limited partnerships should be avoided. These investments are designed to perform best if held three years or longer (10 to 15 years in the case of limited partnerships).

If your time horizon is three years or more, then balanced mutual funds (common stocks and bonds), growth and income funds (conservative, high-dividend-paying U.S. stocks), growth funds, global funds, and international (foreign) funds should constitute at least a moderate part of your holdings. Your time frame needs to be combined with your risk level. A very conservative investor, no matter what the time frame, should refrain from loading up on common stocks, collectibles (rare coins, stamps, gold, silver, etc.), and real estate, with the possible exception of a personal residence.

MAXIMIZING CURRENT INCOME

One of the best ways to safely increase your current income and have a hedge against inflation is what is known as a systematic withdrawal program (SWP). These programs can be set up through one or more mutual fund and/or variable annuity families. You and your investment adviser decide which kinds of investment categories are best suited for you based on time, risk level, tax bracket, and desired level of income.

After you have determined what types of investments suit your personality and situation, the amount of money to be invested into each category needs to be determined. By reviewing the sample portfolios shown in the previous chapters, you will be able to sit down with your financial adviser and determine the specific percentage amounts or dollar figures.

Money is then invested into each of these categories. Accounts are structured so that all dividends, interest, and/or capital gains are automatically reinvested. A systematic withdrawal section on the application (sometimes it is a separate supplemental application) is then completed. The SWP part of the application asks when the income stream is to commence (immediately, six months from now, etc.), the dollar amount or percentage figure you want (e.g., $120 each month or 1% each month), and the frequency of payments (monthly, quarterly, etc.).

As an example, suppose you decide to invest $30,000 in a growth and income fund, a fund that had averaged 15 percent or better over the past 10 to 15 years. Based on your need for current income and concerns about inflation, you decide that you would like a 12 percent income stream sent to you each month. Thus, based on a $30,000 initial investment, $300 will be sent to you each month ($30,000 times 12 percent divided by the 12 months of the year). Every month the mutual fund or variable annuity you invested in would send you a check for $300, whether the stock market, or your investment, is going up, down, or sideways.

A SWP using mutual funds and/or variable annuities provides you with regular income you can depend on. With money market funds or CDs, you are at the mercy of interest rates and are controlled by what someone is willing to offer you. Bonds pay a set rate but are not considered hedges against inflation. An equity-based SWP will pay you more monthly income than bonds, can be altered to provide more income at any time in the future, and has historically been an excellent hedge against inflation.

So far, a SWP may sound too good to be true. After all, we are talking about an investment that involves the following points:

1. It sends us a monthly check.
2. The checks are greater than what our bonds are paying.
3. The amount of the checks does not vary unless we contact

the mutual fund or variable annuity and request an increase or decrease.

4. There is no cost or fee to set up a SWP.

5. There is no cost or fee to change, suspend, or reactivate the SWP.

6. It is a risk reduction tool (if more than one type of fund or portfolio is used).

At this point you are probably saying to yourself, "What's the catch?" To see what the negatives of a SWP are, look at the 59-year example in Exhibit 9–1. Study the far right-hand column carefully ("total value of shares remaining"); notice that the principal goes up and down. This fluctuation is the price that you will pay. To be effective, and make sure you do not go broke, a SWP must be flexible: the withdrawal rate should be less or on parity with the total return of the fund. This last point is not particularly important for a short-term horizon of five years or less, but must be seriously taken into account if you expect the program to last your remaining lifetime.

AN ACTUAL SYSTEMATIC WITHDRAWAL PLAN

Exhibit 9–1 assumes an initial investment of $1 million in a conservative growth and income fund. All dividends and capital gains have been reinvested. This fund, The Investment Company of America, is part of the American Funds family. It is being used in this example because only a small number of mutual funds have been in existence for 50 years or longer and because this fund group has demonstrated tremendous consistency over the past several decades.

Since the investor is income oriented, the account has been structured for a 10 percent annual withdrawal ($100,000 is taken out at the end of the first year). To combat the effects of inflation, annual withdrawals are increased by 4 percent each year thereafter. Since income tax rates have changed over the years and some readers are in different tax brackets than others, the effects of income taxes have not been taken into account. Even though the

EXHIBIT 9–1
Performance of the Investment Company of America SWP over 59 years

Date	Annual Amount Withdrawn	Total Value of Shares Remaining	Date	Annual Amount Withdrawn	Total Value of Shares Remaining
12/31/34	$100,000	$1,153,000	12/31/63	$ 311,865	$ 7,571,000
12/31/35	104,000	2,007,000	12/31/64	324,340	8,478,000
12/31/36	108,160	2,814,000	12/31/65	337,313	10,425,000
12/31/37	112,486	1,620,000	12/31/66	350,806	10,176,000
12/31/38	116,986	1,935,000	12/31/67	364,838	12,752,000
12/31/39	121,665	1,830,000	12/31/68	379,431	14,536,000
12/31/40	126,532	1,659,000	12/31/69	394,609	12,589,000
12/31/41	131,593	1,405,000	12/31/70	410,393	12,508,000
12/31/42	136,857	1,504,000	12/31/71	426,809	14,211,000
12/31/43	142,331	1,855,000	12/31/72	443,881	16,020,000
12/31/44	148,024	2,140,000	12/31/73	461,636	12,865,000
12/31/45	153,945	2,773,000	12/31/74	480,102	10,076,000
12/31/46	160,103	2,547,000	12/31/75	499,306	13,142,000
12/31/47	166,507	2,404,000	12/31/76	519,278	16,513,000
12/31/48	173,168	2,240,000	12/31/77	540,049	15,547,000
12/31/49	180,094	2,271,000	12/31/78	561,651	17,270,000
12/31/50	187,298	2,534,000	12/31/79	584,117	19,997,000
12/31/51	194,970	2,791,000	12/31/80	607,482	23,636,000
12/31/52	202,582	2,929,000	12/31/81	631,781	23,211,000
12/31/53	210,685	2,731,000	12/31/82	657,053	30,393,000
12/31/54	219,112	4,045,000	12/31/83	683,335	35,839,000
12/31/55	277,877	4,845,000	12/31/84	710,668	37,519,000
12/31/56	236,992	5,129,000	12/31/85	739,095	49,307,000
12/31/57	246,472	4,273,000	12/31/86	768,659	59,257,000
12/31/58	256,330	5,930,000	12/31/87	799,405	61,679,000
12/31/59	266,584	6,505,000	12/31/88	831,381	69,074,000
12/31/60	277,247	6,522,000	12/31/89	864,636	88,520,000
12/31/61	288,337	7,740,000	12/31/90	899,222	88,224,000
12/31/62	299,870	6,415,000	12/31/91	935,191	110,706,000
			12/31/92	972,599	117,469,000
		Total Spent		$22,787,565	

management company that oversees the Investment Company of America does a good job when it comes to tax minimization (largely due to a low turnover rate in the portfolio), they are not magicians. Since the cumulative returns and withdrawals on this fund have been great, you should also assume that the aftertax "total value of shares remaining" would be substantially lower if capital gains were paid each year. However, the example is not misleading if such an account were sheltered (part of an IRA, pension plan, variable annuity, etc.).

If you are not certain whether you can live with such variability, ask yourself if you can live with the variability of the continually increasing prices you pay for everything you purchase. Ask yourself if you invest $30,000 in a bank CD or government bond what the purchasing power of your $30,000 will be when the instrument matures in 2, 5, 10, or 20 years from now? Equally important, what will the income from such investments be able to purchase in 5 to 10 years? The answer is probably somewhere between one half to two thirds of what you are currently consuming. Do you really want your standard of living to decrease by 30 to 50 percent every 5 to 10 years?

Getting back to the 59-year example, consider the following points:

- The example represents actual results of a mutual fund that has been in existence for exactly 59 years. No special or "trick" beginning year was used. The example shows an initial investment of $1 million. You can start a SWP with as little as $10,000.
- You cannot hide bad results or assume it is luck if you look at a time frame that is 20 years or longer, particularly when you show results on a year-by-year basis.
- The example shown represents the most conservative U.S. common stock play you can make: a growth and income fund. This particular portfolio comprises over 100 different stocks that pay high dividends.
- The income stream actually increases each year by 4 percent so that purchasing power is maintained (inflation averaged 4 percent over this period).
- No additional investment is ever made. The investor made a single contribution in 1934 and never added any more of his or her money.

- The value of the "remaining shares" (the original $1 mil-
lion plus additional growth) assumes that the income
stream received each year is spent or given away. By the
end of 1992, close to $23 million has been spent, and the
original investment is now worth over $117 million.
- Even better results could be obtained if the initial investment was split up and two or more SWPs were established
with a U.S. portfolio (such as the example of a growth and
income fund) and a foreign or international fund.

To feel completely comfortable with a SWP, do not just look at the
example beginning in 1934 and ending in 1992. Also look at the
example starting with a different year, any year, and then look at
the value of your "remaining shares" three or five years later (e.g.,
start with 1960 and see what the investment has grown to by the
end of 1963 or 1965). Do this with several time periods.

If the concept of a SWP appeals to you, have your financial
adviser contact several mutual funds (or variable annuities) and
ask for examples. To make sure you are not looking at an artificially
good period of time, get examples (known as hypotheticals by
mutual fund and variable annuity groups) that show performance
and withdrawals for at least a 15-year period. Remember, you
cannot hide bad results if lengthy time periods are used.

The amount of income you should request under a SWP depends
on the caliber of the mutual funds you have chosen. Bond funds,
for example, cannot be expected to pay 8 to 12 percent a year and
have any type of net growth to offset inflation. The stock fund you
have selected may have averaged 20 percent a year over the past
decade, but do not expect that kind of return for the next 10 or 20
years.

A SWP works best if equity positions (aggressive growth, small
cap, growth, growth and income, and/or international) within a
mutual fund or variable annuity family are used. If you do your
homework properly, you can structure a 9 to 15 percent annual
income stream. The closer you get to taking out 15 percent per
year, the less growth of principal you will have; the more you tone
down the current income, say, by staying at 9 or 10 percent, the
greater your principal will grow.

Some people set up a SWP in the 14 to 16 percent range because
they desperately need a high level of income to live on. For these

people, principal erosion is not a concern because they are not expecting to live for a long time or because they are expecting other sources of income or principal in the future (e.g., an inheritance, sale of a building, home, or business). Most people who set up a SWP have a finite portfolio that they must depend on for income for the rest of their lives, which may be 30 or 40 more years. These people should start with an annual income stream in the 9 to 11 percent range for a couple of years—a range lower than what stocks have historically returned. As their comfort level or needs change, either due to investment experience or the effects of inflation, this figure can always later be adjusted upwards. A conservative start means that there will be even greater growths of principal, which means a larger base from which to later take out much more money.

CURRENT INCOME FOR HIGH BRACKET TAXPAYERS

There are two disadvantages of a systematic withdrawal program: (1) your principal will probably not go up each year, and (2) most, if not all, of your monthly checks will be taxable. The reason for this is that the income you receive each month includes one or more of the following:

- Dividend income (from those stocks in the mutual fund portfolio that pay dividends).
- Interest (to the limited extent the fund includes interest-bearing instruments such as money market securities and bonds).
- Realized gains (the buying and selling of securities within the fund).
- Unrealized gains (portfolio securities that have increased in value but have not been sold).
- Return of principal (during those periods when gains, interest, and dividends are less than the amount of the withdrawal).

Your monthly check will be included as part of your taxable income for the year to the extent it is composed of the first three items above.

The first disadvantage is easy to counter, simply ask yourself what happens if you go into alternative investments such as bank CDs, government bonds, and money market accounts. These investments give you a predictable return and your principal is generally secure, but how about purchasing power? The value of these investments deteriorates most years because of inflation. Thus, they offer a false sense of security.

The second disadvantage, income taxes, is something that can be minimized if a different investment vehicle is used in conjunction with mutual funds. High monthly income and growth of principal to offset the future effects of inflation can still be accomplished using one of two tax-advantaged investments: variable annuities or variable life insurance. The previous illustration of a systematic withdrawal plan used a mutual fund. Variable annuities and variable life insurance both have a great deal in common with mutual funds. In fact, all three of these investment vehicles provide: (1) professional management, (2) several different investment options to choose from, including conservative, moderate, and aggressive portfolios, (3) the ability to change your investment mix with a telephone call, (4) toll-free telephone numbers to have any questions you might have answered, (5) performance that typically outpaces inflation, depending on your risk level and the portfolio manager selected, and (6) ease and convenience. Let us now look at the tax advantages that make variable annuities and variable life insurance different from mutual funds.

VARIABLE ANNUITIES

As described in an earlier chapter, a variable annuity works like a mutual fund family with two important differences:

Your investments in a variable annuity grow and compound tax deferred.

Variable annuities provide a guaranteed death benefit.

In a variable annuity your contributions are segregated and *you* decide how your money is to be invested. You can choose among stock, bond, government obligation, gold, and money market accounts, just as you would choose among different types of mutual funds.

In addition to offering investment flexibility and segregated accounts, variable annuities include a guaranteed death benefit. The death benefit states that at the time of the annuitant's death, the beneficiary will receive the original investment(s), minus any withdrawals made, or the value of the account on date of death, whichever is greater. The annuitant is similar to the insured in a life insurance policy. The annuitant can be you, your spouse, a child, friend, neighbor, or relative. Most insurers require that the annuitant be age 75 or less.

As an example, imagine that someone invested $100,000 in a variable annuity just before the stock market crash in 1987. Further suppose that the value of the investment dropped by $25,000 due to the crash and right after this drop, the annuitant died. As the beneficiary, you, your spouse, family, and/or living trust would receive a check for $100,000, even though the investment was worth $75,000. If, on the other hand, the annuity was worth $350,000 on the date of the annuitant's death, the beneficiary(s) would receive $350,000. If the person had instead invested $100,000 in a mutual fund and suffered a similar loss, you and your family would not be reimbursed for the decline in value. This, perhaps, is the greatest single risk of a SWP: a loss of principal that takes years to recover or is permanently lost.

There are three ways to take money out of a variable annuity: (1) by written request, (2) use of a systematic withdrawal program (SWP), or (3) annuitization. Since money in an annuity grows and compounds tax deferred indefinitely, you pay taxes only on the money you take out that represents the growth or income portion, not your principal.

Sporadic withdrawals made by telephone or written request are taxed based on the LIFO (last in, first out) method of accounting. This means that your growth and/or income are the first things taxed as money is taken out. As an example, if you invested $20,000 into an annuity and it grew to $30,000, the first $10,000 would be taxed when it was withdrawn, whether or not it was withdrawn all at once or sporadically. The final $20,000 would not be taxed in this example since it is considered a return of principal.

An annuity withdrawn under a systematic withdrawal plan

(SWP), previously described, would be taxed the same way as sporadic withdrawals: all initial withdrawals would be considered growth and/or income and therefore fully taxable. It would only be the final withdrawals, considered principal, that would not be taxed. Money taken out, as described in this and the previous paragraph, would also be subject to a 10 percent IRS penalty unless the owner was at least 59½ or disabled. If such a penalty did exist, it would apply only to the growth and income, not the principal.

Annuitization is the only way to make withdrawals that are tax advantaged. Annuitization means that you are receiving distributions that are considered part interest/growth and part return of principal. The portion considered a return of principal is not taxed. At the time you annuitize, your insurance company will come up with an *exclusion ratio* based on IRS guidelines. This ratio tells the insurance company and you what percentage or dollar amount of each check you receive is free from income taxes. The percentage figure can be quite high. It depends on how much of your contract's current value is composed of your contributions (investments) and how much is based on growth or reinvested interest.

There are disadvantages with annuitization. Once the process begins, you cannot alter the payout schedule; if you opted to have part or all of the account annuitized (liquidated) over, say, an eight-year period, you are stuck with this plan for the entire eight years. If you die or become disabled during this period, nothing changes. The payments would continue to be sent to either you, your estate, or your heirs.

VARIABLE LIFE

Variable life is a form of whole life insurance with two big differences. First, unlike traditional whole life insurance, the investor decides where the money is to be invested; investment options range from conservative to aggresive. Second, the cost of insurance can be significantly lower than other types of coverage. Typically this means that somewhere between 95 and 98 percent of your money is being invested; the balance is used to pay for the insurance coverage. And it is this insurance coverage that makes this type of tax advantaged.

Since variable life qualifies as life insurance, virtually all of the cash buildup can be withdrawn income tax free. The IRS allows this since you are merely borrowing money from your policy. Loans are not taxable. Most insurance companies will charge you a fee to take out such monies; the loan rate is usually between 0 and 2 percent. You never have to pay back the loan. A taxable event is only triggered if you cancel the policy or do not fulfill IRS guidelines (i.e., maintaining the "integrity" of the policy).

When used properly, variable life insurance is a means whereby you can make substantial annual or sporadic withdrawals, a form of monthly income, without paying any income taxes on such income. The key to such tremendous ongoing tax benefits is to make sure that the "seven pay test" (making sure that there is somewhat of a balance between premiums being paid in over a set number of years and withdrawals made during those early years) is met.

HOW LONG YOUR MONEY WILL LAST

Exhibit 9–2 on the following page shows the length of time capital will last using different combinations of withdrawal and interest or growth rates, no matter what type(s) of mutual funds or annuities are used. For example, with an annual withdrawal rate of 9 percent and an interest or growth rate of 7 percent, funds will last for 22 years. If the interest or growth rate equals or exceeds the withdrawal rate, funds will remain constant or grow indefinitely.

You have now learned something that virtually none of your friends and only a small percentage of investment advisers and financial planners know: the attributes of using equity-based vehicles to structure a monthly income stream. But, before you start setting up any of these accounts or repositioning any of your holdings, read the next chapter. It shows you how you should own your assets and the resulting tax, divorce, and death consequences. As you will learn, something that appears so simple, starting an investment, can end up later haunting you if not done properly.

Now that you have gone through all of the trouble of seeing how investments work, the different types of insurance, how public programs can protect you and your family, and have done some

EXHIBIT 9–2
Rate of Withdrawal Table

Annual Withdrawal Rate (Percent)	*Annual Interest or Growth Rate*									
	5	6	7	8	9	10	11	12	13	14
6	36									
7	25	33								
8	20	23	30							
9	16	18	22	28						
10	14	15	17	20	26					
11	12	13	14	16	19	25				
12	11	11	12	14	15	18	23			
13	9	10	11	12	13	15	17	21		
14	9	9	10	11	11	13	14	17	21	
15	8	8	9	9	10	11	12	14	16	20

financial planning, you can begin to complete the picture by learning about living trusts and wills. Some very basic and inexpensive estate planning can preserve your hard work for generations to come. Learning the different forms of ownership is simply the first step of this process.

CHECKLIST OF THINGS TO DO

1. Contact a handful of mutual fund families and have them run computer hypotheticals (which will all be based on actual historical performance) using a systematic withdrawal plan (SWP) at 8, 10, and 12 percent. Some of the top-performing fund families are: American Funds (1–800–421–0180), Phoenix (1–800–243–4361), SoGen (1–800–334–2143) and Vanguard (1–800–662–7447).

2. By using your favorite funds from the growth, growth and income, global bond, short-term international income, and foreign equity categories, you will be able to structure a blended portfolio that will give you the highest possible income stream based on your risk level.

3. If you are in a high tax bracket, use this same SWP strategy by employing a series of variable annuities and/or variable life products. Some of the top-performing variable annuity and life companies are: American Skandia (1-800-541-3087), Equitable (1-800-628-6673), Lincoln National (1-800-443-8137), and Western Reserve Life (1-800-443-9975).

4. Always try to have part of your portfolio invested for growth, no matter how old you are. This means that if you are using a SWP with a series of mutual funds and/or variable annuities that have a blended (or average) rate of return of 13 percent, limit your monthly withdrawals to the 9-11 percent range. The excess total return, 2-4 percent in this example, can be used to partially offset the effects of inflation or a losing year.

5. Heed advice given earlier in the book and "go global" by investing in foreign as well as U.S., stocks, bonds, and money market instruments. Investing some of your money (20 percent to 70 percent depending on your risk level) abroad means that you will:

Own a piece of economic growth in other countries.

Not be at the sole mercy of U.S. economic policymakers.

Be investing in currencies other than just the U.S. dollar.

Have the ability to follow economic trends wherever they occur.

Reduce your overall risk level by 20 to 52 percent (depending on the study cited).

6. If you find that you are in need of additional monthly income, look into a reverse mortgage. It allows you to get monthly income by using the equity in your home. The particulars of each program vary depending on the lender being used. With some firms, your income will last as long as you stay in your home. Three firms that deal in this area are The Individual Reverse Mortgage Account in Mount Laurel, NJ (800-233-4762), The Home Income Security Plan in Louisville (800-942-6550), and The Providential Home Income Plan in San Francisco (800-441-4428). If you would like a more extensive list, send a self-addressed, stamped envelope to the National Center for Home Equity Conversion, 1210 East College Dr., Suite 300, Marshall, MN, 56258.

Chapter Ten

Estate Planning

How You Own Things
Why Title Is Important
Your Will
Probate
Living Trust
Living Will

Stop! Before you dismiss this chapter because it appears to deal only with matters that will go on *after* your death, think again. Estate planning will not only help your loved ones, it will also help you. Do you want to feel like a jerk, knowing that a large part of your estate was given away to Uncle Sam just because you were not willing to spend a few hours to save a lifetime's work? More important, estate planning includes information that will help you while you are alive. Some very "live" issues are raised and answered in this chapter.

At the beginning of the previous chapter, I described a sports team and what they go through at the end of the season. I made an analogy between sports and investing strategies. I also pointed out that although we may no longer play in the game, we still care about what happens to our teammates. Presumably, you care more about your family than you would about fellow team members if you were involved in a sport. By following the advice given in this chapter, you will be helping your loved ones the same way you would help a friend or sports buddy.

The chapter begins by explaining the importance of how assets are titled, not only in the case of death, but in the event of divorce or disability. The different forms of ownership are examined from a legal and tax standpoint. The next sections covers wills—what they mean, what they should include, and how much you should pay for one. A very real part of estate planning is deciding beforehand if your plans will be altered due to divorce, marriage, or children. You probably have some definite views on who you want to get your hard-earned money and which people should get nothing; the section that follows wills deals with this issue. You will want to make sure that after your death your final wishes are carried out and that the estate is distributed or managed in an orderly fashion. This is the responsibility of your executor or trustee. A separate section on executors and trustees is included.

The chapter then moves on to that dreaded topic, probate. You will learn the costs, fees, frustration, and humiliation that probate can bring. Surprisingly, we discover something called a "living probate." Thus, do not think that you will never experience probate. The cure for probate is given in the sections that follow. Several pages are devoted to living trusts, including some cautionary notes for the do-it-yourselfers. Along the same lines, a section on how to select an estate planning attorney has also been included.

The final sections of the chapter cover legal documents that can benefit you while you are alive: durable powers of attorney and living wills.

Your estate is everything you own; it includes your home, automobiles, furniture, bank and brokerage firm accounts, cash, retirement plans, business interests, personal effects, and life insurance. Estate planning is a process to determine who will receive your assets after death. You can also decide when and how the estate is to be distributed.

There are several ways to leave property to those whom you want to have it after death. By properly executing documents such as a will and/or a living trust, as well as naming the right person or people to follow your instructions, you can ensure that your wishes will be carried out. Poor estate planning can result in unnecessary taxes, delays, legal costs, and the distribution of your assets to people you might never have wanted to benefit.

HOW YOU OWN THINGS

Everything you have is owned by either you alone or with someone else. The way in which your assets are titled can have a tremendous impact on you while you are alive and at death. There are seven different ways to title assets: (1) as separate property, (2) tenancy in common, (3) tenancy by the entirety, (4) joint tenancy with rights of survivorship, (5) community property, (6) as trustee, and (7) as custodian. You can also title an asset under the name of a corporation or partnership; these latter two methods are not described in this book. You cannot hold title to the same asset in different ways; you must choose one and only one. Each of these methods is described below.

Separate Property

Separate property includes everything you acquire while single. It also includes items earned or acquired after legal separation or divorce and those things that you receive by gift or inheritance during marriage. Separate property maintains its identity unless it is transferred by the owner to some form of joint ownership. As the sole owner of separate property, only you can decide if and when the asset is to be sold or given to someone else. No other person, including your spouse, can transfer, buy, sell, or give away any of your separate property unless you give them permission.

Tenancy in Common

Tenancy in common is a form of joint or co-ownership. As a cotenant you own the asset with one or more other people or entities (corporation, trust, or partnership). You can sell, transfer, gift, or bequeath (leave in your will or trust) your interest to anyone without the permission of the other co-owners.

Tenancy by the Entirety

Tenancy by the entirety is a form of joint ownership, except it can involve only a husband and wife. It can be terminated only by the joint agreement of both spouses. This form of co-ownership is often used by married couples in separate property states (see "community property" below to determine if you live in a separate property state).

Joint Tenancy with Rights of Survivorship

Perhaps the most common form of co-ownership is joint tenancy with rights of survivorship, often abbreviated as *jtwros*. Like tenancy in common, jtwros means that two or more individuals or entities own the asset and any co-owner is free to dispose of his or her share in any manner while he or she is alive. However, unlike any other form of ownership, upon the death of one of the co-owners under jtwros, the decedent's share automatically passes on to the surviving tenants. Joint tenancy takes precedence over any will or trust.

Community Property

There are seven community property states: Arizona, California, Idaho, Nevada, New Mexico, Texas, and Washington. All other states, except Louisiana and the District of Columbia, are classified as *common law* states. Common law states are also referred to as *separate property* states. Wisconsin is a common law state but has adopted marital property laws that are similar to those in community property jurisdictions. The distinction between community and common law states is important whenever death or divorce occurs.

Community property (c/p) includes everything that you acquire while you are married and reside in one of the seven community property states. It includes all assets, income, salary, personal possessions, and real estate of both spouses. In a community property state, property earned or obtained by *either* spouse during marriage is owned equally by each spouse. Assets acquired by gift or inheritance are considered the separate property of that spouse. Gifts and bequeaths retain their separate property identity unless the person receiving the gift, known as the grantee, decides to make a "gift" of the asset to the other spouse or to the community.

As you will see under the section title a "step-up in basis" below, community property offers a tremendous tax advantage not found with other forms of ownership; but this benefit comes at a cost. Under community property laws, either spouse can sell, transfer, bequeath, or gift his or her share without the permission of the other spouse. Thus, you may own an asset as community property with your spouse and discover that upon that spouse's death his or her share has been left to someone other than you (a child, neighbor, friend, etc.). Thus, in a community property state the decedent's will may say that a secret boyfriend is to receive her share of the community property.

Trustee

Accounts and property that are part of a trust must name one or more trustee(s). Only the trustee(s) has the right to manage, buy, or sell assets within the trust. Trust accounts are easy to identify; title to the account is something like "Ursel Jones, trustee of the Jones Family Trust." The person who creates the trust, known as the *trustor* or *trust maker*, has the ability to change trustees at anytime. People who create trusts usually name themselves as trustee.

Assets placed within a trust maintain their original identity; all separate property remains under the sole ownership of one person. Jointly held property (tenancy in common, jtwros, c/p, tenancy by the entirety) also keeps its co-owner status. These distinctions are normally important only if there is a divorce or death.

Custodian

Accounts set up for minor children or mentally incapacitated people must name a custodian. This is because these categories of people are not considered to have *legal capacity* and therefore cannot normally enter into a binding contract. Only the custodian can trade, buy, or sell assets in the custodial account. Title to these accounts is usually taken as "John Smith, custodian for the benefit of (abbreviated as FBO) Jeff Jones." Even though Jeff Jones is the owner, he lacks legal capacity, due either to age or mental condition. It is for this reason that only John Smith, the custodian listed on the account, can make decisions concerning the asset.

Custodians are similar to trustees in that they are overseeing an account, asset, or property for the benefit of another individual, group, or entity. In the case of a trust, the trustee is also often the trustor (the person who created the trust).

WHY TITLE IS IMPORTANT

Only the person listed as owner or co-owner can control the asset. This is true whether gifts, bequests, sales, purchases, or trades are involved. One of the biggest mistakes people make is naming someone the co-owner of an asset without knowing the full ramifications of such action.

Jointly owned property means that *all* co-owners must agree to the disposition (sale, gift, transfer, etc.) of the item in question. Any co-owner, except in the case of tenancy by the entirety, is always free to sell, gift, trade, or bequeath *his or her interest* in the property; he or she cannot, however, make a decision as to what should happen to the entire property without the consent of everyone listed as co-owner. However, many financial institutions only require one co-owner's consent to buy or sell.

Often, a widow or widower will name a child or children as co-owners of the family home or a bank account. Even though the child has received this asset by gift, the asset cannot be sold without the permission and signature of the new co-owner(s). You may feel that you are still the "true" owner of the property, but no one else will share that opinion.

Jointly held property poses a problem in the event of a lawsuit. If the co-owned property is the subject of a lawsuit, it could be seized, frozen, or sold to satisfy the claims of the person bringing suit. This is true even if only one of the co-owners was allegedly at fault.

Temporary or permanent physical or mental incapacity of a joint tenant also means trouble. If that person is no longer able to sign his or her name or lacks legal capacity, the co-owner(s) must go to court for approval before the asset can be sold, transferred, or given away.

You may say that the points mentioned so far are unimportant to you because you completely trust the co-owner(s) named. Presumably this is true, otherwise you would not have named them as cotenants. However, this feeling of confidence may change when that son or daughter gets married, has children, or their personality is altered due to certain events, religious beliefs, or from drugs or alcohol.

How an asset is titled is important not only for legal reasons, it can also affect your taxes. The next couple of subsections discuss the tax consequences of making gifts and what happens when an asset is inherited.

Tax Ramifications.   Anytime a sale, transfer, gift, or inheritance of an asset is contemplated, always consider any potential income and gift (estate) tax. When you acquire an asset, such as a home, business interest, stock, or bond, you take on what is known as a *cost basis*. This basis is important if the asset is ever disposed of; any and all profits or losses are determined based on the asset's basis. The cost, or basis, is the purchase price minus any depreciation or plus any additions (fix-up expenses, additional contributions, etc.).

When personal property (stocks, bonds, cars, boats, jewelry, furniture, etc.) or real estate is sold for more or less than the purchase price a taxable event can occur. The profit, referred to as gain, is determined by subtracting the purchase price (adjusted for any depreciation or fix-up costs claimed) from the *net* sales price (the selling price minus any costs, fees, or commissions). As an example, if you paid $20,000 for a car, spent $5,000 fixing it up, depreciated $6,000 of it as a business expense, and then paid someone $1,000 to sell it for you for $22,000, the tax consequences would like like this:

Purchase price	$20,000
Fix-up costs	+5,000
Depreciation	−6,000
Adjusted-cost basis	$19,000
Selling price	$22,000
Adjusted-cost basis	−19,000
Selling commission	−1,000
Net (taxable) profit	$ 2,000

This net figure results in a taxable event unless the resulting figure is zero or a negative number or the asset being sold is somehow sheltered (within a retirement plan, part of an annuity, or a tax-free exchange). One of the goals of estate and financial planning is to lower, eliminate, or defer, whenever possible, any tax event.

Unless somehow sheltered, assets sold while you are alive are fully taxable if a net profit results. Assets sold for a loss may result in a tax loss that can be used to offset gains. You can also use a tax loss to offset earned income such as your salary. Death of an owner or co-owner can change the tax consequences by what is known as a *step-up in basis*.

Step-up in Basis

A *stepped-up basis* means that, in the eyes of the IRS, the asset being sold or transferred now costs more than it originally did. This means that any resulting profit will be reduced and any possible loss will be enhanced. A step-up in basis occurs only upon the death of a sole owner or co-tenant in the case of community property or joint tenancy with rights of survivorship.

The best way to show how a new basis is calculated is by example. Suppose that you were the sole owner of some stocks, bonds, personal property, or real estate that originally cost you $100,000. For sake of illustration, let us assume that the cost basis is not altered by any depreciation, additional contributions, or fix-up costs. The asset is now worth $300,000 and you decide to sell it. If the asset were sold for $300,000, you would have a $200,000 profit. Unless somehow sheltered, taxes on the $200,000 gain would be due for the year in which the asset was sold.

Change the set of facts slightly and assume that just before the sale occurred, you died. Your heir(s) would receive a step-up in basis equal to the fair market value of the asset as of the date of your death ($300,000 in this example). If the heirs later sold the asset, any profit or loss would be determined based on the new cost basis. If, in our example, the property you paid $100,000 was worth $300,000 at your death and the heirs later sold it for $300,000, there would be no taxable gain. This is because the new basis is $300,000; your heir(s) received a 100 percent step-up in basis. This is one of the few ways in which income taxes can be avoided, but death must occur to get this tax advantage.

Let us change the facts again. Assume that you and someone else own the property as joint tenants with rights of survivorship (jtwros). If a sale occurred while both of you were alive, there would be a taxable gain of $200,000, just as if you owned the asset as separate property. If, however, either tenant died before the sale, there would be an adjustment in the cost basis of the decedent's share. Half of the property would get a step-up in basis equal to that share's value at the date of death.

In our example, upon the death of a joint owner his or her share is now considered to have an original purchase price of $150,000 (one half the fair market value at death), even though he or she paid only $50,000 for that interest. Any profit or loss is based on the new cost basis. In this case the new cost basis is the decedent's share, adjusted upward to $150,000, and the surviving tenant's original cost $50,000, or one half of the original purchase price. Now any profit or loss is based on a purchase price, also referred to as the *adjusted basis*, of $200,000. If the property were sold for $300,000, the surviving tenant would pay taxes on a gain of $100,000 (unless there was some exclusion, tax-free exchange, or the sold asset was part of a qualified retirement plan or annuity).

Let us change the facts one more time. Assume everything is the same except this couple is married, they live in a community property state, and the asset is titled as community property (e.g., "Robert and Cathy Perkins, c/p"). Upon the death of either spouse, the property will receive a 100 percent step-up in basis *on both halves*, even though only one spouse has died. If the property had been sold while both spouses were alive, there would have been a potential taxable gain of $200,000 (the $300,000 sale price minus the $100,000 purchase price). However, in this particular example, wherein one or both spouses have died, there is no taxable event since the property has a new cost basis of $300,000. Any profit or loss is based on the new basis, $300,000, being subtracted from the sale price. In our example where the sale price is assumed to also be $300,000, no taxes are due since $300,000 minus $300,000 results in a gain of zero.

Keep in mind the following points concerning community property and a step-up in basis:

1. The property must be titled as "community property" prior to the sale and death of either spouse; living in a community property state is not enough.
2. Death must occur to receive the stepped-up basis.
3. The 100 percent step-up basis also occurs if both spouses die at the same time. All items titled as community property will receive a 100 percent step-up in basis upon the death of either the husband or wife, even though such

items have been retitled under the name of the trust (living trusts are discussed in detail below).

Most people in community property states take title to their homes, savings accounts, and securities as "jtwros" with their spouse. As you can now see, this may be the biggest mistake you have ever made. Fortunately, you can go out and retitle the asset tomorrow for little or no cost. You do not need a lawyer or court order to make such a change. Simply contact the savings institution, brokerage firm, or county recorder's office and find out what form they require.

YOUR WILL

A will spells out who gets your property when you die. A trust can do the same thing, but there are things that only a will can do:

- If you have *minor* children, a will is necessary to name a guardian.
- If you acquire property before you have had a chance to amend your will or trust, provisions commonly found in a will can make sure that such an asset will be inherited by the person you want to receive it.
- If you have a trust but have forgotten to title an asset under the name of the trust, your will can make sure such items are disposed of according to the terms of the will or trust.
- In the rare event that you have been left an asset from someone else's estate and that asset is being probated and you die before title has been changed to your name, the asset will pass to the person named as the residuary beneficiary in your will.
- A will can be used to disinherit a child, spouse, or relative.
- A will names the executor of your estate. This is the person who supervises the distribution of assets; he is your estate's legal representative.
- Some states either do not require probate (a topic explained below) or they simplify the process for small estates; in these cases a will can be an easier and less expensive alternative to a living trust.

If you die without a will, your state of residence already has one prepared for you; this is what is known as dying *intestate* (without a valid will). The problem with intestate succession is that your estate may not be distributed according to your desires.

In separate property states, if two people are married with children, the surviving spouse will receive a third and the children will evenly divide the remaining two thirds. If there is only one child, the surviving spouse gets half and the child gets half. If there is one or more minor children, the court must create a trust to handle the minor's share until he or she reaches age 18. Once the child attains legal age, which is 18 in most states, his or her share is distributed outright, regardless of the child's experience, maturity, or judgment. If there are no children, the surviving spouse gets the decedent's share of the estate.

In community property states, if you are married, with or without children, and do not have a valid will, all community assets will go to the surviving spouse. Separate property will also go to the surviving spouse unless there are children. If there is only one child, the remaining spouse will get half; if two or more children exist, the survivor gets a third of the separate property and the children evenly divide the remaining two thirds.

Who Should Have a Will?

Virtually every adult should have a will. In fact, the only people who should not have a will are people who are certain that they understand the laws of their state of residence as it pertains to intestate succession (how your estate will be distributed if you do not have a will). As you can see from the previous sections, merely titling property so that the co-owner inherits your share may be very unwise from the point of view of income taxes, estate taxes, gift taxes, and marketability. Besides, there is always the chance that you have forgotten one or more assets, and these items, particularly personal property, may be left to an unintended heir or may subject your estate to probate.

Cost of Will Preparation

The cost of having a will prepared ranges from zero to a few thousand dollars. The type of will you have prepared will be the greatest determinant of how much it will cost. The cost can escalate quite a bit depending on the complexity of your estate. Using a lawyer is certainly not the cheapest way but it is the recommended course of action for most people.

You can get a list of lawyers and law firms that deal in estate planning from your city or county's bar association. An alternative would be to get a list of the 3,000 lawyers and law professors who have at least 10 years of active practice in estate planning and an "outstanding reputation, exceptional skill, and have made substantial contributions to the field by lecturing, writing, teaching, and participating in bar activities." To receive a free list of members in your area, write to The American College of Trust and Estate Council, 2716 Ocean Park Blvd., Suite 1080, Santa Monica, CA, 90405.

What Property Cannot Be Transferred by Will

All property titled as joint tenancy with rights of survivorship (jtwros) will automatically go to the surviving co-owner(s), regardless of what your will says. The same thing is true with life insurance and retirement plans; proceeds will go to the named beneficiary(s). All property in a living trust will go to the beneficiaries named in the trust instrument. And finally, certain bank accounts or pay-on-death accounts will pass directly to the person designated as beneficiary or co-owner.

Having Your Will Contested

Close to a fourth of all wills are successfully contested. This is because after a will has been written, it is usually put in a safe place and never seen again until death. As time passes and conditions change, events occur that might have caused the will to be changed.

Usually, the legal grounds for contesting a will are limited to age, mental incapacity, fraud, duress, or undue influence. If you were an adult when your will was prepared, age is not an issue. Mental incapacity is very difficult to prove. The court will presume that the decedent was of sound mind; forgetfulness or even being unable to recognize one's friends do not, by themselves, prove incapacity. The charge of fraud, duress, or undue influence is also difficult to prove. The person(s) challenging your will must show that some person was able to take advantage of the decedent when he or she was confused or emotionally distraught and that property was left to people who would not otherwise have inherited anything.

Consequences of Divorce, Marriage, and Children

Depending on your state of residence, a divorce does not automatically revoke bequests to a former spouse. If you have a child or get married after you have already had a will prepared, it should be revised. If you do not amend your will to at least acknowledge the existence of a new spouse or child, it may later be successfully contested according to laws designed to protect children and spouses.

Disinheriting and Choosing Your Heirs

You can leave anything you own to anyone you like; in common law (separate property) states, your spouse has a right to a certain percentage of your property. In community property states, your spouse is entitled to at least half of the community assets. Also keep in mind that assets titled as ''jtwros'' will automatically pass to the surviving tenant(s), which may or may not be what you wanted.

Aside from the spousal rights described above, you can disinherit anyone you choose, including any or all of your children. Aside from your family, a person receives nothing from your estate by simply not being mentioned in the will or trust. If you have a child, or there is a grandson or granddaughter from a deceased child, disinheritance must be specifically stated by naming that child or grandchild and stating ''I leave X nothing'' or ''I leave Y one dollar.''

Moving to Another State

Your will is valid in any state you move to except Louisiana. Keep in mind that if you move from a common law to a community property state or vice versa, marital ownership laws of your new state of residence may affect your will.

Your Executor

An executor is the person or persons you name to oversee the distribution of your estate after you have died. The executor administers all assets except those listed in your living trust (if you have one). The executor is also necessary if there is a probate.

The job of executor requires more work than many people realize. An executor is required to assemble and value all of the decedent's assets, file income tax and estate tax returns, pay these taxes from the estate's assets, distribute the remaining assets to heirs, and account for everything that has been done. The executor can be held personally liable if assets are depleted without leaving sufficient amounts to pay taxes. Oftentimes, the executor will have several meetings with attorneys and accountants.

Your executor should either be a responsible member of the family or a professional, such as a lawyer, accountant, or financial adviser. If no suitable family member is available, or if there is contention or rivalry among family members, it is better to avoid the potential for conflict and go outside the family. Whomever you select as your executor, make sure he or she understands the job's scope and nature before naming that person in your will. Designate a substitute in case the person you select dies, is incapacitated, or otherwise turns out to be unable to perform his or her responsibilities.

PROBATE

The purpose of probate is to establish clear title to, or ownership of, an asset. A decedent's assets cannot be transferred to any heirs until all claimants to those assets have been eliminated, either by coming forward or by passage of time. The process of eliminating all claimants is called probate. Your estate will go through this process unless all of your personal property and real estate are titled under "jtwros," or a living trust, or your estate is limited to life insurance policies, annuities, and/or qualified retirement plans

EXHIBIT 10–1
Probate Fees in California and New York

Gross Estate Value	California	New York
$ 100,000	$ 6,300	$ 10,000
200,000	10,300	18,000
500,000	22,300	38,000
1,000,000	42,300	68,000
2,000,000	62,300	118,000
5,000,000	122,300	268,000

such as IRAs, pension plans, and Keoghs. Probate can occur whether or not you have any creditors. There are four negative aspects of probate: costs, time, frustration, and ongoing reminder of the loss of a loved one.

Costs of Probate

The cost of probate depends on the decedent's state of residency, whether real estate was owned in multiple states, and the size of the gross estate. Every state has its own schedule of probate fees. These are fees that go to the court and the attorney probating your estate. In some states, legal fees for probate can be negotiated; other states have a chart that must be followed. One of the unfair parts about probate is that in many states the fee is based on gross value. For example, if your entire estate consisted of a home with a fair market value of $500,000 and a $400,000 mortgage, the probate fees would be based on $500,000, not the $100,000 equity in the house. Shown in Exhibit 10–1 is a schedule for probate fees in California and New York. In the case of California, the figures shown are a minimum; fees shown for New York are average costs.

Probate costs usually exceeded the fees shown in Exhibit 10–1. The attorney and lawyer involved can petition the court for what is known as *extraordinary* expenses. These requests for additional fees are usually granted.

Time Required to Probate an Estate

Probate usually takes 18 months to complete. Some of this time is specified by law, such as the amount of time public notices must appear in newspapers and how long creditors have to come forward. Other time periods cannot be easily calculated. The area you live in may have an overbooked court system; it could take your executor several months just to get a court date. Or the estate's executor (called the administrator if you did not name an executor in your will) may need additional time to track down the location of assets or find certain papers. It took close to 20 years to probate the estate of Howard Hughes and over 10 years to settle John Wayne's estate.

Frustration and Loss of Control

The probate process means your heirs lose control. Your family or other heirs may not be able to sell or transfer any assets without court approval. In short, you will end up paying the court to tell you who gets what and when they can get it. Oftentimes, the surviving spouse and children must petition the court for an allowance until probate is finalized. After death, there is a natural period of grieving. The probate process may extend this sorrow for one or several years. Probate is a constant reminder of death.

Probate: Not Just for the Dead

When people think of death, one of the first things that comes to mind is probate. However, most people do not know that they will go through probate while they are still alive if they become physically or mentally incapacitated. This is true no matter how your assets are titled and even if you have a valid will (since a will can only go into effect after death). This type of incapacity results in what is known as conservatorship.

Conservatorship. A conservatorship means that the court has taken control of your affairs and names a conservator to act on your behalf. A conservatorship is not just for the elderly. You could be in an accident or contract an illness that would temporarily or permanently leave you physically or mentally incapable of handling your own affairs.

The conservator may or may not be your spouse, child, or friend; the court makes the appointment. Even if a family member is named as the conservator, the court still controls your money and other assets. All expenses incurred by your estate or transactions conducted on your behalf are reported to the court annually for review.

The chances of you being part of a conservatorship are doubled if you own property with someone else. Since joint ownership requires signatures of all co-owners for sales, transfers, and encumbrances, if one of the co-tenants becomes incapacitated, the court will take his or her place via a conservatorship. You will then find yourself with a new co-owner: the probate court. Once involved, the court remains an active participant until the person dies or recovers.

A conservatorship can be expensive, time consuming, and humiliating. Expenses are incurred since there are court and attorney fees; the amount of time involved depends on the availability of a court date and the number of witnesses; and it is humiliating to be forced to appear in court with someone who is trying to prove your physical or mental handicap.

The costs, delays, and humiliation of a conservatorship and probate can be avoided. There is only one way to ensure that both are eliminated: a living trust.

LIVING TRUST

Like a will, a living trust is something you create while you are alive. Unlike a will, it is something that can help administer your personal and financial affairs while you are alive and after death. It allows you to transfer ownership of real estate and personal property from your name into the name of a legal entity called a living trust. Since you create the trust, you control it. Living trusts are usually revocable, which means that you can alter, amend, or revoke it while you are alive and legally competent. There are three parties to every living trust: trustor, trustee, and beneficiary.

Trustor

When you set up a trust, you are known as the trustor, also referred to as the grantor, settlor, creator, or trust maker. If you and your spouse have a living trust, each of you is a grantor, trustor, etc. As the trustor, you decide what your trust will include and what will be left out. You decide who will manage your estate while you are alive and after death. You also decide who will inherit your assets and when and how they are to receive these items. As previously mentioned, you can change the parties or provisions to your trust at anytime. You do not need the approval of a lawyer, court, or anyone else.

Trustee

The trustee is the person who manages the assets listed in the trust. Most people act as their own trustee while they are alive. If you are married, you and your spouse can be co-trustees. A co-trustee can buy, sell, transfer, gift, or dispose of any trust asset without the permission of the other co-trustee. In the case of married couples, most people include the provision that if they die or become incapacitated, the other spouse, usually already named as co-trustee, will immediately have control of all trust property.

Beneficiary

While you are alive, you are the beneficiary of your trust assets. You can buy, sell, transfer, or gift any of your assets to anyone you like. After your death, trust assets will be managed or distributed to the other beneficiary(s). These are the people, charities, or other organizations that receive part or all of your estate according to the provisions of your trust. It is the responsibility of the then acting trustee(s) to make sure your instructions are carried out. No supervision or court intervention is necessary.

Funding Your Trust

Perhaps the biggest mistake made by people who set up living trusts is not properly funding the trust. All assets that are not titled under the name of the trust cannot be managed or distributed by the trust agreement. Furthermore, personal property and real estate left outside of the trust are subject to probate unless they are titled as jtwros or have a designated beneficiary (life insurance and retirement plans).

Assets are placed into your trust by a simple name change. Your house will no longer be owned under the name Steve Zank; title will now be "Steve Zank, trustee of the Zank Family Trust, dated 5/26/91." Whenever you retitle assets, the name of the trustee, trust, and date of the trust must be indicated. Your joint account with your spouse will no longer say "Roger and Cathy Perkins, jtwros;" it will be titled as "Roger and Cathy Perkins, trustees of the Perkins Trust, dated 2/3/86."

If you later decide to remove an asset from the trust, you simply reconvey it back to your individual or joint names. The trustor (you and/or your spouse) always has the power to add or take things out of the trust.

Cost of a Living Trust

The cost of a living revocable trust can range anywhere from a few hundred to a few thousand dollars. The price depends on the complexity of the trust and how involved you want to be. If your living trust is not complex and you are willing to change title to assets from your name to the name of the living trust, the cost should be less than $1,000; it can actually be as low as $400 depending on the area you live in and the competition among local attorneys.

Some people feel most comfortable dealing with a large, well-established law firm. There is certainly nothing wrong with this approach, but keep in mind that you may be paying dearly for this feeling of security. The documents prepared by expensive firms may not be as good as those prepared by a lawyer who limits his or her practice to living trusts. Nevertheless, there is something to be said for any existing relationship you may have with a specific firm or lawyer.

Most attorneys will give you an initial consultation for free. The following should be discussed:

1. What their trust "package" provides.
2. What the costs will be.

3. What the attorney will do for you.
4. What the costs will be if changes ever need to be made in the future.
5. How long it will take to have the documents completed and signed.

If You Do Not Have a Living Trust

Almost everyone should have a living revocable trust. If you do not have a living trust, there is a good chance your estate will go through probate. You may also go through a probate proceeding while you are still alive if you become incapacitated. Probate can be avoided by titling assets in a certain way, but this usually just postpones and compounds the problem. If you do not have a living trust or a valid will, your estate may be distributed in a way contrary to your wishes. A will virtually guarantees that your estate will be probated; this is also true if you have a *testamentary trust* (this is a type of trust that becomes active after your death). Remember that the probate process is costly, time consuming, and frustrating.

Durable Power of Attorney for Health Care

Although we never expect to be in an accident or become ill, it can happen. And when it happens, we may not be in a physical or mental condition to make a decision. A durable power of attorney for health care gives another person the power to make health care decisions for us if we are unable to. Such a power can be very narrow or broad in nature. You may wish to give someone the power to make any such decisions short of life or death. You can also specify what kind of life support is acceptable.

If a durable power of attorney for health care is something that interests you, check into the following:

1. Does your state recognize such a document?
2. Will your doctor abide by the contents of the document?
3. Will the person you give the power to abide by your wishes?

The durable power of attorney has value only if someone knows of its existence and comes forward with the document. If such a situation arises, you will probably not be in a position to make sure that it is executed. It is not the sort of document you can have drawn up after the fact. If surgery or other medical decisions need to be made, make sure you have previously made your wishes known.

Durable Power of Attorney for Property

If your state recognizes durable powers of attorney, consider having one for property decisions. This power allows the person named to sign your name if you are physically or mentally unable to. Married couples usually grant the other spouse such powers; however, you can name anyone you choose. A durable power of attorney for property is usually done for convenience, but it also may be a cost saver. Suppose you have a stock or piece of property you want to sell because you feel the price has either peaked or is about to drop in value. You want to sell the asset immediately, but you are unable to do so because of some physical or mental inability; you might be on vacation or confined to a hospital bed. The person with such a durable power can sell, buy, or transfer that asset for you. In short, they can act on your behalf, giving verbal orders or signing your name to documents.

Two potential disadvantages may result from a durable power of attorney. First, the person you give such a power to may abuse it. This problem can be solved by giving limited and narrow authority (e.g., "you can only buy and sell my blue chip stocks at Merrill Lynch; all proceeds must go into a money market account and remain in my name"). Second, not all institutions may recognize or act on such a power without a court order. There is no real solution to this problem except getting such a court order or trying to convince the person or institution that they should follow your wishes.

LIVING WILL

Also known as a *pull-the-plug* provision, this is a document that you sign while you are still competent. It lets your doctor know that you do not wish to be kept alive under certain specific conditions. It is a statutory document, which means that the wording must be very specific and cannot be tailored or altered in any way.

The living will is not always adhered to by hospitals, and some states do not recognize it. However, most advisers agree that it is better to leave such instructions than to have nothing at all. It is recommended that you give copies to your lawyer, clergyman, and the person to whom you give your power of attorney. The living will can be revoked easily at any time.

In some states, a doctor or hospital that does not honor a living will must withdraw from your case. In other states, the document is not binding and serves only as a "directive" to the hospital. A living will is short and standard; you can get a copy from an attorney, doctor, hospital, or other medical association.

A living will, like a durable power of attorney for property or health care, living trust, or community property agreement can be revoked by you at any time; you must simply be mentally competent when such a cancellation occurs.

Thirty-eight states and the District of Columbia have passed laws authorizing residents to provide instructions to family and physicians about what should be done, or not done, in the event they are unable to make or communicate a decision about their medical treatment. An organization called Choice in Dying can give you information about your specific state. The group can be contacted by writing to 200 Varick St., New York, NY 10014 (telephone 212–366–5540).

This chapter has described the different ways accounts can be titled and what can later happen if a mistake is made. The focal point of this chapter was to point out how important it is to have a will *and* a living trust. As you can now see, estate planning does not have to be complex or costly. This does not mean that you should try to save several hundred dollars by bypassing an attorney for a do-it-yourself approach. An estate-planning lawyer can save you tens, perhaps hundreds, of thousands of dollars.

This would be a good time to review how all of your assets are titled. For a quick summary of everything you own, refer to the net worth worksheet you filled out in the first chapter. If you live in a community property state and have assets titled under joint tenancy, you may wish to make a title change. If you own an asset with one or more of your children, you might want to reconsider such an arrangement if estate simplification or avoidance of probate was your motive for adding someone as a co-owner.

As you begin the last chapter, you have only one task left: interviewing and choosing the professionals who will advise and help you make your insurance, investment, financial, and estate planning decisions. This final chapter provides an approach to successfully selecting your team members. The process described will take you several hours to complete but will be most rewarding. The difference between a good adviser and a mediocre one is just as extreme and important as having a good teacher instead of a poor one.

CHECKLIST OF THINGS TO DO

1. Review how your assets are titled. If you live in a community property state, consult an estate planning attorney and fully explore the pros and cons of having any property titled under joint tenancy (jtwros) changed to community property (c/p).

2. If your will was drafted before the early 1980s, have an attorney review it. If you have married or had children since your will was drafted, have it amended to reflect such changes. A review is also in order if one of your beneficiaries dies, you get a divorce, you move to another state, a major asset is sold, lost, or added, or when estate tax laws change.

3. Most parts of the country are now saturated with living trust seminars; look in your local newspaper for upcoming seminars in your area. Go out and purchase the book, *Your Living Trust* (New York: Perigee Books, 1992), 200 pp.

4. If you plan to leave money to your children or want to make gifts to them while you are alive, consider the following:

- Name a guardian for each minor child.
- Set up accounts for minor children under the Uniform Transfer to Minors Act (UTMA). Gifts under UTMA are managed by the person you name as custodian for the child until the child becomes an adult (up to age 25 in California). You do not need a lawyer or any special form to open up such an account at a bank, brokerage firm, or

through a mutual fund group. UTMA is in use in many states, other states follow a similar act, known as the Uniform Gifts to Minors Act (UGMA).

- Gain more lasting control by leaving money or assets for your children (adult and/or minor) by having a will drafted.

5. Set up and fund a revocable living trust. You can alter, amend, or destroy all or part of the trust at anytime prior to death or mental disability. Your trust package should include all of the following: (a) revocable living will, (b) durable power of attorney for health care, (c) durable power of attorney for finances, (d) a living will (the "pull-the-plug" provision)—depending on your beliefs, (e) community property agreement (if you live in one of the eight states that follow community property law), and (f) a pourover will (for those items intentionally or unintentionally left outside of the living trust).

6. According to one of the nation's leading authorities on estate planning, some of the biggest errors made in estate planning are: (a) lacking adequate records for those who follow in your footsteps, (b) leaving everything to your spouse if you have children and an estate worth several hundred thousand dollars, (c) improperly titling all property under joint tenancy, (d) naming a financially immature person as beneficiary of your life insurance policies, (e) choosing an executor or successor trustee who is not financially savvy, and (f) failing to update or review your will and trust.

Chapter Eleven

Choosing a Professional

Interviewing a Stockbroker
Selecting a Financial Planner
Getting Good Insurance
Hiring a Tax Preparer

It is always surprising how quickly some people select an individual or company to manage their money. People who have spent years accumulating a savings account will turn it over to a broker after attending a single seminar, relying on the recommendation of a friend, or reading an advertisement. The selection process described below will take a few hours to complete. At times it may seem like an inconvenience. But ask yourself, "How long did it take to earn this money I'm ready to invest?" We are all trained for jobs and professions, but few take the time to learn how to invest the fruits produced from that work.

A broker is someone who is paid a fee or commission in return for buying or selling a security or piece of real estate for a client. A broker must have a license before conducting any such transaction. Getting a license entails studying for and successfully passing an exam. Some broker or agent exams can be passed with as little as 25 hours of preparation (along with a four-month waiting period after the exam is passed). Other licenses, such as those that involve the selling of stocks, bonds, limited partnerships, and REITs, take over three months of intensive studying and then passing a six-hour exam.

Having passed a test or exam does not mean that your adviser or broker is completely knowledgeable in the areas he or she is dealing in. It simply means that the person has basic knowledge—competence and experience come with time.

By the time you finish this short chapter, you will learn: (1) how to interview a stockbroker, (2) what questions you should be asking, (3) what questions the broker should be asking you, (4) how to select a financial planner, (5) how to get good insurance rates, and (6) how to hire an accountant who is the proper match for you. The chapter ends with a discussion of the pitfalls of taking advice from your friends and relatives.

INTERVIEWING A STOCKBROKER

When telephoning or walking into a brokerage firm, you are greeted by the receptionist. When you ask to speak to a broker, he or she will page the "broker of the day." By talking to the broker of the day, you are playing a form of Russian roulette because the broker is selected from a pool of brokers, also referred to as registered representatives. This pool of brokers is composed either of trainees, relatively new recruits, or a mix of seasoned as well as inexperienced advisers.

The experience and expertise of the broker you will be talking to can be anywhere from zero to extremely sophisticated. To protect yourself from poor or dangerous advice, ask the broker you are introduced to these questions:

1. How long have you been a broker?
2. What areas do you specialize in?
3. What areas are you weak in?
4. How do you stay abreast of new investment opportunities?
5. What type of formal training or education have you had?
6. What financial groups or organizations do you belong to?

The importance of each one of these questions is expanded upon below.

Brokerage Experience

The first question is asked to find out the amount of experience the broker has; after all, if you were to go in for surgery, you would not want to hear the doctor say, "Oh boy. This is my first case!"

You do not want someone learning about investing with *your* money. Deal only with a broker who has at least five years' experience *as a broker*. The learning curve in the brokerage business is steep, but fortunately quite a bit can be learned in five years. Having several years of experience means that the broker has seen good and bad markets come and go. He or she has also seen how certain programs promoted by the parent firm have turned out. And the broker has also seen the results of all of the "hot tips" overheard during the past years.

Areas of Specialization

Every stockbroker has certain areas of particular interest. As lawyers tend to specialize in one or two areas, registered representatives have expertise with a select number of investments. After all, there are thousands of different stocks and bonds, not to mention the large number of convertible and preferred securities. Along with traditional stocks and bonds, there are over 3,700 different mutual funds. Add to this the several dozen current limited partnership offerings, real estate investment trusts, options, commodities, and so on, and you have a tremendous number of different investment opportunities. No broker can be expected to keep fully abreast of even one or two dozen different stocks and bonds.

By asking the broker his or her strengths, you can see if this person follows the same areas that you have an interest in. The broker may be brilliant with lots of experience, but if she specializes in commodities and you are interested in mutual funds, she is not the person for you.

Areas of Weakness

We all have strengths and weaknesses. By pointing out his weaknesses, the broker is showing honesty. More important, you now know the area in which you should not rely on the broker for advice.

The broker you end up using can later help you interview advisers who specialize in other areas. Your broker can help coordinate your overall game plan. It is also likely that your broker knows other brokers who are experts in the areas you later become interested in.

Staying Abreast of Developments

You should use a stockbroker not only because she keeps track of your investments, but also because she is learning about new investments and techniques to better serve her clients. There is no reason to pay a broker a commission if she knows as much or less about the investment than you do. Seek out someone who is constantly looking at new opportunities, whether these opportunities are in the area of specific investments, financial planning, estate planning, or income tax reduction.

Find out what periodicals and other sources the registered representative is using. A broker should not confine her universe of information only to in-house research reports, which may or may not be biased.

Seeing how the broker stays updated can give you a sense of whether or not this person views the business only as a means of making commissions or as an interesting profession in which something can be learned every day. A love of knowledge translates into a smarter broker; that smart broker will have an edge over her peers that can translate into more profit in your portfolio.

Education and Training

When a brokerage firm hires a registered representative, its chief concern is whether or not the person is good in sales. Product knowledge is not considered important since this will be taught to the trainee during orientation. In the financial services industry, "good in sales" means that the person is generating a lot of fees or commissions for the firm. This is in direct conflict with the interests of you, the client.

Ask the broker what his or her educational background is. Extensive training and education not only shows dedication and a certain degree of intelligence, it is also an indication of someone who is really trying to service the client.

The vast majority of brokers and agents do not have any of the designations listed below. This does not mean that they are incompetent. It simply means that they have not taken the time or incurred the expense of going through a formal program. It is also quite commonplace to meet with a designated adviser who is not a broker. Such a person is compensated on an hourly rate, by a retainer, or with a flat fee for the preparation of a financial plan or other investment summary. The most practical designations in the brokerage community are the following:

CFP (Certified Financial Planner)—a six-part program that takes approximately two years to complete. The graduate ends up with a great deal of breadth. There are approximately 36,000 CFPs in the nation, a small number in comparison to the people who call themselves a "financial planner."

CLU (Chartered Life Underwriter)—a 10-part program that takes approximately four years to complete. This is the highest designation one can obtain in the life insurance industry. The graduate ends up with a strong grounding in the different aspects of life insurance and estate planning. This designation has been around for over 60 years.

ChFC (Chartered Financial Consultant)—a 10-part program that takes approximately two to three years to complete. This is the insurance industry's answer to the financial planning designation, CFP. Graduates end up with quite a bit of breadth with an emphasis in the area of insurance products.

CFS (Certified Fund Specialist)—a 60-hour program that leads to the only designation in the area of mutual funds. Graduates have an extensive knowledge of mutual funds, variable annuities, matching client objectives with specific funds, modern portfolio theory (MPT), and a strong overview of financial and estate planning. There are fewer than 500 CFS graduates.

Registry member (The Registry of Financial Planning Practitioners)—the upper echelon of financial planning. Successful graduates must have several years of experience in financial planning, obtain client endorsements, possess one or more of the designations listed above, pass a comprehensive exam, and have a thorough financial plan scrutinized by a board of examiners. There are about 1,400 Registry members in the nation.

All of the designations described above require continuing education. This ongoing learning process helps to ensure that the adviser is constantly being exposed to new ideas, concepts, and products that may better your lot as an investor.

Formal degrees are less important than these designations since such education is usually theoretical. All of the designations described above use current information that is both practical and topical. Nevertheless, undergraduate and graduate degrees are a definite plus if the degrees were earned in areas that relate to financial services. A Ph.D. in history has no value to a client looking for a fixed-income specialist, whereas an MBA graduate who took some investment classes could end up being a plus.

Questions the Broker Should Ask You

No one can properly advise you about investing unless that person knows something about you. If the broker you are interviewing has done a good job answering the questions you posed in the previous section, sit back and see if he or she asks you the questions listed below. These are questions you may have answered in earlier chapters; here we are trying to discern how knowledgeable the broker or financial planner is.

1. What are your current holdings?
2. Are you looking for current income and/or growth?
3. What is your risk level?
4. Is there a time frame we must work within?
5. What is your tax bracket?

There is no such thing as the "perfect" investment. Every legitimate investment is designed to fill part of some people's portfolios at certain times. No matter how strongly a broker recommends a security or program, it simply may not be appropriate for you.

SELECTING A FINANCIAL PLANNER

A financial planner can have a great impact on your retirement. This person may end up coordinating a plan that introduces you to investments you had never previously considered and a means of reducing risk. A good planner can make your retirement goals easier to obtain, resulting in less stress. Finally, the planner can add a sense of objectivity that you do not have.

The process of selecting a financial planner is not much different from selecting a broker. However, in this case, since you will be working much more closely with an individual, two areas need particular scrutiny: background and references.

Your financial planner may end up not only being your central money manager, but it is also likely that he or she will end up implementing your retirement plan. Therefore, individual skill and experience as a broker are important. A financial planner is like a coach on a team. He or she is expected to know quite a bit about a lot of different things. Extensive knowledge of investments, insurance, taxes, and estate planning are required.

Financial planners are not experts in every aspect of investments, insurance, taxes, or estate planning. They should have good grounding in each of these areas and perhaps be specialists in one or two areas. Financial planners should also admit to those areas in which they are not particularly strong, and they should have access to one or more experts in those areas. If necessary, these outside experts can be brought in to coordinate and implement a specific part of your financial plan.

The financial planner you are interviewing should stand ready to give you a list of references. By contacting two or three of these people, you will get a good sense as to the planner's knowledge, attention, and sensitivity to his or her clientele.

Interview at least two or three financial planners. Pay particular attention to their educational and job backgrounds. You want someone working with you who has the experience you do not have, someone who has spent years learning and who continues to keep abreast of new developments in the profession.

GETTING GOOD INSURANCE

Your insurance agent should help you with insurance products and only insurance products. Agents are not usually trained in the area of securities. They can possess good estate planning skills, but usually fall short in the area of financial planning. If you are going to use an insurance agent or broker in areas other than risk transference or estate planning, interview that person the same way you would a financial planner or stockbroker.

Ideally, the insurance agent you choose will represent a number of carriers. Being offered products from different companies will result in competitively priced policies.

Insurance decisions should be based on three things: quality, price, and service. You want to make sure the company that represents you is rated highly by the A.M. Best Company; deal only with companies rated either A+ or A++ by Best. The A+ and A++ rating represent the two highest ratings from this neutral source. As an added precaution, seek out companies that are also highly rated by another outside rating service, such as Moody or Standard & Poor.

HIRING A TAX PREPARER

The accountant, tax preparer, or enrolled agent who prepares your taxes can end up saving you hundreds, if not thousands, of dollars for one or more years. These dollars, which would normally have gone to Uncle Sam can now be invested, resulting in a larger nest egg at retirement. The person who prepares your taxes can also provide you with ideas as to how your taxes can be minimized in future years.

When interviewing prospective accountants, narrow your search to tax preparers who match your needs. That is, you do not need a CPA who is also a tax attorney to prepare a simple return. On the opposite end of the spectrum, a quickie tax preparation outfit should not be used if you have multiple business interests or properties.

Get price quotes from two or three accountants who fit your needs. The savings they may generate can easily offset your tax preparation bill.

Do not invest through an accountant unless that person also possesses additional degrees or, better yet, designations in the areas of investments, financial planning, or insurance. Keeping abreast of the Internal Revenue Code (IRC) is more than a full-time job. Expecting that your tax preparer knows the ins-and-outs about the IRC and is also a whiz when it comes to stocks and bonds is ridiculous. You would not ask your stockbroker to prepare your taxes, so do not ask your accountant about investments.

Once you have completed the interviewing process, you can sit back and relax. The time you have invested will now begin to pay off and will continue to pay large dividends for the rest of your life. Hopefully, you will have assembled a talented team that is on your side, a group of professionals who are concerned about your well-being and not the amount of fees or commissions.

The retirement planning process is now complete. By following the checklists and advice given throughout this book, you have done your homework and made the necessary commitment to a successful future. You are to be congratulated for doing something that very few of your friends or neighbors have done or will do: to learn about the different options and courses of action available and to act in a prudent and informed manner.

CHECKLIST OF THINGS TO DO

1. Ask about your planner's background. For a list of financial planners or advisers in your area, contact one of the following organizations:

Institute of Certified Fund Specialists, 7911 Herschel Ave., Suite 201, La Jolla, CA, 92037 (800-848-2029).

IAFP Registry, Two Concourse Parkway, Suite 800, Atlanta, GA, 30328 (404-395-1605).

The Institute of Certified Financial Planners, 7600 East Eastman Ave., Suite 301, Denver, CO, 80231 (800-282-7526.

The National Association of Personal Financial Advisors, 1130 Lake Cook Rd., Suite 105, Buffalo Grove, IL, 60089 (800-366-2732).

The American Institute of Certified Public Accountants, Personal Financial Planning Division, 1211 Avenue of the Americas, New York, NY 10036.

2. Check out any unfamiliar securities firm you are thinking of doing business with. The National Association of Securities Dealers (NASD) (301-590-6500) and the Securities Investor Protection

Corporation (SIPC) (202–371–8300) are good sources of information about member firms.

3. Verify your broker's history. State security regulators keep track of brokers registered to sell securities in individual states and whether these people have any past violations. The North American Securities Administrators Association (202–737–0900) can tell you how to contact the securities commission in your state. The NASD can also provide information about violations by brokers. Find out the backgrounds and designations of those you deal with.

4. Get a second opinion. If an investment product sounds unfamiliar or unusual, call a broker or financial adviser at another firm and find out what he or she knows about it.

5. Whether or not you have an existing stockbroker, financial planner, or investment counselor, go out and interview at least three other similar advisers by using a list provided in this chapter. No matter how good you think your broker or planner is, it is very likely that you might find someone even better during this interview process.

6. As a final precaution, ask your prospective adviser (broker, planner, counselor, etc.) for a list of at least three references you can talk to.

7. Make sure that you are not being taken advantage of by following these rules:

Have the broker or adviser draft you a letter or financial plan that restates your goals, objectives, and suggested strategy.

Read any account or advisory agreement before you sign it.

Keep written notes of your meetings and conversations with your adviser—periodically send him or her a letter confirming recent activities or statements (e.g., "you stated that this is a conservative investment and I should expect X rate of return. . . .").

Keep all paperwork, brochures, and prospectuses.

Financial Tables

To be fully informed about retirement planning and general investment principles, you need to know how to use certain tables. The pages that follow are the guts of any financial plan; these tables are also an integral part of any financial planning software. The tables show you how to make projections into the future, showing what you will end up with, whether you start with $10 or $47 million. The tables enable you to determine how inflation will affect your purchasing power, how long a certain amount of money will last, what a specific lump sum will grow to, and the effects of making annual contributions to a savings plan.

As you glance through the following pages, you will see four columns on each page. The column headings on each page are identical; only the assumed interest rate changes. These tables cover rates ranging from 1 to 20 percent. Each page also covers time periods from 1 to 25 years.

Since there are actually a total of four tables showing values from 1 to 20 percent over 1 to 25 years, once you understand how to use each of these four tables for one time period and one interest rate, you will know how to use them for any other time period or any other interest rate. First, let us see when a certain table is to be used.

TABLE 1

Table 1, identified as "Compounding Factor for 1 (what an initial amount becomes when growing at compound interest)," is used only when the following two circumstances apply:

1. You are using a specific amount.
2. That lump-sum figure is growing at a positive figure (adjusted for inflation and/or taxes).

As an example, suppose you have $6,000 to invest for 11 years; you have further assumed that your money will earn 9 percent, on average, over those 11 years. Finally, you have calculated that you are in the 33 percent tax bracket (state and federal combined) and that inflation will average 5 percent over the next 11 years. Your real rate of return is calculated as follows:

Assumed rate of return	9%
Minus income taxes (one third of your 9 percent return is being eaten up by taxes)	−3
Equals the aftertax return	6%
Minus the rate of inflation	−5
Equals real rate of return	1%

Thus, what began as a 9 percent return ends up being an actual 1 percent rate of return. By turning to the first page of the tables, the one titled "Rate 1%" in bold type, we can see what we will end up with in 11 years. We are using the "1%" page because this is the rate of true growth for this particular investment, if taxes and inflation have been factored in.

Since we are dealing with a lump-sum figure that we will not be adding to, $6,000 in this example, and that figure is growing at a positive number (1 percent is a positive number), only Table 1 is needed. Look under the column marked Table 1 and match it with the row marked 11 years. The number shown by matching this column and this row is 1.12. Simply take this factor and multiply by the lump-sum figure (1.12 × $6,000). The resulting figure, $6,720, is the answer. The original $6,000 will have an ending value of $6,720 at the end of 11 years, assuming a 9 percent rate of return reduced by 3 percent for income taxes and further reduced by another 5 percent for inflation.

TABLE 2

Table 2, identified as "Compounding Factor for 1 per Annum (growth of equal year-end deposits all growing at compound interest)," is used only when the following two circumstances apply:

1. You can save/invest the same amount each year.
2. That annual figure is growing at a positive figure (adjusted for inflation and/or taxes).

As an example, suppose you have $6,000 to invest each year for the next 11 years; you have further assumed that your money will earn 9 percent, on average, over those 11 years. Finally, you have calculated that you are in the 33 percent tax bracket (state and federal combined) and that inflation will average 5 percent over the next 11 years. Your real rate of return is calculated as follows:

Assumed rate of return	9%
Minus income taxes	−3
(one third of your 9 percent return is being eaten by taxes)	
Equals aftertax return	6%
Minus the rate of inflation	−5
Equals real rate of return	1%

Since we are dealing with a series of savings or investments that will be made annually, $6,000 in this example, and that figure is growing at a positive number (1 percent is a positive number), only Table 2 is needed. Look under the column marked Table 2 and match it with the row marked 11 years. The number shown by matching this column and this row is 11.57. Simply take this factor and multiply by the lump-sum figure (11.57 × $6,000). The resulting figure, $69,420, is the answer. The $6,000 that can be saved each year will have an ending real value of $69,420 in 11 years.

TABLE 3

Table 3, identified as "Sinking Fund Factor (level deposit required each year to reach 1 by a given year)," is used only when the following two circumstances apply:

1. You are trying to end up with a certain amount.
2. The amount that can be saved each year to end up with that lump-sum figure is growing at a positive figure (adjusted for inflation and/or taxes).

As an example, suppose you had a goal of trying to end up with $6,000 and that you had 11 years to reach that goal. You have further assumed that the money you save will earn 9 percent, on average, over those 11 years. Finally, you have calculated that you are in the 33 percent tax bracket (state and federal combined) and that inflation will average 5 percent over the next 11 years. Your real rate of return is your "unknown" annual savings, which will grow as follows:

Assumed rate of return	9%
Minus income taxes	−3
(one third of your 9 percent return is being eaten by taxes)	
Equals aftertax return	6%
Minus the rate of inflation	−5
Equals real rate of return	1%

Your question is simply, "Given these assumed rates, how much will I have to save each year?" Since we are dealing with a series of savings that we will not be adding to and that figure is growing at a positive number, only Table 3 is needed. Look under the column marked Table 3 and match it with the row marked 11 years. The number shown by matching this column and this row is .087. Simply take this factor and multiply by the lump-sum figure (.087 × $6,000). The resulting figure, $522, is the answer. By saving $522 each year, you will have exactly $6,000 at the end of 11 years, assuming a 9 percent rate of growth on these annual savings, reduced by 3 percent for income taxes and further reduced by another 5 percent for inflation.

TABLE 4

Table 4, identified as "Discount Factor (how much 1 at a future date is worth today)," is used only when the following two circumstances apply:

1. You are using a specific amount.
2. That lump-sum figure is "growing" at a negative rate (adjusted for inflation and/or taxes).

An an example, suppose you have $6,000 to invest for 11 years; you have further assumed that your money will earn 9 percent, on average, over those 11 years. Finally, you have calculated that you are in the 33 percent tax bracket (state and federal combined) and that inflation will average 7 percent over the next 11 years. Your *real rate of return* is calculated as follows:

Assumed rate of return	9%
Minus income taxes	−3
(one third of your 9 percent return is being eaten by taxes)	
Equals aftertax return	6%
Minus the rate of inflation	−7
Equals real rate of return	−1%

We are trying to find out what the effects of inflation and taxes are on this amount of money. Thus, what began as a 9 percent return ends up being an actual 1 percent loss in value per year. By turning to the same first page of the tables, the one titled "Rate 1%" in bold type, we can see what we will end up with in 11 years. We are using the "1%" page because this is the rate of true "growth" for this particular investment, if taxes and inflation have been factored in.

Since we are dealing with a lump-sum figure that we will not be adding to, $6,000 in this example, and that figure is growing at a negative number (−1 percent is a negative number), only Table 4 is needed. Look under the column marked Table 4 and match it with the row marked 11 years. The number shown by matching this column and this row is .896. Simply take this factor and multiply by the lump-sum figure (.896 × $6,000). The resulting figure, $5,376, is the answer. The original $6,000 will have an ending value of only $5,376 at the end of 11 years, assuming a 9 percent rate of return reduced by 3 percent for income taxes and further reduced by another 7 percent for inflation. This means that our investment is not keeping pace with the projected rate of inflation, once taxes have been factored in.

USING THE TABLES

To make sure you understand how to use these tables, let us go through an illustration and see what answers you come up with. Assume the following facts:

- You have $50,000 in bank CDs averaging 8 percent.
- You can save an additional $4,000 each year.
- You were going to put the $4,000 of annual savings into a tax-deferred annuity that should average 9 percent.
- You are looking at a time horizon of 20 years.
- You have assumed that inflation will average 5 percent over the next 20 years and you are in a 15 percent tax bracket.
- You want to know what you will have at the end of 20 years.

For this particular problem, some of the calculations will be the same. See if you can fill in the blanks for the CD investment (all answers are given at the end of the example):

Assumed rate of return	_%
Minus income taxes	−_
(_____ of your __ percent return is being eaten by taxes)	
Equals aftertax return	_%
Minus the rate of inflation	−_
Equals real rate of return	_%

Now do the same thing for the $4,000 that is to be invested in a tax-deferred annuity:

Assumed rate of return	_%
Minus income taxes	−0
(your return here is not being currently taxed)	
Equals aftertax return	_%
Minus the rate of inflation	−_
Equals real rate of return	_%

For this particular illustration, only Table 1 and Table 2 will be used. Simply go to the page that equals the real rate of return that you ended up with (a different page for each investment). Look under the column Table 1 for the lump-sum figure (the CD money). Match this column with the time period being used (20 years in this example). The resulting factor is then multiplied by the original lump-sum figure ($50,000). This amount is what you will end up with at the end of 20 years, assuming the real rate of return you have calculated.

Repeat the process for the money that is to be invested each year in the tax-deferred annuity. Look under the column under Table 2 since a certain amount can be saved each year (the annuity money). Match this column with the time period being used (20 years in this example). The resulting factor is then multiplied by the amount that can be saved each year ($4,000). The resulting figure is what you will end up with at the end of 20 years, assuming the real rate of return you have calculated.

To see if you ended up with the correct answers, let us go through the same examples together.

For the CD investment:

Assumed rate of return	8%
Minus income taxes	−1.2
(15 percent of your 8 percent return is being eaten by taxes)	
Equals aftertax return	6.8%
Minus the rate of inflation	−5
Equals real rate of return	1.8%

Now do the same thing for the $4,000 that is to be invested in a tax-deferred annuity:

Assumed rate of return	9%
Minus income taxes	−0
(your return here is not being currently taxed)	
Equals aftertax return	9%
Minus the rate of inflation	−5
Equals real rate of return	4%

For the CD figure, simply go to the page that equals the real rate of return that you ended up with (round up 1.8 percent to 2 percent and then go to that page). Look under the column under Table 1 and match this column with the 20-year row. The resulting factor, 1.49, is then multiplied by $50,000. The resulting amount, $74,500, is what the $50,000 in CDs will grow to at the end of 20 years, assuming a real rate of return of 2 percent.

Repeat the process for the money that is to be invested each year in the tax-deferred annuity. First, go to the page titled "Rate 4%." Look under the column under Table 2 since $4,000 can be saved each year (the annuity money). Match this column with the 20-year row. The resulting factor, 29.78, is then multiplied by $4,000. The resulting figure, $119,120, is what $4,000 will grow to at the end of 20 years, assuming a 4-percent rate of growth.

Of course, you can use any dollar figure, any time frame, and any rate of return you want. This last example used only Table 1 and Table 2; these will be the two tables that you will be using the most. The nice thing about all four of these tables is that they never go out of date. You will be able to use these tables today, tomorrow, and 50 years from now. They give you the power to make your own projections. Take a few minutes to review the beginning of this appendix on how all four tables are used.

Rate **1%** Year	Table 1 Compounding Factor for 1 What an initial amount becomes when growing at compound interest	Table 2 Compounding Factor For 1 per annum Growth of equal year-end deposits all growing at compound interest	Table 3 Sinking Fund Factor Level deposit required each year to reach 1 by a given year	Table 4 Discount Factor How much 1 at a future date is worth today
1	1.01	1.00	1.00	.990
2	1.02	2.01	.498	.980
3	1.03	3.03	.330	.971
4	1.04	4.06	.246	.961
5	1.05	5.10	.196	.952
6	1.06	6.15	.163	.942
7	1.07	7.21	.139	.933
8	1.08	8.29	.121	.924
9	1.09	9.37	.107	.914
10	1.10	10.46	.096	.905
11	1.12	11.57	.087	.896
12	1.13	12.68	.079	.887
13	1.14	13.81	.072	.879
14	1.15	14.95	.067	.870
15	1.16	16.10	.062	.861
16	1.17	17.26	.058	.853
17	1.18	18.43	.054	.844
18	1.20	19.62	.051	.836
19	1.21	20.81	.048	.828
20	1.22	22.02	.045	.820
21	1.23	23.24	.043	.811
22	1.24	24.47	.041	.803
23	1.26	25.72	.039	.795
24	1.27	26.97	.037	.788
25	1.28	28.24	.035	.780

Rate **2%** Year	Table 1 Compounding Factor for 1 What an initial amount becomes when growing at compound interest	Table 2 Compounding Factor For 1 per annum Growth of equal year-end deposits all growing at compound interest	Table 3 Sinking Fund Factor Level deposit required each year to reach 1 by a given year	Table 4 Discount Factor How much 1 at a future date is worth today
1	1.02	1.00	1.00	.980
2	1.04	2.02	.495	.961
3	1.06	3.06	.327	.942
4	1.08	4.12	.243	.924
5	1.10	5.20	.192	.906
6	1.13	6.31	.159	.888
7	1.15	7.43	.135	.871
8	1.17	8.58	.117	.854
9	1.20	9.76	.103	.837
10	1.22	10.95	.091	.820
11	1.24	12.17	.082	.804
12	1.27	13.41	.075	.789
13	1.29	14.68	.068	.773
14	1.32	15.97	.063	.758
15	1.35	17.29	.058	.743
16	1.37	18.64	.054	.729
17	1.40	20.01	.050	.714
18	1.43	21.41	.047	.700
19	1.46	22.84	.044	.686
20	1.49	24.30	.041	.673
21	1.52	25.78	.039	.660
22	1.55	27.30	.037	.647
23	1.58	28.84	.035	.634
24	1.61	30.42	.033	.622
25	1.64	32.03	.031	.610

Rate **3%** Year	Table 1 Compounding Factor for 1 What an initial amount becomes when growing at compound interest	Table 2 Compounding Factor For 1 per annum Growth of equal year-end deposits all growing at compound interest	Table 3 Sinking Fund Factor Level deposit required each year to reach 1 by a given year	Table 4 Discount Factor How much 1 at a future date is worth today
1	1.03	1.00	1.00	.971
2	1.06	2.03	.493	.943
3	1.09	3.09	.324	.915
4	1.13	4.18	.239	.889
5	1.16	5.31	.188	.863
6	1.19	6.47	.155	.838
7	1.23	7.66	.131	.813
8	1.27	8.89	.113	.789
9	1.31	10.16	.098	.766
10	1.34	11.46	.087	.744
11	1.38	12.81	.078	.722
12	1.43	14.19	.071	.701
13	1.47	15.62	.064	.681
14	1.51	17.09	.059	.661
15	1.56	18.60	.054	.642
16	1.61	20.16	.050	.623
17	1.65	21.76	.046	.605
18	1.70	23.41	.043	.587
19	1.75	25.12	.040	.570
20	1.81	26.87	.037	.554
21	1.86	28.68	.035	.538
22	1.92	30.54	.033	.522
23	1.97	32.45	.031	.507
24	2.03	34.43	.029	.492
25	2.09	36.46	.027	.478

Rate **4%**	Table 1 Compounding Factor for 1 What an initial amount becomes when growing at compound interest	Table 2 Compounding Factor For 1 per annum Growth of equal year-end deposits all growing at compound interest	Table 3 Sinking Fund Factor Level deposit required each year to reach 1 by a given year	Table 4 Discount Factor How much 1 at a future date is worth today
Year				
1	1.04	1.00	1.00	.962
2	1.08	2.04	.490	.925
3	1.12	3.12	.320	.889
4	1.16	4.25	.236	.855
5	1.22	5.42	.185	.822
6	1.27	6.63	.151	.790
7	1.32	7.90	.127	.760
8	1.37	9.21	.109	.731
9	1.42	10.58	.095	.703
10	1.48	12.01	.083	.676
11	1.54	13.49	.074	.650
12	1.60	15.03	.067	.625
13	1.67	16.63	.060	.601
14	1.73	18.29	.055	.578
15	1.80	20.02	.050	.555
16	1.87	21.82	.046	.534
17	1.95	23.70	.042	.513
18	2.03	25.65	.039	.494
19	2.11	27.67	.036	.475
20	2.19	29.78	.034	.456
21	2.28	31.97	.031	.439
22	2.37	34.25	.029	.422
23	2.47	36.62	.027	.406
24	2.56	39.08	.026	.390
25	2.67	41.65	.024	.375

Rate 5% Year	Table 1 Compounding Factor for 1 What an initial amount becomes when growing at compound interest	Table 2 Compounding Factor For 1 per annum Growth of equal year-end deposits all growing at compound interest	Table 3 Sinking Fund Factor Level deposit required each year to reach 1 by a given year	Table 4 Discount Factor How much 1 at a future date is worth today
1	1.05	1.00	1.00	.952
2	1.10	2.05	.488	.907
3	1.16	3.15	.317	.864
4	1.22	4.31	.232	.823
5	1.28	5.53	.181	.784
6	1.34	6.80	.147	.746
7	1.41	8.14	.123	.711
8	1.48	9.55	.105	.677
9	1.55	11.03	.091	.645
10	1.63	12.58	.080	.614
11	1.71	14.21	.070	.585
12	1.80	15.92	.063	.557
13	1.89	17.71	.057	.530
14	1.98	19.60	.051	.505
15	2.08	21.58	.046	.481
16	2.18	23.68	.042	.458
17	2.29	25.84	.039	.436
18	2.41	28.13	.036	.416
19	2.53	30.54	.033	.396
20	2.65	33.07	.030	.377
21	2.79	35.72	.028	.359
22	2.93	38.51	.026	.342
23	3.07	41.43	.024	.326
24	3.23	44.50	.023	.310
25	3.39	47.73	.021	.295

Rate 6% Year	Table 1 Compounding Factor for 1 What an initial amount becomes when growing at compound interest	Table 2 Compounding Factor For 1 per annum Growth of equal year-end deposits all growing at compound interest	Table 3 Sinking Fund Factor Level deposit required each year to reach 1 by a given year	Table 4 Discount Factor How much 1 at a future date is worth today
1	1.06	1.00	1.00	.943
2	1.12	2.06	.485	.890
3	1.19	3.18	.314	.840
4	1.26	4.38	.229	.792
5	1.34	5.64	.177	.747
6	1.42	6.98	.143	.705
7	1.50	8.39	.119	.665
8	1.59	9.90	.101	.627
9	1.69	11.49	.087	.592
10	1.80	13.18	.076	.558
11	1.90	14.97	.067	.527
12	2.01	16.87	.059	.497
13	2.13	18.88	.053	.469
14	2.26	21.02	.048	.442
15	2.40	23.28	.043	.417
16	2.54	25.67	.039	.394
17	2.69	28.21	.036	.371
18	2.85	30.91	.032	.350
19	3.03	33.76	.030	.331
20	3.21	36.79	.027	.312
21	3.40	39.99	.025	.294
22	3.60	43.39	.023	.278
23	3.82	47.00	.021	.262
24	4.05	50.82	.020	.247
25	4.29	54.86	.018	.233

Year	**Rate 7%** Table 1 Compounding Factor for 1 What an initial amount becomes when growing at compound interest	Table 2 Compounding Factor For 1 per annum Growth of equal year-end deposits all growing at compound interest	Table 3 Sinking Fund Factor Level deposit required each year to reach 1 by a given year	Table 4 Discount Factor How much 1 at a future date is worth today
1	1.07	1.00	1.00	.935
2	1.15	2.07	.483	.873
3	1.23	3.22	.311	.816
4	1.31	4.44	.225	.763
5	1.40	5.75	.174	.713
6	1.50	7.15	.140	.666
7	1.61	8.65	.116	.623
8	1.72	10.26	.098	.582
9	1.84	11.98	.084	.544
10	1.97	13.82	.072	.508
11	2.11	15.78	.063	.475
12	2.25	17.89	.056	.444
13	2.41	20.14	.050	.415
14	2.58	22.55	.044	.388
15	2.76	25.13	.040	.363
16	2.95	27.89	.036	.339
17	3.16	30.84	.032	.317
18	3.38	34.00	.029	.296
19	3.62	37.38	.027	.277
20	3.87	41.00	.024	.258
21	4.14	44.87	.022	.242
22	4.43	49.01	.020	.226
23	4.74	53.44	.019	.211
24	5.07	58.18	.017	.197
25	5.43	63.25	.016	.184

Rate **8%** Year	**Table 1** **Compounding** **Factor for 1** What an initial amount becomes when growing at compound interest	**Table 2** **Compounding** **Factor For 1** **per annum** Growth of equal year-end deposits all growing at compound interest	**Table 3** **Sinking Fund** **Factor** Level deposit required each year to reach 1 by a given year	**Table 4** **Discount** **Factor** How much 1 at a future date is worth today
1	1.08	1.00	1.00	.926
2	1.17	2.08	.481	.857
3	1.26	3.25	.308	.794
4	1.36	4.51	.222	.735
5	1.47	5.87	.171	.681
6	1.59	7.34	.136	.630
7	1.71	8.92	.112	.585
8	1.85	10.64	.094	.540
9	2.00	12.49	.080	.500
10	2.16	14.49	.069	.463
11	2.33	16.65	.060	.429
12	2.52	18.98	.053	.397
13	2.72	21.50	.047	.368
14	2.94	24.21	.041	.341
15	3.17	27.15	.037	.315
16	3.43	30.32	.033	.292
17	3.70	33.75	.030	.270
18	4.00	37.45	.027	.250
19	4.32	41.45	.024	.232
20	4.66	45.76	.022	.215
21	5.03	50.42	.020	.199
22	5.44	55.46	.018	.184
23	5.87	60.89	.016	.170
24	6.34	66.77	.015	.158
25	6.85	73.11	.014	.146

Rate **9%** Year	Table 1 Compounding Factor for 1 What an initial amount becomes when growing at compound interest	Table 2 Compounding Factor For 1 per annum Growth of equal year-end deposits all growing at compound interest	Table 3 Sinking Fund Factor Level deposit required each year to reach 1 by a given year	Table 4 Discount Factor How much 1 at a future date is worth today
1	1.09	1.00	1.00	.917
2	1.19	2.09	.479	.842
3	1.30	3.28	.305	.772
4	1.41	4.57	.219	.708
5	1.54	5.99	.167	.650
6	1.68	7.52	.133	.596
7	1.83	9.20	.109	.547
8	2.00	11.03	.091	.502
9	2.17	13.02	.077	.460
1 0	2.37	15.19	.066	.422
1 1	2.58	17.56	.057	.388
1 2	2.81	20.14	.050	.356
1 3	3.07	22.95	.044	.326
1 4	3.34	26.02	.038	.299
1 5	3.64	29.36	.034	.275
1 6	3.97	33.00	.030	.252
1 7	4.33	36.97	.027	.231
1 8	4.72	41.30	.024	.212
1 9	5.14	46.02	.022	.195
2 0	5.60	51.16	.020	.178
2 1	6.11	56.77	.018	.164
2 2	6.66	62.87	.016	.150
2 3	7.26	69.53	.014	.138
2 4	7.91	76.79	.013	.126
2 5	8.62	84.70	.012	.116

Rate **10%** Year	Table 1 Compounding Factor for 1 What an initial amount becomes when growing at compound interest	Table 2 Compounding Factor For 1 per annum Growth of equal year-end deposits all growing at compound interest	Table 3 Sinking Fund Factor Level deposit required each year to reach 1 by a given year	Table 4 Discount Factor How much 1 at a future date is worth today
1	1.10	1.00	1.00	.909
2	1.21	2.10	.476	.827
3	1.33	3.31	.302	.751
4	1.46	4.64	.216	.683
5	1.61	6.11	.164	.621
6	1.77	7.72	.130	.565
7	1.95	9.49	.105	.513
8	2.14	11.44	.087	.467
9	2.36	13.58	.074	.424
10	2.59	15.94	.063	.386
11	2.85	18.53	.054	.351
12	3.14	21.38	.047	.319
13	3.45	24.52	.041	.290
14	3.80	27.97	.036	.263
15	4.18	31.77	.032	.239
16	4.60	35.95	.028	.218
17	5.06	40.55	.025	.198
18	5.56	45.60	.022	.180
19	6.12	51.16	.020	.164
20	6.73	57.28	.018	.149
21	7.40	64.00	.016	.135
22	8.14	71.40	.014	.123
23	8.95	79.50	.013	.112
24	9.85	88.50	.011	.102
25	10.84	98.35	.010	.092

Rate **11%** Year	Table 1 Compounding Factor for 1 What an initial amount becomes when growing at compound interest	Table 2 Compounding Factor For 1 per annum Growth of equal year-end deposits all growing at compound interest	Table 3 Sinking Fund Factor Level deposit required each year to reach 1 by a given year	Table 4 Discount Factor How much 1 at a future date is worth today
1	1.11	1.00	1.00	.901
2	1.23	2.11	.474	.812
3	1.37	3.34	.299	.731
4	1.52	4.71	.212	.659
5	1.69	6.23	.161	.594
6	1.87	7.91	.126	.535
7	2.08	9.78	.102	.482
8	2.31	11.86	.084	.434
9	2.56	14.16	.071	.391
10	2.84	16.72	.060	.352
11	3.15	19.56	.051	.317
12	3.50	22.71	.044	.286
13	3.88	26.21	.038	.258
14	4.31	30.10	.033	.232
15	4.79	34.41	.029	.209
16	5.31	39.19	.026	.188
17	5.90	44.50	.023	.170
18	6.54	50.40	.020	.153
19	7.26	56.94	.018	.138
20	8.06	64.20	.016	.124
21	8.95	72.27	.014	.112
22	9.93	81.21	.012	.101
23	11.03	91.15	.011	.091
24	12.24	102.17	.0098	.082
25	13.59	114.41	.0087	.074

Rate **12%** Year	Table 1 Compounding Factor for 1 What an initial amount becomes when growing at compound interest	Table 2 Compounding Factor For 1 per annum Growth of equal year-end deposits all growing at compound interest	Table 3 Sinking Fund Factor Level deposit required each year to reach 1 by a given year	Table 4 Discount Factor How much 1 at a future date is worth today
1	1.12	1.00	1.00	.893
2	1.25	2.12	.472	.797
3	1.41	3.37	.296	.712
4	1.57	4.78	.209	.636
5	1.76	6.35	.157	.567
6	1.97	8.12	.123	.507
7	2.21	10.09	.099	.452
8	2.48	12.30	.081	.404
9	2.77	14.78	.068	.361
1 0	3.11	17.55	.057	.322
1 1	3.48	20.66	.048	.288
1 2	3.90	24.13	.041	.257
1 3	4.36	28.03	.036	.229
1 4	4.89	32.39	.031	.205
1 5	5.47	37.30	.027	.183
1 6	6.13	42.75	.023	.163
1 7	6.87	48.88	.021	.146
1 8	7.69	55.75	.018	.130
1 9	8.61	63.44	.016	.116
2 0	9.65	72.05	.014	.104
2 1	10.80	81.70	.012	.093
2 2	12.10	92.50	.011	.083
2 3	13.55	104.60	.0096	.074
2 4	15.18	118.16	.0085	.066
2 5	17.00	133.33	.0075	.059

Rate 13% Year	Table 1 Compounding Factor for 1 What an initial amount becomes when growing at compound interest	Table 2 Compounding Factor For 1 per annum Growth of equal year-end deposits all growing at compound interest	Table 3 Sinking Fund Factor Level deposit required each year to reach 1 by a given year	Table 4 Discount Factor How much 1 at a future date is worth today
1	1.13	1.00	1.00	.885
2	1.28	2.13	.470	.783
3	1.44	3.41	.294	.693
4	1.63	4.85	.206	.613
5	1.84	6.48	.154	.543
6	2.08	8.32	.120	.480
7	2.35	10.41	.096	.425
8	2.66	12.76	.078	.376
9	3.00	15.42	.065	.333
10	3.40	18.42	.054	.295
11	3.84	21.81	.046	.261
12	4.34	25.65	.039	.231
13	4.90	29.99	.033	.204
14	5.54	34.88	.029	.181
15	6.25	40.42	.025	.160
16	7.07	46.67	.021	.142
17	7.99	53.74	.019	.125
18	9.02	61.73	.016	.111
19	10.20	70.75	.014	.098
20	11.52	80.95	.012	.087
21	13.02	92.47	.011	.077
22	14.71	105.49	.0095	.068
23	16.63	120.20	.0083	.060
24	18.79	136.83	.0073	.053
25	21.23	155.62	.0064	.047

Rate **14%** Year	Table 1 Compounding Factor for 1 What an initial amount becomes when growing at compound interest	Table 2 Compounding Factor For 1 per annum Growth of equal year-end deposits all growing at compound interest	Table 3 Sinking Fund Factor Level deposit required each year to reach 1 by a given year	Table 4 Discount Factor How much 1 at a future date is worth today
1	1.14	1.00	1.00	.877
2	1.30	2.14	.467	.770
3	1.48	3.44	.291	.675
4	1.69	4.92	.203	.592
5	1.93	6.61	.151	.519
6	2.20	8.54	.117	.456
7	2.50	10.73	.093	.400
8	2.85	13.23	.076	.351
9	3.25	16.09	.062	.308
10	3.71	19.34	.052	.270
11	4.23	23.05	.043	.237
12	4.82	27.27	.037	.208
13	5.49	32.09	.031	.182
14	6.26	37.58	.027	.160
15	7.14	43.84	.023	.141
16	8.14	50.98	.020	.123
17	9.28	59.12	.017	.108
18	10.58	68.39	.015	.095
19	12.06	78.97	.013	.083
20	13.74	91.03	.011	.073
21	15.67	104.77	.0096	.064
22	17.86	120.44	.0083	.056
23	20.36	138.30	.0072	.049
24	23.21	158.66	.0063	.043
25	26.46	181.87	.0055	.038

Rate 15% Year	Table 1 Compounding Factor for 1 What an initial amount becomes when growing at compound interest	Table 2 Compounding Factor For 1 per annum Growth of equal year-end deposits all growing at compound interest	Table 3 Sinking Fund Factor Level deposit required each year to reach 1 by a given year	Table 4 Discount Factor How much 1 at a future date is worth today
1	1.15	1.00	1.00	.870
2	1.32	2.15	.465	.756
3	1.52	3.47	.288	.658
4	1.75	4.99	.200	.572
5	2.01	6.74	.148	.497
6	2.31	8.75	.114	.432
7	2.66	11.07	.090	.376
8	3.06	13.73	.073	.327
9	3.52	16.79	.060	.284
10	4.05	20.30	.049	.247
11	4.65	24.35	.041	.215
12	5.35	29.00	.035	.187
13	6.15	34.51	.029	.163
14	7.08	40.51	.025	.141
15	8.14	47.58	.021	.123
16	9.36	55.72	.018	.107
17	10.76	65.08	.015	.093
18	12.38	75.84	.013	.081
19	14.23	88.21	.011	.070
20	16.37	102.44	.010	.061
21	18.82	118.81	.0084	.053
22	21.65	137.63	.0073	.046
23	24.89	159.28	.0063	.040
24	28.63	184.17	.0054	.035
25	32.92	212.79	.0047	.030

Rate **16%**	Table 1 Compounding Factor for 1 What an initial amount becomes when growing at compound interest	Table 2 Compounding Factor For 1 per annum Growth of equal year-end deposits all growing at compound interest	Table 3 Sinking Fund Factor Level deposit required each year to reach 1 by a given year	Table 4 Discount Factor How much 1 at a future date is worth today
Year				
1	1.16	1.00	1.00	.862
2	1.35	2.16	.463	.743
3	1.56	3.51	.285	.641
4	1.81	5.07	.197	.552
5	2.10	6.88	.145	.476
6	2.44	8.98	.111	.410
7	2.83	11.41	.088	.354
8	3.28	14.24	.070	.305
9	3.80	17.52	.057	.263
10	4.41	21.32	.047	.227
11	5.12	25.73	.039	.195
12	5.94	30.85	.032	.169
13	6.89	36.79	.027	.145
14	7.99	43.67	.023	.125
15	9.27	51.66	.019	.108
16	10.75	60.93	.016	.093
17	12.47	71.67	.014	.080
18	14.46	84.10	.012	.069
19	16.78	98.60	.010	.060
20	19.46	115.38	.0087	.051
21	22.57	134.84	.0074	.044
22	26.19	157.42	.0064	.038
23	30.38	183.60	.0055	.033
24	35.24	213.98	.0047	.028
25	40.87	249.21	.0040	.025

Rate **17%** Year	Table 1 Compounding Factor for 1 What an initial amount becomes when growing at compound interest	Table 2 Compounding Factor For 1 per annum Growth of equal year-end deposits all growing at compound interest	Table 3 Sinking Fund Factor Level deposit required each year to reach 1 by a given year	Table 4 Discount Factor How much 1 at a future date is worth today
1	1.17	1.00	1.00	.855
2	1.37	2.17	.461	.731
3	1.60	3.54	.283	.624
4	1.87	5.14	.195	.534
5	2.19	7.01	.143	.456
6	2.57	9.21	.109	.390
7	3.00	11.77	.085	.333
8	3.51	14.77	.068	.285
9	4.11	18.29	.055	.243
10	4.81	22.39	.045	.208
11	5.62	27.20	.037	.178
12	6.58	32.82	.031	.152
13	7.70	39.40	.025	.130
14	9.01	47.10	.021	.111
15	10.54	56.11	.018	.095
16	12.33	66.65	.015	.081
17	14.43	79.98	.013	.069
18	16.88	93.41	.011	.059
19	19.75	110.29	.0091	.051
20	23.11	130.03	.0077	.043
21	27.03	153.14	.0065	.037
22	31.63	180.17	.0056	.032
23	37.01	211.80	.0047	.027
24	43.30	248.81	.0040	.023
25	50.66	292.11	.0034	.020

Year	Rate 18% Table 1 Compounding Factor for 1 What an initial amount becomes when growing at compound interest	Table 2 Compounding Factor For 1 per annum Growth of equal year-end deposits all growing at compound interest	Table 3 Sinking Fund Factor Level deposit required each year to reach 1 by a given year	Table 4 Discount Factor How much 1 at a future date is worth today
1	1.18	1.00	1.00	.848
2	1.39	2.18	.459	.718
3	1.64	3.57	.280	.609
4	1.94	5.22	.192	.516
5	2.29	7.15	.140	.437
6	2.70	9.44	.106	.370
7	3.19	12.14	.082	.314
8	3.76	15.33	.065	.266
9	4.44	19.09	.052	.226
10	5.23	23.52	.043	.191
11	6.18	28.76	.035	.162
12	7.29	34.93	.029	.137
13	8.60	42.22	.024	.116
14	10.15	50.82	.020	.099
15	11.97	60.97	.016	.084
16	14.13	72.94	.014	.071
17	16.67	87.07	.012	.060
18	19.67	103.74	.010	.051
19	23.21	123.41	.0081	.043
20	27.39	146.63	.0068	.037
21	32.32	174.02	.0058	.031
22	38.14	206.34	.0049	.026
23	45.01	244.49	.0041	.022
24	53.11	289.50	.0035	.019
25	62.67	342.60	.0029	.016

Rate 19% Year	Table 1 Compounding Factor for 1 What an initial amount becomes when growing at compound interest	Table 2 Compounding Factor For 1 per annum Growth of equal year-end deposits all growing at compound interest	Table 3 Sinking Fund Factor Level deposit required each year to reach 1 by a given year	Table 4 Discount Factor How much 1 at a future date is worth today
1	1.19	1.00	1.00	.840
2	1.42	2.19	.457	.706
3	1.69	3.61	.277	.593
4	2.01	5.29	.189	.499
5	2.39	7.30	.137	.419
6	2.84	9.68	.103	.352
7	3.38	12.52	.080	.296
8	4.02	15.90	.063	.249
9	4.79	19.92	.050	.209
10	5.69	24.71	.041	.176
11	6.78	30.40	.033	.148
12	8.06	37.18	.027	.124
13	9.60	45.24	.022	.104
14	11.42	54.84	.018	.088
15	13.59	66.26	.015	.074
16	16.17	79.85	.013	.062
17	19.24	96.02	.010	.052
18	22.90	115.27	.0087	.044
19	27.25	138.17	.0072	.037
20	32.43	165.42	.0061	.031
21	38.59	197.85	.0051	.026
22	45.92	236.44	.0042	.022
23	54.65	282.36	.0035	.018
24	65.03	337.01	.0030	.014
25	77.39	402.04	.0025	.013

Rate	Table 1	Table 2	Table 3	Table 4
20%	**Compounding Factor for 1** What an initial amount becomes when growing at compound interest	**Compounding Factor For 1 per annum** Growth of equal year-end deposits all growing at compound interest	**Sinking Fund Factor** Level deposit required each year to reach 1 by a given year	**Discount Factor** How much 1 at a future date is worth today
Year				
1	1.20	1.00	1.00	.833
2	1.44	2.20	.455	.694
3	1.73	3.64	.275	.579
4	2.07	5.37	.186	.482
5	2.49	7.44	.134	.402
6	2.99	9.93	.101	.335
7	3.58	12.92	.077	.279
8	4.30	16.50	.061	.233
9	5.16	20.80	.048	.194
10	6.19	25.96	.039	.162
11	7.43	32.15	.031	.135
12	8.92	39.58	.025	.112
13	10.70	48.50	.021	.094
14	12.84	59.20	.017	.078
15	15.41	72.04	.014	.065
16	18.49	87.44	.011	.054
17	22.19	105.93	.0094	.045
18	26.62	128.12	.0078	.038
19	31.95	154.74	.0065	.031
20	38.34	186.69	.0054	.026
21	46.01	225.03	.0044	.022
22	55.21	271.03	.0037	.018
23	66.25	326.24	.0031	.015
24	79.50	392.48	.0026	.013
25	95.40	471.98	.0021	.010

Index